The 10 Principles for Fearless Success

---

1   Make one idea your life

2   Arise, awake and stop not till the goal is reached

3   Work relentlessly

4   Be fearless—face the brutes!

5   The darkest night brings the brightest dawn

6   Pure in thought, word and deed

7   Character is established through a thousand stumbles

8   Everyone is great in their own place

9   Create your own destiny

10 All power is within you

Maha Sinnathamby is one of the most inspirational people I have ever met. Here is a man who against all odds converted a tract of 'worthless' bush land into a thriving city. Despite opposition that would deter most people, he persevered with his vision. His story contains invaluable lessons for anybody who is serious about becoming successful.

Noel Whittaker—investment expert, journalist and author

When I met Maha for the first time I could see in his eyes, in his demeanour, and in his language that here was a man who was committed to a vision. He was relentless; he was positive; he had a schoolboy effervescence that was infectious. The politicians, bureaucrats, councillors, bankers and others whom he had to persuade along the way never stood a chance. He was always going to win them over.

Bernard Salt—trend forecaster and economic commentator

Life is about the communities we belong to and our contribution to them; our rugby club, our children's school, our family or our church. Maha has created a whole city with hundreds of thriving communities which will influence hundreds of thousands of lives for generations to come. This is a story of a man who through his belief and persistence has created something extraordinary. Australians often celebrate our sporting achievements above their due. Our history should also recognise and celebrate our pioneers just as fervently, as men like Maha Sinnathamby are few, but they are truly great Australians.

John Eales—World Cup-winning Wallabies captain and author

This is a wonderful story of perseverance, self-belief and a real life lesson to us all. I have known Maha Sinnathamby for quite a few years and have seen first-hand how his dream has become a reality via the Springfield project. Being a keen golfer I was immediately drawn to the brilliant golf course Brookwater, which was my initial contact with Maha and his massive overall undertaking. The project is still a work in progress but Maha and his team should be extremely proud of what has been achieved and what will ultimately become a testimony to the vision and never-say-die attitude of its creator.

Allan Border—former Australian cricket captain

STOP NOT TILL THE GOAL IS REACHED

THE 10 PRINCIPLES FOR FEARLESS SUCCESS
THAT INSPIRED **MAHA SINNATHAMBY** TO BUILD A CITY

KAREN McCREADIE

WILEY

John Wiley & Sons Australia, Ltd

First published in 2012 by
John Wiley & Sons Australia, Ltd
42 McDougall St, Milton Qld 4064

Office also in Melbourne

Typeset in Bembo 11.5/13.5pt

© Karen McCreadie 2012

The moral rights of the author have been asserted

National Library of Australia Cataloguing-in-Publication data:

Author:	McCreadie, Karen.
Title:	Stop Not Till the Goal is Reached: The 10 Principles for Fearless Success That Inspired Maha Sinnathamby to Build a City/Karen McCreadie.
ISBN:	9781742468563 (pbk.)
Notes:	Includes index.
Subjects:	Sinnathamby, Maha.
	Sharpless, Bob.
	Real estate development – Queensland – Springfield.
	Land use – Queensland – Springfield.
	Springfield (Qld.) – History.
Dewey Number:	333.33092

Cover design by Xou Creative

Cover photograph: Rob J. Williams

Printed in China by Printplus Limited

10 9 8 7 6 5 4 3 2 1

Disclaimer
The material in this publication is of the nature of general comment only, and does not represent professional advice. It is not intended to provide specific guidance for particular circumstances and it should not be relied on as the basis for any decision to take action or not take action on any matter which it covers. Readers should obtain professional advice where appropriate, before making any such decision. To the maximum extent permitted by law, the author and publisher disclaim all responsibility and liability to any person, arising directly or indirectly from any person taking or not taking action based on the information in this publication.

To my wife and best friend in life, Yoga Sinnathamby.

Foreword

Sometimes we meet people and share experiences that define our lives. Whether in our professional, social, religious or political pursuits, we remember people who have had a profound effect on our thinking and have moved us to action.

I have known Maha Sinnathamby for more than 27 years as both business partner and friend. He is a unique human being. Persistence, courage and infectious enthusiasm are character traits found in many successful people, and he has these traits in abundance. But he is much more complex than most. He has a keen sense of social justice and a strong desire to back the underdog and prove the establishment wrong. He has enormous energy, which is generated by his constant thirst for information and intellectual stimulation. And he is driven by his spirituality and his admiration for inspirational leaders who changed the world—Mahatma Gandhi and Nelson Mandela are his favourites. I can't help think that, had he not come to Australia, Maha might have pursued a political career, such is his passion for social issues and encouraging everyone to live productively.

Understanding what drives Maha is the subject of this book. From an extremely humble childhood and with an educational record as, by his own admission, an 'average student', Maha has achieved enormous success as a property developer. This success has been hard-earned. There have been many periods of financial uncertainty caused by property cycles, the changing political environment and, more recently, the global financial crisis. But Maha recognises no obstacles to achievement.

To this day I am in awe of Maha's vision for Springfield and his audacity and persistence in promoting an idea that was universally ridiculed by the establishment in its early years. Complementing his enormous determination with hard work, skilful financial management and a talent for building strategic partnerships has helped reduce the inherent risks and persuade others to share his vision.

Meeting Maha and becoming his business partner were life-changing events. As in all long-term relationships we have had our disagreements, particularly over some of the financial challenges we have faced, but I could not have asked for a more committed and loyal business partner. I congratulate Maha on all he has achieved in both his business and his community involvement. He has been a wonderful mentor to me and in the Springfield development he has created a legacy that will be admired by generations to come.

Bob Sharpless
Managing Director
Springfield Land Corporation

Contents

About the author

Karen McCreadie is a freelance ghostwriter and author. Following a previous career in marketing and personal development in the UK and Australia, Karen established herself as a ghostwriter in 2000 and has been writing professionally ever since. So far she has written over 35 books on topics as diverse as property and stockmarket investing, personal development, sports psychology, personality profiling, change management and business coaching. As well as writing under her own name she also works with busy professionals including business leaders, CEOs and renowned international speakers. Many of the books Karen has written have become bestsellers and many have been translated into several different languages. For more information on Karen visit <www.wordarchitect.com>.

Acknowledgements

Of the many hundreds of people I have come to know well during my lifetime, I can truly say I've learned something valuable from each and every one of them. My parents of course had the greatest influence on me. My father and mother were strong and focused individuals who gave me a good education and an enduring set of values to take forward in life. Also important, they evoked in me a strong sense of self-belief. My seven brothers and sisters, all great in their own right, also gave me lots of valuable guidance and inspiration. Growing up together, we all benefited greatly from the value of a united family.

To Yoga, my wife of 44 years, you have filled the role of best friend, reliable adviser and calming influence supremely well. You've stuck with me through thick and thin throughout my working life. You have endured a lot of pain and some joy along the way. You've been a source of inspiration and strength when I needed it most. You stood by me during the tough times when all was nearly lost. And you always kept the home fires burning and did a magnificent job of bringing up our children when I was off chasing my goals.

To our four loving children, you are the light and inspiration of my life. Thank you for your great support, and for your understanding through the times when you needed me and I was not there. It gave me great joy and happiness to watch you grow into the fine adults you are now.

There are many others to whom I want to extend my heartfelt thanks.

To Bob Sharpless, my business partner these past 27 years. No-one else would have had the foresight to join me at my lowest ebb, yet you did. You had the strength of will and the patience to stick with me through all the ups and downs. I can only hope you would now say the journey has been worth it. And to Belinda, who at great personal sacrifice was prepared to back your decision to leave Perth and join us in Brisbane, who never gave up on us, even when we were struggling and close to losing it all, and who has always been a real source of strength. Belinda, you are a great woman.

To my first business partner in Perth, Ken Law-Davies, who joined me on the Murdoch Constructions journey. Your faith in me that persuaded you to quit a steady government job to join me in building a business from scratch was very much appreciated. I value our friendship to this day.

To David Henry, Barry Alexander, Malcolm Finlayson and all the others who were prepared to do their utmost to keep going from the start of Springfield. And to my current and loyal team of dedicated staff who continue to strive and give their best.

To my good friend and close confidant John Genner, who went out on a very long and fragile limb in backing us both financially and in negotiations during the difficult early stages of Springfield. It's probably easy now in hindsight to say you backed a winner, but you certainly took a big risk on us then.

To the mayors, councillors and staff of Moreton and Ipswich City councils, and to all the premiers, ministers, members of Parliament and bureaucrats at all levels of the Queensland and federal governments who had the vision and foresight to see something special in Springfield over the past 20 years, and who helped us to bring that vision to reality. You all had a job to do, but your support and encouragement was gratifying.

To all my supporters in private enterprise who were with me from day one of the Springfield journey and stayed with me all the way, I thank you. In one form or another, the collective input of about a hundred or so individuals made a huge contribution at the coal face to Springfield's success today.

Of the utmost importance, I thank the many thousands of families who moved to Springfield because they believed in the new city that was being built. I also pay tribute to the hundreds of businesses that operate at Springfield for their faith in the vision.

Acknowledgements

To the great country that my family and I have had the good fortune to call home these past 40 years or so—a country with an enduring and consistent democratic tradition of equity, equality and fairness to all citizens.

I thank Karen McCreadie who has done her utmost to ensure this work reflects my motive to inspire the reader to action. In telling the Springfield story and in exploring the success principles that have guided me on my life's journey, Karen had open access to Bob and me, and also to my family. Her many quotes and supporting examples of amazing achievements throughout history serve to demonstrate the strength of the adage that 'success leaves clues'.

Karen and I would like to acknowledge Greg Bourke for the extensive time he devoted to assembling all my personal historical records and all those relating to the Springfield journey, and for the invaluable contribution he made to this book.

My gratitude also goes to my editorial committee—Con Galtos, John Goddard and our daughter Meera Honan. Each has given me invaluable advice and guidance on our journey to produce this book. Finally I thank Kristen, Katherine and the rest of the team at John Wiley & Sons for their guidance and great support.

Maha Sinnathamby
January 2012

Introduction

Have you ever wondered what makes one person succeed and another fail? Does it simply come down to luck, talent or family connections? Have you ever been entranced by a biography but been unable to get behind the myth to synthesise the lessons and understand what *you* need to do to be successful in your own life?

Why is it that some born to poverty resign themselves to the conditions and circumstances of their birth while others use the experience to redefine their future? What inspires one person to never give up despite repeated failure while another will throw in the towel at the slightest setback? What makes some people claim their skin colour, gender, religion, language or location disadvantages them, while others refuse to acknowledge or be handicapped by such distinctions?

What makes some individuals feel entitled to government handouts, happy to take all they can get, while others turn their back on the safety net, determined to forge their own path through hard work and perseverance? What makes one individual with financial problems declare bankruptcy and walk away without a backward glance and another stay and fight to pay off their debts?

What drives some to focus purely on wealth creation and others to see further and do what's right rather than what's profitable? What is it that motivates one person to always say 'Yes' and to relentlessly seek a solution and another to constantly say 'No' and to never even look?

What makes one person sell his soul for a dollar and another refuse to sell out for hundreds of millions, holding fast to the integrity of his vision? What drives one man to take on the biggest challenge of his life at a time when most people are thinking of slowing down and buying a pair of slippers? And how is it even possible to create a truly remarkable legacy while always putting family first?

Stop Not Till the Goal is Reached is the story of Maha Sinnathamby—migrant, property developer, community builder, visionary and one of Australia's top 100 most wealthy businessmen. It also tells the story of Springfield, a fully master-planned city 23 kilometres west of Brisbane in Queensland, Australia.

US anthropologist Margaret Mead famously said, 'Never doubt that a small group of thoughtful, committed citizens can change the world. Indeed, it is the only thing that ever has'. This book relates how a small group of committed individuals achieved something extraordinary after taking on a project so massive that most public companies with unlimited resources and hundreds of staff wouldn't even have contemplated it. Never before in the history of development had a small, privately owned company taken on a project of Springfield's size and survived.

When other developers looked at that 2860 hectares of land, which the owner refused to subdivide, they saw insurmountable problems. Most people who viewed the property were intimidated by its scale—equivalent to over 4085 rugby pitches. The land itself was hard, inaccessible and hilly, much of it covered in dense forest, with limited access and almost nonexistent services. It was located in an economically depressed region with high unemployment and welfare dependency, with a prison, a psychiatric hospital and an army training base nearby. Part of the land came with coal exploration rights. Only a small section was suitable for development; the rest wasn't remotely viable without extortionate infrastructure investment and complex state and local government approvals. And to top it off, Maha and his business partner, Bob Sharpless, didn't have the money to buy or develop the land.

But Maha saw something different. He saw a new city rising up out of the Australian scrub. A city, designed to the highest technological and environmental specifications, where people could take joy in living, learning, working and playing. A city with state-of-the-art schools and university, cutting-edge hospitals and healthcare facilities, a vibrant city centre, abundant parklands and world-class leisure facilities.

Stop Not Till the Goal is Reached tells of how this vision became a reality—how the impossible was made possible through the dedication, commitment, self-belief and sheer bloody-mindedness of a small group of thoughtful, committed citizens, and how, with Maha Sinnathamby at the helm, they did change the world. It is both a story of fierce perseverance, resilience and sheer hard work, and an exploration of what drives someone to deliberately choose the hardest path because it was the right thing to do.

A few heart-whole, sincere, and energetic men and women can do more in a year than a mob in a century.

The city did indeed rise up out of the Australian scrub. In 2010 Springfield won the prestigious FIABCI Prix d'Excellence Award for World's Best Master Planned Community.

But the book is not just about property development, business deals and how to become a multimillionaire. Nor is it just a biography of an extraordinary individual and an equally extraordinary business partnership. It's also about courage, commitment and fierce determination, about what can be achieved when you refuse to give up.

This book is a call-to-arms for anyone who wants to achieve something great, be it to win gold at the Olympics, to write a novel or to build a business empire. You are what you want to be, and you have more control over your life's outcomes than you might think. It doesn't matter what you want to achieve, or who you are, there are hallmarks to success, and this book identifies those hallmarks so you can use them as guideposts in your own adventure.

Stop Not Till the Goal is Reached unpacks Maha's 10 principles for fearless success. Each principle has its roots in the practical yet ancient philosophy that has inspired and supported Maha throughout his life, and every unattributed quote that appears through the book is drawn from the same philosophy, which will be explained in more detail in chapter 10. Maha's 10 principles are explored through his own personal story and through other examples of astonishing personal achievements from around the world. These stories, all true, demonstrate what is possible with the right mindset, the right people and the right action, and how thinking big, audacious, even impossible thoughts has led to real world transformation.

Chapter 1

Make one idea your life

Take up one idea. Make that one idea your life—think of it, dream of it, live on that idea. Let the brain, muscles, nerves, every part of your body, be full of that idea, and just leave every other idea alone. This is the way to success, and this is the way great spiritual giants are produced.

The idea of having one single central focus in life is not new. If you were to look back on every major achievement through the course of human history you would find that someone, somewhere took one idea and made it their personal mission. Successful entrepreneurs, political leaders, inventors, scientists, philosophers, spiritual gurus and famous authors have long talked about the importance of pursuing one central objective. The ancient Sufi mystic Rumi said, 'There is one thing that we all must do. If we do everything else but that one thing, we will be lost. And if we do nothing else but that one thing, we will have lived a glorious life'.

Every successful business has at its heart a single, clear and tangible idea. For Microsoft it was to have a computer on every desk in every home. For Google it was to organise the world's information and make it universally accessible and useful. John F. Kennedy committed a nation to the idea of 'landing a man on the moon and returning him safely to the Earth'.

Napoleon Hill, author of *Think and Grow Rich*, a book that influenced and inspired Maha as he struggled through university, called it your 'definite major purpose'. Hill wrote, 'There is one quality which one must possess to win, and that is definiteness of purpose, the knowledge of what one wants, and a burning desire to possess it'.

Our conscious mind has a finite capacity to process data yet we are bombarded with vast amounts of information all the time. Having a definite purpose allows us to cut through the clutter and direct our focus, energy and attention. Success takes time, commitment and a kind of obsession. The principle of one central purpose is therefore the starting point of all achievement.

Maha's life has been built on a series of single ideas, each of which has added to his knowledge base and led him naturally to the next. It all began in Rantau, Malaysia.

Rantau, Malaysia 1939

Mahalingam Sinnathamby (or Maha as he is now known) was born at the start of the Second World War. From his first moments Maha was a feisty, energetic and restless child. He wouldn't settle and refused to be confined to his cot. He demanded almost constant attention and cried throughout the night, so that his exhausted mother, who already had four children, found it increasingly difficult to cope.

The Sinnathamby home was not a particularly happy one. The family lived in a hut in the rural village of Rantau built around a rubber plantation about 60 kilometres south of Kuala Lumpur in Malaysia. It was a basic existence. A few mats covered the dirt floor, water was collected from a well on the plantation and there was no electricity in the home. Like many of the other villagers Maha's father, Valipuram, worked on the plantation seven days a week. Because of earlier training as a hospital assistant he also managed the village dispensary.

But it wasn't poverty and overwork that caused the unhappiness. Maha's parents were joined not by love but by duty. In their culture arranged marriages were the norm, but Valipuram felt a deep sense of loss and longing for a life he felt he should have been living but couldn't.

Valipuram had had aspirations to be a Hindu monk. He had grown up in Sri Lanka and his own father had died when he was quite young. In

Indian culture then there was no worse fate than becoming a widow. Even *sati*, the now banned practice whereby a woman would throw herself on her husband's funeral pyre, was considered a better option than living as a widow. Without their father, life was extremely tough and Valipuram's mother struggled to feed her children. At home she would bake cakes and traditional sweets to sell on the streets, earning barely enough to support her family. Often as a boy Valipuram would wait by his mother in the kitchen, hoping that one of the cakes would break so he could eat the crumbs.

In 1920 Valipuram, along with most of his extended family, was granted a transfer within the British colonies from Sri Lanka to Malaysia. In Kuala Lumpur he got a job in the General Hospital. He studied hard to become a grade one hospital assistant, then considered equivalent to 'half a doctor'. Around this time he and his best friend became engrossed in the teachings of Sri Ramakrishna, a 19th-century Bengali mystic. When not working at the hospital the two were utterly focused on their desire to become monks. They resolved to dedicate their lives to spiritual study and enlightenment.

Valipuram's mother became increasingly concerned about his religious aspirations. She desperately wanted to see her son and daughter marry, but he was determined to pursue his spiritual quest. After years of study Valipuram and his friend decided it was time to act. They shaved their heads as a symbol of renunciation of their worldly lives, packed their bags and travelled discreetly to Penang to board a ship to Calcutta, India, where they planned to join the Ramakrishna Mission. Just before the ship was due to leave, however, Valipuram was seized by his uncles, who had learned of his plans and dashed to Penang to bring their nephew home. Valipuram was instructed forcefully that his mother and sister needed him more than any Indian monastery. He was devastated.

According to Indian culture it was it was a father's responsibility to ensure that his daughter is married. In his absence the responsibility fell to Valipuram as the only son. Their mother, anxious to ensure her daughter was properly looked after, had chosen a family who also had a brother and sister ready for marriage. When Valipuram was brought home against his will his mother pleaded with him: 'The families need to exchange daughters for marriage. They won't take your sister unless you agree to marry their daughter. You must do it for *your* sister's sake!'

So in 1925, to ensure his sister's honour and security, Valipuram sacrificed his own hopes and dreams and married Maha's mother, Pavalaratnam, while his sister married Pavalaratnam's brother. Only 14 at the time, his new bride was equally upset by the match and the prospect of leaving home to spend her life with a man she didn't love and who she knew didn't love her. Valipuram made no secret of his feelings and in the early years of their marriage they frequently lamented the forced match.

As a result, the two lived almost separate lives. Valipuram, bitterly disappointed at not being able to travel to India, would return from work to immerse himself in study and prayer. This effectively left Pavalaratnam to raise their growing family alone. Unsurprisingly the household was not a happy one. The two young people had been forced into a situation neither had wanted. It wasn't fair for either of them, and each harboured resentment against the other.

Then Maha came along.

~

A resourceful and resilient woman, Pavalaratnam had converted her sense of loss and isolation into maternal love and immersed herself in her role as a mother. But Maha tested her in a way that even she struggled to handle. His volatility and restlessness made family life so difficult she was finally forced to reach out to her husband for help.

Perhaps this is part of Maha's legacy: he's a fighter, but his warrior instinct is born not from division but from the recognition that sometimes fighting is a necessary part of life. Whether people like it or not, he will bring them together and force a resolution—to create something bigger and better as a result. And that's what he helped to do, even as an infant, within his own family.

The first four Sinnathamby offspring were model children—quiet, respectful and compliant. Then Maha arrived and it was simply no longer possible for Pavalaratnam to manage the family alone. He needed two committed parents and Valipuram reluctantly accepted his wife's pleas for help.

As any parent will confirm, one awkward child alone can be difficult to deal with, but when he or she disturbs other young children the pressure can be multiplied. So Valipuram would often take Maha off for a walk to give the Sinnathamby household some peace. Pavalaratnam could then settle the other children while her husband endeavoured to calm the youngest member of the family. He would walk endlessly around the plantation murmuring Hindu verses and prayers and singing to his struggling, bright-eyed son as the family dog followed behind. Some nights Valipuram walked for many hours. As the only person in the area with any medical experience he was effectively the local GP, so on occasion he would take a short cut to the village dispensary for a sedative for Maha so everyone could get some sleep!

One evening, while a tropical storm was brewing and the trees in the plantation creaked and strained, Valipuram took his restless son on one of their nightly walks. As the wind whipped and whistled through the trees Maha clung to his father, his little face searching his father's eyes for reassurance. Looking down at his feisty son, Valipuram realised, perhaps for the first time, that this little person needed him.

A deeply spiritual man, Valipuram believed he had missed his calling and had been denied his true destiny. It was this sense of loss that was the root cause of unhappiness in his marriage. But looking at his difficult, volatile son snuggling into him for protection from the dangers of the world, Valipuram finally realised that he was not in the wrong place after all. He was exactly where he should be. He was a husband and a father. He had a wife who was pregnant again and who needed him. As the darkness closed in around him he finally accepted his life, recognising at last that the resentment and distress he felt over a life unlived was actively stopping him from living the life he had.

Maha's father had thought that his one idea was to become a monk. His inability to follow that path had wasted 10 years of his life spent mourning at a door that had closed. And yet, as playwright Tom Stoppard once said, 'Every exit is an entry somewhere else'. Once Valipuram realised this, his life changed. After 10 years of marriage, with five children and another on the way, Valipuram returned home that evening a changed man and thereafter became a fully committed husband and father.

By doing so he fulfilled his own destiny as a powerful teacher and inspiration. There can be little doubt that Maha Sinnathamby would not be the man he is today and would not have achieved what he has achieved had his father not committed himself to his one idea of being a supportive husband, spiritual guide and inspiration to his own children. The family became much happier, although their material conditions did not improve — if anything they got worse.

~

Valipuram's brother-in-law was a clerk working at the same British-run rubber plantation, and the two were close. At great personal risk to himself and his family, he had harboured three Gurkha soldiers from the Japanese occupiers, who suspected Valipuram of guilt by association. Valipuram's cause was not helped by the fact that he had been educated in a British-run school. As one of the only English speakers in the area, he would relay what he heard on the BBC news broadcasts to local soldiers and villagers and was therefore considered an informant. In July 1944 a truckload of Japanese soldiers drove up to the Sinnathamby home.

Before the truck stopped, a soldier brandishing a rifle jumped down and approached the hut. The family dog leapt to his feet. The soldier took aim and fired. The gunshot broke the silence and the children began to cry as their beloved Alsatian yelped and fell to the ground. Approaching Maha's father, the soldier slammed the rifle butt into his face, knocking him to the ground. Bloodied and semi-conscious, Valipuram was hauled into the back of the truck as his family screamed and his dog bled to death outside their home. Maha was just four years old.

During the war a breakaway group of Indian rebels had supported the Japanese. As a result, the Japanese were more lenient towards Indian prisoners and Valipuram was sentenced to just five years in prison. Had he been Chinese he would have been executed. Valipuram was taken to a makeshift prison 18 kilometres away that would eventually house 142 local prisoners of war. The Japanese were notoriously cruel and brutal in war and the prisoners were regularly beaten and tortured for information. They were fed little and Valipuram spoke of eating leaves or anything edible he could find in the compound. He and nine other prisoners slept on the floor of a cell 10 feet by 10 feet. Many were left to die without food or water.

Pavalaratnam then had seven children under 13 years old. They had no money saved and the sole breadwinner had just been dragged away to prison. Faced with this nightmare the Sinnathamby family's *definite major purpose* became very simple: 'Survive and find food for father'. Pavalaratnam would travel to the prison once a month to take food to her husband. This meant leaving her children to fend for themselves while she made the 36-kilometre round trip by bicycle. The prospects for the children were bleak enough without contemplating the loss of their father. She would do whatever she must to ensure that her husband stayed alive and the family remained together.

Maha's mother was an extremely strong woman. Indeed Maha's life has been defined by the constant presence of strong women. Pavalaratnam was a model of resilience, indomitable strength and perseverance; his wife Yoga's quiet strength and loyalty have been fundamental to his accomplishments and, most importantly, to the unity and stability of the family; and the loyalty, strength of character and sacrifices made by Belinda Sharpless, wife of Maha's business partner, Bob, have been instrumental to the success of Springfield. Ask Maha about any of these women and you will quickly appreciate the respect and reverence he has for each.

Perhaps Maha's idol and inspiration Gandhi said it best: 'If by strength is meant moral power, then woman is immeasurably man's superior. Has she not greater intuition, is she not more self-sacrificing, has she not greater powers of endurance, has she not greater courage? Without her, man could not be'.

During the day the Sinnathamby children would share the household chores to help their mother, then they would focus on finding food for her to take to the prison. Young Maha helped look after the little vegetable garden and tend to the chickens. He still remembers opening the hutch in the morning and wondering why it was always the same chicken that was first to race into the yard. His elder brother caught and sold fish to provide them with a basic income. The family lived on tapioca, with the occasional bowl of rice considered a luxury.

Through sheer necessity the children grew to be independent and resilient individuals. Maha's formative years were hard. Eventually there would be eight children and their parents living in a small hut on the edge of the rubber plantation. There was no electricity, no running water, little food and even less money. 'Looking back, life really was tough', Maha recalls, 'but I believe it was the best thing that ever happened to me. Those early hardships taught me how to fight life's battles and survive—often against the odds. I am really proud of my humble beginnings and I think it proves that it doesn't matter where you start, it's what's in your heart that really counts'.

The biggest battle in those early years was keeping Valipuram alive. Often when Pavalaratnam arrived at the prison she was not allowed inside. It came down to what mood the soldiers were in: on a good day they would let her in; on a bad day she would be turned away. Sometimes Valipuram went for days without food, but Pavalaratnam was a determined woman and this rarely happened. After she had struggled so hard to find food and had made the arduous journey to deliver it, no petulant soldier was going to stand in her way. On one occasion a Japanese soldier drew his pistol, aimed it at her head and yelled in her face, 'One more step and I'll shoot you!' Pavalaratnam stood for a moment, pulled out the gold chain that hung around her neck and said, 'Let me in and you can have this'. The chain was the only thing of value she owned.

Sometimes she would bring one of the children with her to the prison in the hope that the child's presence would help her secure access and lift her husband's spirits. Maha recalls, 'One of my earlier memories is when Mum took me to visit Dad in prison. I was about four years old. It was a long journey. The road from Rantau to the prison in Seremban was very steep in sections so we would have to get off the bike, walk up the hills and cycle down and it would take four to five hours to get there. I remember seeing Dad and he immediately asked me how I was. I replied rather indignantly that I was getting very poor food and it wasn't the same as when he was at home. Of course I didn't realise that my very poor food was a great deal better than his no food'. Yet even when he was starving he would often share the food Pavalaratnam brought with other prisoners who had nothing.

There can be little doubt that Pavalaratnam's regular pilgrimage saved his life. All around him people in the camp were dying. Once when he had been sent to the hospital to die Maha's mother stood over her unconscious husband and prayed. In the end starvation and disease claimed 140 of the 142 inmates. Only Valipuram and one other man survived the ordeal.

In September 1945 the Japanese surrendered and Maha's father was allowed to go home. He had served 14 months of his five-year sentence and would surely have died had the war not ended. Although barely more than skin and bones his spirit was unbroken. Valipuram survived against impossible odds because of the selfless commitment of his wife and his own inner determination. He later received a commendation from Lord Louis Mountbatten on behalf of the British government for his services to the British during the war.

If the mind is intensely eager, everything can be accomplished—mountains can be crumbled into atoms.

Despite being weak and desperate to see his family, as soon as he was released Valipuram went straight to the local schools and enrolled each of his children. In prison Valipuram had been plagued by fears for his children's welfare and became utterly committed to the next *definite major purpose* of the Sinnathamby family—education. The only way his children could secure a better life was to increase the value of their human capital through education—the acquisition of skills and knowledge.

~

Growing up in this environment it is perhaps a little easier to understand Maha's drive towards achievement and success, and his perseverance long after most sane people would have walked away. Maha has faced and overcome many obstacles, he has experienced countless rejections, his plans have met with ridicule, and through it all he has steadfastly refused to quit. If anything these obstacles have increased his resolve and commitment. From the moment he announced that he would build a city in the Australian bush everyone thought he was crazy, laughing at him openly. But when you put those challenges in the context of his early life, it is perhaps easier to appreciate just why he was not discouraged. When you have watched your dog bleed to death in front of you, when you have endured your father's imprisonment and your mother's frequent absences, when you have had to muster all your resources to find food just to keep the family together and help each other survive—all before you were six years old—then being rejected by bureaucrats or bankers probably doesn't seem that intimidating.

Maha was born into conditions that in the west might be described as 'abject poverty', but he will tell you that in fact he had something far more valuable than material possessions—two extraordinary parents who loved him, instilled in him a steely determination and were singularly dedicated to the education and betterment of their eight children.

A passion for education

The ideal of all education, all training, should be man-making. But, instead of that, we are always trying to polish up the outside. What use in polishing up the outside when there is no inside? The end and aim of all training is to make the man grow. The man who influences, who throws his magic, as it were, upon his fellow-beings, is a dynamo of power, and when that man is ready, he can do anything and everything he likes; that personality put upon anything will make it work.

Both parents taught all the Sinnathamby children the value of education. From a spiritual perspective, Maha's father believed strongly that all intelligence and skill should be used both to purify the soul and to contribute to the betterment of society—an idea that Maha still strongly adheres to today. He was never very happy in school, though.

The main reason for this was that he lived about 35 minutes away by bus. When school broke up for lunch and the other students dashed off to their homes nearby or played together outside, Maha would travel all the way home to Rantau for lunch and return for the afternoon session. So he never really had the opportunity to make friends or play sport and he often felt distanced from his schoolmates. The advantage, however, was that he used the opportunity of the long bus trips to read biographies of inspirational leaders such as Lincoln and Roosevelt that he borrowed from the school library.

The years passed and each child in turn finished local school, sat the assessment exam and moved on to high school. One day Valipuram lined up his sons and announced that the two eldest would be doctors, 'and you, Maha, will be a civil engineer'. The die was cast. The eldest, however, insisted he wanted to be a vet and completed his studies at the University of Queensland. The second son did become a doctor after studying at the University of Sydney, and Maha took his degree at the University of New South Wales.

Valipuram had been adamant that his children study in an English-speaking country. Australia was ideal both because it was close and it enjoyed an excellent reputation for its university education. Ultimately, six of Valipuram's children studied overseas.

Maha's own educational journey was far from illustrious, though. Having passed the entry course with a 'C' grade, in 1959 Maha started his engineering degree in Sydney. In reality, he didn't know exactly what engineers did but he assumed they built bridges, dams, roads and buildings. The course, however, was almost pure mathematics and physics and he was very much out of his depth.

To make matters worse, Sydney was not the multicultural city it is today. There were very few foreign students and most of his fellow students struggled even with his name. Maha felt sure this was getting in the way of his making friends, so he decided to adopt a common Australian name and began calling himself Eddie. Although he did not perceive himself as different, he was keen to assimilate and felt that changing his name would help him do that. Even back then Maha refused to think negatively, and his approach and attitude evidently worked. Unlike his school days, university was fun and he had plenty of friends. His best friend was Ho, a Chinese student from Singapore. Although bright in maths and physics, Ho too struggled with the assigned coursework.

It was Maha's experience at university that first taught him that being talented at something was never as important as just getting on with it. As the ancient wisdom that has guided him his whole life reminds us, 'Even the greatest fool can accomplish a task if it were after his or her heart. But the intelligent ones are those who can convert every work into one that suits their taste'. In other words, any fool can do something they want to do, but it takes real intelligence to tackle something you don't want to do or are *not* good at and still get it done. Sometimes we don't have the luxury of choosing the task that is a perfect fit for our abilities. Sometimes we just have to see what needs to be done and do it.

Engineering was like that for Maha. It was a constant struggle, but he had an obligation to complete his course and he certainly didn't want to let his parents down, so he did what he needed to do. He was able to convert every assignment into one that suited his taste and while driving his taxi he would repeat over and again 'I am the best engineer in the world'. It wasn't easy and it wasn't necessarily enjoyable, but he proved to himself he could do it, and in doing so he helped demonstrate that anything is possible, even when it's not 'your thing'!

~

Aldous Huxley once said, 'The most valuable of all education is the ability to make yourself do the thing you have to do, when it has to be done, whether you like it or not'. Life is not meant to be smooth sailing. Our times of real growth and development come when we are under pressure. The strongest, purest diamonds are the ones created under the greatest pressure.

Maha was always aware of how much importance his parents placed on education, but it was only when he became a father himself that he came to appreciate the life-changing opportunities education presents.

Less than a year before he was sworn in as the 44th US President, Senator Barack Obama gave a speech called 'What's Possible for Our Children' at Mapleton Expeditionary School of the Arts in Thornton, Colorado. In his address he said, 'At this defining moment in our history, they've never needed that chance [education] more. In a world where good jobs can be located anywhere there's an internet connection — where a child in Denver is competing with children in Beijing and Bangalore — the most valuable skill you can sell is your knowledge. Education is the currency of the Information Age, no longer just a pathway to opportunity and success but a prerequisite. There simply aren't as many jobs today that can support a family where only a high-school degree is required. And if you don't have that degree, there are even fewer jobs available that can keep you out of poverty'.

This is the reality for everyone living in the modern world. For Maha, education is not just the currency of the future, it is our passport to the future, and we can't get where we want to go without it. Education can be cashed in anywhere in the world. It can never be lost, stolen or forced from you, and the more you have the more valuable you become, for no other reason than that you become more resourceful and resilient. When you are open to learning new things you expand your mind to new possibilities, and it is that openness and expansion that can be transformational. As the American writer Oliver Wendell Holmes once said, 'A mind once stretched by a new idea never regains its original dimensions'. If we are to survive in the future, and our children are to survive in the future, we need education to lift everyone up and provide real possibilities for everyone.

Maha's passion for education is not merely rhetorical; he is a living example of how education can transform a life, not just through the formal education gained at school and university, but through his constant drive to immerse himself in his one idea or chosen area of interest. He has also passed on his passion for education and disciplined effort to his own children. If you ask his kids what life in the Sinnathamby household was like, they will tell you it was loving, but strict and very disciplined. The girls, who are several years older than their brother, vividly remember their daily routine, which shaped their lives from the age of about six.

At 4.45 am they would be woken by their father and told they had 15 minutes to get up, wash their face, clean their teeth and get dressed. At 5.00 am on the dot they would begin various learning activities. Uma, Maha's eldest daughter, remembers they would have to read a book such as *Enjoying English*, which she hated! Or they would play a word game in which Maha would choose a positive word, such as 'determination' or 'concentration' and the girls would have to make up as many words as possible from the letters of that word. As the oldest, Uma would have to find words with four letters or more,

Raynuha three letters or more and Meera, the youngest, two letters or more. Sometimes Maha would set them each a topic and they would have to write and deliver a speech on that topic.

At 6.30 am, after an hour and a half of learning activities, they would all go for a jog for half an hour followed by a shower, breakfast and off to school at 8.00 am. And this happened whether they were at school or on holidays. The only difference was that during the holidays Uma would go to work with her dad at 8.00 am instead of going to school. She still remembers the quiet dread as the school holidays approached, and how all her friends would be talking excitedly about what they were going to do or what exotic places they would be visiting with their family. Uma would remain silent, because she knew what she would be doing in the holidays and was already looking forward to going back to school!

Maha has always worked long hours, so this routine was his way of staying connected and involved with his children as they grew up while also making sure they were fully aware of his aspirations for their education. It was also his way of supporting Yoga with the family while he was trying to build a business. Perhaps most important, with a little hardship in their lives he believed they would learn the most important characteristics of success—discipline, perseverance and the ability to do what needs to be done regardless of whether you feel like it or not!

Although Naren, Maha and Yoga's son, came along six years after their youngest daughter and didn't automatically slot into the same routine, he still remembers his father's drive to squeeze the maximum value out of each day. All the children were expected to write a five-year plan. To an outsider this sounds punishing, especially for little children, but if you talk to any of Maha's children today there is never even a hint of anything other than love and admiration for both their parents. They will readily admit there were times they didn't enjoy the routine, but as adults they acknowledge its value.

Live for an ideal, and that one ideal alone. Let it be so great, so strong, that there may be nothing else left in the mind; no place for anything else, no time for anything else…Every man should take up his own ideal and endeavour to accomplish it.

The principle in action

A unique example of what can be achieved with one idea and a deep determination to see that idea through to fruition is found in the life and achievements of Mahatma Gandhi. Although Maha was aware of who Gandhi was through his own father's reverence for him, it wasn't until he read Gandhi's biography at the age of 22 that Maha realised for himself what a remarkable man he was. Maha recalls, 'I was absolutely amazed how a person who had such similar origins to me had managed to secure independence for India without money, army or family connections. The British Empire was the biggest empire that had ever existed and Indian Independence was the catalyst for its eventual breakup. Gandhi has had a profound influence on my life and his accomplishments served as a constant reminder to me that you can achieve anything if you go about it the *right* way — with courage, dignity and fearlessness'.

What makes Gandhi's story so powerful is not just that he won independence for his country but that he achieved this end not through force but through civil disobedience and nonviolent resistance.

Gandhi's 'one idea' was social justice. Trained as a lawyer in London, he received his first real taste of social injustice while in South Africa. He doubtless would have experienced discrimination and harassment as an Indian student studying in London, the heart of Imperial Britain, but it was his experiences in British-controlled South Africa that really planted the seeds for his social activism. He was outraged by how badly Indians were treated. One of his first experiences in South Africa was of being thrown off a train for sitting in the first-class carriage, even though he had a valid ticket for that compartment. As a 'coloured' he was not permitted to travel first class.

As his experience of injustice grew, Gandhi began to organise politically on behalf of the Indian community. He developed a method of direct civil disobedience based on the principles of nonviolent resistance, truthfulness and endurance that played an important part in securing civil rights for Indian people in South Africa over some 21 years. These efforts helped to inspire Nelson Mandela to take up the fight against apartheid many years later.

Within 15 years of returning to India Gandhi was the leader of the Indian nationalist movement. Using the tactics of nonviolence and civil disobedience, he worked tirelessly to end British rule in India. During this struggle he was arrested and beaten many times, but he never wavered. His approach was so novel and incomprehensible to the British that they were at a loss as to how to respond. They couldn't work out how to defeat him. He was a small, slight, gently spoken man with great charismatic appeal to the people, but he refused to fight. If he had taken up arms, then the British could have crushed the rebellion. If he had used violence they could have used his actions to justify increased repression, but when the British used violence against peaceful demonstrators it simply made Gandhi stronger.

Regardless of the violence inflicted on him and his followers they did not fight. And when the Indian people finally did retaliate violently in protest and despair, Gandhi went on a hunger strike until they stopped. He had no money, no family connections and no army to call on, but he had a powerful single vision and commitment—to make the British leave of their own accord and on good terms. And he achieved just that. India was granted independence in 1947.

Gandhi's courage and strength of character inspired some of the world's most significant leaders. Civil rights activist Martin Luther King Jnr, Nelson Mandela and more recently Barack Obama have all cited Gandhi as a major influence in their lives. The great physicist Albert Einstein exchanged letters with Gandhi, and on hearing of his death he wrote, 'Generations to come will scarce believe that such a one as this walked the earth in flesh and blood'.

Maha, too, was greatly influenced by Gandhi's ethical strength, persistence and resolution to do what was right.

In business we are taught that the end always justifies the means. It doesn't. Assuming the goal is always more important than the way you achieve that goal is a fundamental mistake. Gandhi believed the way people behave is more important than what they achieve. What made Gandhi's accomplishments so extraordinary was not that he forced the British to leave India but the *way* he got the British to leave India. Gandhi taught the world the value of the pursuit of a single aim, but perhaps more importantly he taught the world that the way in which you achieve your aim is every bit as important as the aim itself. When millions of Indians were mobilised against the British, they might have pressed their numerical advantage, taken up arms, fought and won. But he didn't want to achieve independence through violence, and he went on a hunger strike in protest until armed resistance ended.

If the price of success is your integrity and moral character, then no matter what the success, or how much money or power is at the end of the rainbow, the price is too high. Gandhi showed the world that when the cause is just and meaningful and benefits the majority of people involved, and you hold fast to that vision, then the outcome is assured.

There can be little doubt that some of Maha's darkest and most painful times have been illuminated by the courage and resilience of a man many have called 'the most powerful man who has ever lived'.

When once you consider an action, do not let anything dissuade you. Consult your heart, not others, and then follow its dictates.

What this principle means for you

Making one idea your life is a vital principle for success. It doesn't mean you will only ever have one idea. Life for most of us is a series of one ideas that take us progressively towards a larger vision.

For Maha, Springfield was his last and boldest definite major purpose, and it would draw on all his previous ideas. Here was a project that would call on his warrior spirit and every scrap of persistence he possessed. It was a project that could be realised only through commitment, passion and force of will in the face of all obstacles. And it was a place where he could bring his passion for education to life so that it would affect a far wider community. At the time of writing, Springfield hosts eight schools, colleges or further education facilities and one university catering for more than 8700 students. Many refer to Springfield as Maha's fifth child. Bringing it to fruition is the culmination of a lifetime of smaller achievements and hard-won lessons and battles.

If you don't choose one idea and make it your life, you will never understand what it takes to be successful. If you never commit yourself to anything or if you quit as soon as it gets a little tricky, you will never achieve anything meaningful.

> There is the danger of frittering away your energies by taking up an idea only for its novelty, and then giving up for another that is newer. Take one thing up and do it, and see the end of it, and before you have seen the end, do not give up. He who can become mad with an idea, he alone sees light. Those that only take a nibble here and a nibble there will never attain anything. They may titillate their nerves for a moment, but there it will end.

Life is too short to fritter away your energies. If you sit around waiting for someone else to fix your problems or tell you what to do, you may be sitting around a very long time. Alternatively, if you try everything you will master nothing and will end up equally frustrated.

We look at people who are successful and assume they must have had a lucky break or they were born with money or God-given abilities that the rest of us just don't have. People point to the dazzling talents of extraordinary individuals, from Mozart to golfer Rory McIlroy, as evidence that innate ability exists. Yet the truth is different. Mozart's father was a famous composer in his own right, passionate about music and how it was taught to children. His definite major purpose and personal obsession was to train his son, and he started his tuition when Mozart was only three years old. The compositions that Mozart made at five years of age, which are the stuff of legend, were not in his own hand. They were impressive, but his first real demonstration of genius was his Piano Concerto No. 9, which was composed when he was 21 years old, some 18 years after he started his intensive study.

Similarly, golfer Rory McIlroy was introduced to golf at an exceptionally young age. His father Gerry, also a fine golfer, who had played at scratch handicap, started coaching his son when Rory was just 18 months old. At 22 he won his first major—the US Open—by eight shots with a record-breaking 16 under par. But this exceptional performance occurred some 20 years after he began his instruction.

These individuals, and many more like them, are undeniably talented. The point is, what is talent? Scientists have been trying to answer that question for more than 150 years. In the past three decades there has been a vast amount of research into this area and yet every study has concluded that *there is no such thing as natural talent.*

Certainly people have different skill levels and abilities but they were not born that way. Talent is nothing more than the natural consequence of persistent and disciplined practice over the long term. What makes Mozart and Rory McIlroy exceptional is that by the time the world came to know them they had honed their skills for thousands and thousands of hours over many years.

The researcher K. Anders Ericsson, who led one particular study into what it takes to reach mastery in any field, noted that while he and his team could not find evidence of natural gifts they did notice something else: no matter what the activity, excellence took years of disciplined practice to achieve. He concluded that excellence in any field takes 10 000 hours of deliberate practice. Neurologist Daniel Levitin agrees, stating, 'No-one has yet found a case in which true world-class expertise was accomplished in less time. It seems that it takes the brain this long to assimilate all that it needs to achieve true mastery'.

This is why it's so vital to take one idea and make it your life. As human beings, we have a finite amount of time to live. If we truly want to achieve something meaningful, then we must use our finite time constructively and back that one idea to the end. It doesn't matter whether we want to be a great golfer, musician, concert pianist or city builder, there is no short cut to mastery and there is no short cut to success. Success in anything demands time, attention and deliberate, real world action over the long term.

So forget about finding your 'thing'. Choose something that you enjoy and that you can get your teeth into right now and turn your back on everything else.

> It is a great thing to take up a grand ideal in life and then give up one's whole life to it. What otherwise is the value of life, this vegetating, little low life of man?

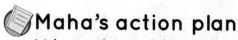Maha's action plan

Make *one idea* your life! In order to help you shift your thinking and incorporate this principle into your life you will need to:

➤ dedicate yourself to one thing

➤ make a start

➤ find others who align with your vision.

Dedicate yourself to one thing

If you ask Maha about his one big idea he will tell you it has been real estate and property development, and specifically the creation of Springfield as a fully master-planned city. But he will also tell you that it could have been anything. In university he was inspired by Nelson Mandela's fight to end apartheid in South Africa. He was incensed by racial division and he had read about Gandhi's work in South Africa too. Had he been in South Africa and not Australia, and had someone asked him to make social justice his definite major purpose, then he readily admits his life would have been very different. As it was, he married and decided that his aspirations to be a revolutionary or freedom fighter were unrealistic, and he turned his formidable focus on becoming successful in other ways.

Right now, what is it that you enjoy doing or dream of doing? Forget about some mysterious possible hidden talent; think about your life as it is right now. Do you like physical activity or mental activity? What are you already interested in? What are your strengths and weaknesses—what 'one idea' could tap into the strengths and minimise the weaknesses?

When Maha first read the self-help bible *Think and Grow Rich* by Napoleon Hill he was studying engineering at the University of New South Wales. This was his first exposure to the importance of having a definite major purpose and of focusing all your activity on one goal.

Above all be of single aim; have a legitimate and useful purpose, and devote yourself unreservedly to it.

—James Allen (American author of *As a Man Thinketh*)

For well over 20 years now Maha's definite major purpose has been the delivery of Springfield as a city and his determination to maintain the integrity of the vision and create a legacy that will positively affect hundreds of thousands of lives. This is not possible without full-time, round-the-clock commitment. Maha says, 'You have to go all out on one thing—you can't be a part-time anything and expect to be successful at it'. And it is this crucial first step that is central to Maha's personal philosophy: take a stand and choose one thing today; forget about every other possibility and dedicate yourself to mastering that one area.

Can you have more than one major MISSION pervading your life? NO. That could be like coming to a fork in the road and trying to go both ways by straddling it.

—Charles A. Garfield (American authority on high achievement)

Make a start

You have a finite amount of time in this life. If success is a consequence of at least 10000 hours of deliberate, disciplined practice and real-world experience, then you don't have time to be searching for the 'perfect idea'. Even if you threw yourself into something today and spent 10 hours a day every day immersed in this activity it would take you nearly three years to achieve mastery!

Spending precious time dipping in and out of things in the hope of uncovering some innate talent is a waste of time and energy. Talent will emerge in almost anything you do if you just make a commitment to it and put everything into it. What you choose is not of first importance; that you consciously choose something to dedicate yourself to is. Then you must make a start. There is no point thinking about what you plan to do forever. You have to get into action and break the inertia.

Maha remembers being greatly influenced by a Chinese colleague at his first job in Malaysia after graduating. Keen to soak up knowledge and learn from other people's experience, Maha was on the lookout for people who could teach him things that could accelerate his progress. Maha recalls, 'I have always been a very restless person and

I was amazed to find this other really restless character and how he just jumped into action. It didn't matter if he really knew what he was doing, he just did it and worked out how to make it better on the move. It was he who really showed me how important it was to make a start'.

---

*Though no-one can go back and make a brand new start,
anyone can start from now and make a brand new ending.*

—Carl Bard (American academic)

There is no doubt that Maha could have been successful in a number of areas. He chose property development because he came upon it during his journey. But he had the perseverance and drive to succeed that he could have applied in just about any area. And the same is true for you. So stop searching for the perfect idea, stop procrastinating and just make a start.

The secret of success is constancy of purpose.

—Benjamin Disraeli (British Prime Minister)

Find others who align with your vision

One of Maha's greatest gifts is his uncanny ability to work out what someone is capable of and how he can enlist those strengths for mutual gain while at the same time inspiring that person to deliver on their potential for their *own* motives. He is constantly seeking mutual benefit for everyone involved.

Think of this ability in terms of a Russian babushka or nesting doll. On the outside you will see one doll, but if you open it up you will find another inside it, and if you open that one you will find yet another, and so on. Springfield is like that. On the outside is an incredibly impressive city being constructed with full planning approvals for the future. If you open Springfield up, however, you will find a whole bunch of people each fulfilling their own unique ambitions and aspirations, which happen to align with the goals of the entire project. This is no accident but points to one of Maha's fundamental strengths—being able to find, and retain the commitment of, people whose own 'one idea' aligns with his. Where his idea was to create a magnificent city, his land and planning expert Barry Alexander, for example, wanted to secure ground-breaking planning approvals for a new city. That was his motivation and drive and he did just that. Sadly Barry passed away in 2011, but what he achieved through his own drive, determination and passion was unprecedented, and without those approvals the Springfield master plan would not exist.

To the person with a firm purpose, all men and things are servants.

—Johann Wolfgang von Goethe (German poet)

By finding other highly motivated, passionate people, Maha created an environment that allowed others to achieve their own personal goals within the context of the overall objective. Most people don't work just for money. They work for pride and a sense of achievement in what they have been able to accomplish. Maha is an expert at tapping into such motivations. His own people are driven for their own reasons, not just the company's, and that combination is an incredibly powerful force. So make sure you enlist the right people whose goals are aligned with the collective vision.

Individual commitment to a group effort—that is what makes a team work, a company work, a society work, a civilisation work.

—Vince Lombardi (famous American Football coach)

Chapter 2

Arise, awake and stop not till the goal is reached

Let us proclaim to every soul: Arise, awake and stop not till the goal is reached. Arise, awake! Awake from this hypnotism of weakness. None is really weak; the soul is infinite.

In the modern world the idea of longevity, of persistence and tenacity over the long term, seems to have gone out of fashion in favour of the quick fix, pseudo-celebrity and get-rich-quick schemes. We don't want distant goals, we want instant gratification—and as a result we end up with nothing. Or, as physicist and author E. H. Walker so eloquently put it, 'Think of the plans we make for our lives, and then we talk to ourselves within our minds about these plans. Our plans feed our day dreams. We stare out windows imagining loves fulfilled, futures blessed with success, riches, fame, recognition and respect. We hope, and we build ever more elaborate plans to hide our disillusionment as each hope slips away. Then one day, we awake to find ourselves buying lottery tickets to patch those ludicrous fantasies together as they turn to nothing'.

Unless you take the principle of long-term persistence to heart, all your plans will end as nothing more than ludicrous fantasies that turn to nothing. Nothing is achieved without effort and sacrifice, no matter how much we might wish it were otherwise.

When Maha and Bob Sharpless first moved to Brisbane in September 1985 they rented a little house in Spring Hill on the city fringe, which would be Bob's home and also double as their office. On the wall hung a wooden plaque and it was this second principle that was etched into it. It is a principle that has served Maha well, and the original plaque now hangs in the chairman's office on the tenth floor of Springfield Tower, corporate HQ for the Springfield Land Corporation (SLC), the privately owned company set up by Maha and Bob to develop Springfield.

Time is the only genuinely finite resource we have. Whether you're a king or a pauper, you have just 24 hours in every day. It is important that you use those precious hours effectively to make your one idea a reality, and that means you must get up — whether or not you want to or are fully awake — get into action and *stop not till the goal is reached*.

BE Engineering

His time at the University of New South Wales gave Maha perhaps his first adult experience of this principle. He knew the importance his parents placed on education and he was acutely aware of the sacrifices they had made to ensure that he and his siblings were educated well. But university was tough. He and his friend Ho would be at the library every morning as soon as it opened and rarely left until it closed. It appeared to be so much easier for local students. They seemed to do a fraction of the studying and there was always time for socialising and having fun. Maha and Ho, on the other hand, found the course extremely hard going and had little time for recreation.

At that time, if you failed any subject in a semester you had to repeat all subjects, not just the one you failed. As the course progressed the mathematics and physics units got harder and harder, and Maha and Ho failed on a number of occasions, finally having to repeat both the first and second years. Maha knew it was not easy for his father to find the money to support him. By the end of each month, without fail, Valipuram would send Maha a bank draft for £35, and Maha felt guilty about failing his subjects. In his regular letters home he explained his results, even though he knew it would distress his parents to learn the truth.

His father replied to every letter and Maha still remembers one particular reply...

'Son, I love you very much and I am sad that you have failed another exam. It is of no comfort, I know, but understand; only you can do it. I can finance you or pray for you but only you can sit for the exams. Like a woman who has to give birth, I can only stand by and help as I can. I cannot have that baby for her. She must do it. I cannot do your exam, or the next one, for you. Son, you can do it, and while I cannot do it for you, I love you and have faith in you.'

Maha took this message to heart. He knew he was the only one who could make it happen. 'This was a major turning point for me', he remembers. 'I wasn't talented in maths, physics or engineering but I wasn't going home without that degree, not after everything my parents had sacrificed to put me there.' Maha resolved to arise, awake and stop not till the goal was reached! The next day, he announced to Ho, 'This semester, it's going to be all-out war'.

One late afternoon Maha and Ho took a break from the library to sit outside in the sunshine. Maha remembers turning to Ho and cursing the course: 'Bloody hell, this course is a bastard. I don't know how we are going to make it, but I will tell you something, Ho. I am going to stay here until my cock hair is white if that's what it takes to finish this!' Ho now lives in Canada and he and Maha still laugh at this colourful description of determination and reminisce about how hard it was to get their respective qualifications. 'Getting into university was hard', recalls Maha. 'But getting out was even harder.'

In the end it took Maha six years to complete his degree. He knew it was *he* who had failed the subjects and it was therefore up to him to find a way to pay for the extra time at university. He asked if he could complete the degree part time so he could earn the money necessary to pay the fees himself. Although his father had told Maha he was happy to continue supporting him, he proudly acknowledged his son's growing independence. In pursuit of his engineering degree Maha worked as a taxi driver, studying in his breaks and time off as he juggled payment for the course as well as his rent. And he stopped not till his goal was reached.

~

At last he completed his degree and at graduation took his place alongside his fellow graduates, most of whom had completed the course in four years. Maha recalls, 'When my name was called, I could not believe that I had finally got my degree. It was the most momentous occasion in my life'.

The keynote speaker at the ceremony, an engineer and former graduate, described his 25 years' professional experience. He put the view that the most successful engineers were students who had struggled throughout their studies and refused to give up. In his experience, they made far better employees and carved out far more impressive careers than students with honours qualifications or exceptional grades who cruised through the course on intelligence alone. He described students who succeeded through sheer grit and force of will and who then carried these qualities into their careers. They stuck at difficult tasks until they were finished and they never quit. They made fewer mistakes because they doubted their ability and were much more likely to check and recheck their work, which always produced a higher standard. They sought innovative solutions to problems because they were more familiar with problems. And they had made enough mistakes in the past not to be scared of them but to understand that they offered an opportunity to learn even more. 'A good education', it has been said, 'is not so much one which prepares a man to succeed in the world, as one which enables him to sustain a failure'.

Maha was mesmerised. It was as though the engineer was talking directly to him, encouraging him to have faith in himself. He had thought that taking six years to complete his course instead of four was a failure or showed weakness, and yet here was a successful man telling him it may just reveal his greatest strength. He had done something uncommon: he had refused to give up. Maha recognised that you never fail *until you give up*. For the first time in his young life he realised that he possessed something that most people didn't—a fierce determination to see something through to the end. His failures had not been weaknesses but rather opportunities to develop his strengths. The qualification itself had not been the prize; the journey, with all its highs and lows, was the real reward. It was the means, not just the end, that was important.

Often we are so focused on the end that we forget about how that result is achieved.

Pay as much attention to the means of work as to its end ...With the means all right, the end must come. We forget that it is the cause that produces the effect; the effect cannot come by itself; and unless the causes are exact, proper and powerful, the effect will not be produced. When the cause is there, there is no more difficulty about the effect, the effect is bound to come. If we take care of the cause, the effect will take care of itself. The realisation of the ideal is the effect. The means are the cause: attention to the means, therefore, is the great secret of life.

The 'means' for Maha while at university (as ever since) was determination, tenacity and perseverance. Because he never gives up, the 'effect' or outcome is assured.

Education raises the bar for people. Learning new things is always useful, but when it also allows you to learn new things about yourself it is exponentially so. The power of education is not just in the certificate that tells the world you have qualified; it is becoming the person you need to become in order to get that certificate that is transformational.

Maha realised that through his struggles he had become a stronger man and he was reminded of a passage of ancient wisdom he'd read: 'You know how pearls are made. A parasite gets inside the shell and causes irritation, and the oyster throws a sort of enamelling round it, and this makes the pearl.' The pearl would not have been possible had the oyster not first been irritated, just as Maha's valuable engineering degree would not have been possible without all the difficulties he experienced.

Opossum Creek

The biggest and boldest goal Maha embraced in his life was the creation of a city on the land that was originally known as Opossum Creek, situated between Brisbane and Ipswich in Queensland, Australia.

Maha and Bob arrived in Brisbane in September 1985. Bob had started working with Maha in November 1984. He was told at the interview that there was no real vacancy and no money, and if he wanted to work with Maha he would be paid only on results. Bob, who was 27 at the time, accepted. He was young and ambitious and wanted to learn about property development from someone successful, although he now admits he didn't realise how bad Maha's financial position really was! What Bob did know, though, was that Maha was a fiercely determined, resilient and resourceful individual with a 'wicked' smile. And, perhaps more important, he liked him. So when Maha asked Bob to join him in Brisbane to rebuild the business Bob agreed. They have been business partners ever since.

It was a good 12 months before they began to make any money at all. Brisbane was a new city for Maha. They needed to foster new connections and extend the ones they already had, and it all took time. Eventually they got a few runs on the board and things really started to pick up. But Maha was increasingly restless. The business was growing well but he talked about his desire to do something really dramatic. A firm believer in the importance of mobilising all your skills and abilities to bring about an outcome that will uplift humanity, not just yourself, Maha was concerned that he was not using all his human capital.

In business planning meetings, the possibility of doing something big was stirring—an idea fuelled and encouraged by David Henry. Although Maha and Bob had employed an administrative assistant, David was the first development professional they hired in 1987. Maha had got wind that another entrepreneur was buying up land in Brisbane's Fortitude Valley and managed to secure one of the parcels he needed. The developer was livid, but he wanted the land so he negotiated with Maha and Bob to swap it for three other sites and some cash. When they decided to develop a couple of those sites they recognised that they needed a project manager to make it happen. David, who had a building degree, became an integral part of the Springfield team. Bob became good friends with David, whom he affectionately describes as a 'blue-arsed fly', because he was always on the move, would leap into action very quickly and powered through a huge amount of work. He had great organisation skills and was a brilliant project manager. He also worked well with Maha. They were kindred spirits, bound together by a shared love of land and development. The pair would travel around looking for larger and larger land parcels, and they saw the effects of unplanned development as Brisbane edged outward in an ad hoc and uncoordinated way. 'Look around you', David enthused. 'It's a mess already. I tell you, go to the States. They've built whole communities where all the land is zoned *en masse* for planned development stretching years into the future.'

Columbia, Maryland, between Baltimore and Washington, DC, was one such US development. Home to some 85 000 residents and 2500 businesses, Columbia was the brainchild of businessman-developer James Rouse and its creation was the greatest adventure of Rouse's life. In his famous speech in 1963 at the Metropolitan Future Conference held at University of California Berkeley, Rouse criticised the lack of planned growth and urban sprawl, warning, 'In our American cities today we do not have prepared or in-process plans that will account for the orderly growth of our population over the next 20 years. If we did have the plans, we would lack the powers to enforce them. If we had the plans and the powers, we would lack architects and urban designers with the sensitive concern—the people-centered attitude—required to fulfil their hope'.

According to Rouse, 'The biggest hole in the planning process … is right at the beginning of it. We aren't coming up with the right answers because we aren't asking the right questions at the outset. Planning deals with highways, land uses, public buildings, densities, open spaces, but it almost never deals with people. So seldom as to be never, in my experience, do you find in a planning study or report any serious discussion of the problems that people face in an urban society or how plans are directed at relieving those problems'. He suggested, 'We can't plan effectively for the future … unless we start at the beginning—and that beginning is people'.

This perspective inspired Maha, and he and David set out to visit 15 master-planned communities around the world. They went to Robina on Australia's Gold Coast, Joondalup in Western Australia and similar communities such as Reston in the US and Milton Keynes in the UK. Rouse talked of 'communities in which people feel important and uplifted'. That was inspiring. To create a city from scratch, built around the people who would use it so they feel important and uplifted—that was dramatic!

Imagine building a new city, applying the best planning principles to guide a high-quality development where people could live, learn, work and play. A place that would effectively combine residential neighbourhoods and schools, all forms of tertiary education, businesses and recreational areas, where roads were planned and built early, where public transport corridors were created to allow for future capacity. It would take guts and a great deal of money to build a four-lane freeway to a cow paddock miles outside the existing city boundary, but when that city grew out around it, as it surely would, people would praise the intelligence and foresight of the planners. Imagine a place where the developer could say, 'Come and live in a city where there are no traffic problems and you can live, study, shop and go to work all within just a few minutes of your home'. Yes, that really would be leading edge!

As he and David drove through the outskirts of Brisbane on their hunt for more land Maha began to see the landscape with fresh eyes. For years he had been focused on individual lots, but now he saw the blight that smaller, uncoordinated development left on the landscape. For years he had built hotels, shopping centres, houses and commercial buildings and sold land parcels. For years, like so many other developers, he had simply tacked onto what was already there. And the result was a haphazard urban sprawl that put increasing pressure on the infrastructure and services that were already there. Maha could see that like so many cities the world over Brisbane, and eventually Queensland, would be a mess if the growth continued to ooze outwards in a disorganised way. Growth was inevitable, but there had to be a better way to manage and plan for that growth.

George Bernard Shaw once said, 'Some men see things as they are and say, "Why?" I dream of things that never were, and say, "Why not".' Author James Allen went further: 'For true success ask yourself these four questions: Why? Why not? Why not me? Why not now?' Maha Sinnathamby also dreams of things that never were and asks, 'Why not, why not me and why not now'. Here was a project—to build a new city from scratch—that would need all his human capital to bring to fruition. It was the ultimate test of his perseverance and will, a chance to do something unique, to forge a legacy. It was an opportunity to do good business that also brought significant benefit to society.

> *Look here—we shall all die! Bear this in mind always, and then the spirit within will wake up. Then only, meanness will vanish from you, practicality in work will come, you will get new vigour in mind and body, and those who come in contact with you will also feel that they have really got something uplifting from you.*

Maha was hooked. And the search was on for a parcel of land big enough to accommodate a master-planned city.

~

When Associated Forest Holdings (AFH) decided to sell their six Queensland plantations in 1990, just such an opportunity presented itself. Comprising around 10 117 hectares and valued at many millions, the six forestry plantations had generated very little income in the previous year and the board instructed the AFH CEO to liquidate the assets. Initial interest was strong and all the parcels sold except one. Unfortunately for AFH, the one that didn't sell, known as Opossum Creek, was the largest. At 2860 hectares (7067 acres), Opossum Creek represented nearly a third of their total Queensland assets but no offer was tendered for the land. Although there was plenty of initial interest, the overwhelming economic realities soon extinguished any serious contenders. For a start it was a vast parcel of raw land—about 4.5 kilometres by 9 kilometres. There was only one regional road along one edge of the property and there was no water or other services to support development.

Everyone who had expressed interest asked whether they could purchase just a section of the land closest to the road. This section, they believed, was the only part where development was viable. The rest of the land was too isolated and almost worthless because of the lack of access or services. From the road the far reaches of the land were kilometres away and could not be developed for years, possibly decades. This had financial implications because the new buyer would effectively have to hold 'non-performing land' that would chew up resources needed elsewhere for what would surely be a long-term, capital-intensive development project. AFH was adamant that there could be no cherry picking, however. They knew that if they agreed to sell the best section they could be left with the rest for decades. This was an unusual piece of land, and AFH and their sales agent realised that they might have to wait for an equally unusual buyer.

Maha loved land. To him it was like a blank canvas whose only limits were his own imagination. Like an artist constantly searching for the perfect light or the perfect landscape to paint, Maha was constantly searching for the perfect land parcel that could ignite his dreams. Of course he knew of the AFH properties and had looked at all of them, including Opossum Creek. Although he couldn't see much of the property from Old Logan Road, the parcel looked promising on paper. It was reasonably close to existing development, but it was definitely the most daunting. The road where Maha had parked offered the only access to the land, and he wondered if it was wise to tackle such a monster without the necessary capital or experience. Maha recalls, 'I knew we didn't have the money but I kept thinking about it. I'd keep pulling out sales information and having another look. I kept seeing it being advertised so I knew it hadn't sold'.

The only way to make it viable would be to take an option contract on the land dependent on gaining suitable approvals for development. This strategy had worked well for Maha in the past; he secured the land for a period of time by paying the owner an option fee that was a fraction of the purchase price. This gave him the right but not the obligation to buy the land before or on an agreed date in the future for an agreed amount. He would then seek approvals to establish whether or not the project was viable. If it was, he could then exercise the option and buy the land. If it was not, then he would let the option expire and move on to the next project. Sometimes he and Bob would develop the property themselves; other times they would on-sell the development with approvals in place and bank the profit.

Maha and Bob owned some valuable assets but they had debts and there was little money in the bank. Buying in this way limited the outlay and significantly reduced the risk. It was a smart and profitable way to develop, especially for projects with a lifespan of one to two years. But using the same strategy for a project that would take decades to complete could be, at best, unpredictable. Holding land was expensive and there were sure to be one, possibly two, real estate downturns before the city was complete. If the land was not rising in value because of one of those downturns, then the cost of servicing the debt would escalate and everything could so easily come crashing down. Indeed this scenario is the cause of many large-scale development failures. Bold, audacious long-term developments are rarely completed by the company that starts them. The first company almost always goes broke and the project is sold on, with approvals in place, to another developer, who finishes the project and takes the glory and the profit. As for a master-planned city, there was no precedent anywhere in the world of a private enterprise successfully starting and completing such an ambitious project.

It was corporate suicide.

Like other developers before him, Maha had approached the sales agent regarding the possibility of dividing the land and buying only part of it but was told it was all or nothing. So he waited. After nine months he learned that Opossum Creek had still not sold. It was hardly surprising considering the challenges, yet had it not been for those challenges the land parcel *would* have sold and Springfield would not exist. To Maha, Opossum Creek's lack of appeal was a blessing rather than a curse. He and Bob did not have the money to buy the land outright and they could not afford to get into a price war over the property.

On impulse, in January 1991 Maha called the agent responsible for selling Opossum Creek. Perhaps the vendor would be more flexible now that developer after developer had turned their backs on this impossible prospect and all interest had apparently dried up. The agent seemed happy that Maha had called and the two agreed to meet to view the land together. The agent then encouraged the AFH CEO to meet directly with Maha, now the only interested party, and another site meeting was arranged. By now Bob was concerned, especially when Maha enthusiastically recounted how he had stood on the hill, looked out over the property and saw the 'beautiful face of a city' looking back at him. Despite this lofty vision Maha laid out a strategy that, while bold, was sound. They agreed to proceed, but to tread lightly.

~

Maha was energised by the words of his idol Gandhi, who said, 'You have to stand against the whole world although you may have to stand alone. You have to stare the world in the face although the world may look at you with bloodshot eye. Do not fear. Trust that little thing in you which resides in the heart and says: forsake friends, wife, all, but testify to that for which you have lived and for which you have died'. Opossum Creek was just the dramatic project Maha was looking for. It was bold—some would say insane—but Maha felt sure it was the right thing to do. As the ancient wisdom reminded him, 'Each work has to pass through these stages—ridicule, opposition, and then acceptance. Those who think ahead of their time are sure to be misunderstood'.

Several meetings and nine months later Maha called Bob from Melbourne Airport. 'Get David in the room', he said excitedly. A few moments later David and Bob were on speakerphone and Maha exclaimed, 'Listen up chaps! I've got it! I have got the land!'

In the end, with no other buyers in sight, AFH had agreed to Maha's terms. He would pay what AFH had asked for the property—it was $7.84 million with an additional option fee of $300 000, which would secure the land for a period of one year during which time Maha and Bob would seek approvals on the land most suitable for immediate development. If they got the approvals they would complete the sale contract, paying $3 million with the balance of $4.84 million to be paid five years after that. On top of this Maha and Bob would have to pay just under $400 000 a year in interest payable on the outstanding $4.84 million at 8 per cent per annum.

Maha yelled down the phone in delight: 'Over seven thousand acres! This is the largest piece of real estate in the country. We can do great things with this amount of land!' There was no response. Crestfallen that his excitement was clearly not shared, Maha shouted, 'What is wrong with you bastards? Why aren't you excited?' And before hanging up Maha added, 'Well, you blokes had better get your minds around this. Tomorrow, we are going to attack this hard. It's going to be all-out war!'

As the phone fell silent Bob and David looked at each other. But it wasn't delight *they* felt. Both had been aware of the possibility of the deal and knew it was progressing steadily, but now it was real. 'Shit', said Bob. 'Now it's over to us to make this work.' As David left the office he wondered whether he should feel guilty about encouraging Maha.

~

So began the biggest challenge of Maha's and Bob's lives. This was not a project that would be completed in two years. It wouldn't be completed in 20, possibly not even in 40 years. They had hardly any money in the bank and would have to borrow the $300 000 option fee from a friend. There was no way of knowing where or how they could raise the $3 million in a year, and there was going to be considerable expense involved in gaining the approvals. Now more than ever before everyone in the team would need to arise, awake and stop not till the goal was reached.

Opossum Creek became known as Greater Springfield and in 2011, some 20 years after the land was initially secured, the site was home to 23 000 residents while still only 13 per cent developed. It was never a project that was going to happen overnight. To bring a city to life when no-one else thought it was needed, smart or even possible was a long-term vision. And what has made Springfield unique is that what would be major goals in their own right—building projects such as roads, residential communities, shopping centres, schools and a university campus—were nothing more than stepping stones on the way to the realisation of the fully conceived vision.

On that very ridge overlooking Opossum Creek Maha Sinnathamby saw a new city. Today, through the combined efforts of Maha, Bob, Raynuha and their team and their collective commitment to arise, awake and stop not till the goal is reached, you can go to that same ridge and see the city that Maha imagined back in 1991.

Perseverance will finally conquer. Nothing can be done in a day.

The principle in action

There are countless historical examples of what can be achieved with determination and a willingness to arise, awake and stop not till the goal is reached. Perhaps one of the most ambitious was sending a man to the moon.

On 25 May 1961 President John F. Kennedy, in a Special Message to the Congress on Urgent National Needs, asked the US Congress for an increase in funds to send a man to the moon, to increase unmanned space exploration, to develop a nuclear-powered rocket and to advance satellite technology.

In his now famous speech, Kennedy said, 'I believe that this nation should commit itself to achieving the goal, before this decade is out, of landing a man on the moon and returning him safely to the earth. No single space project in this period will be more impressive to mankind, or more important for the long-range exploration of space; and none will be so difficult or expensive to accomplish'.

This was indeed a bold objective. He acknowledged that the Soviets had a head start. They had already developed large rocket engines, which gave them a lead time of many months over the Americans. But this did not dissuade him. 'We nevertheless are required to make new efforts on our own—for while we cannot guarantee that we shall one day be first, we can guarantee that any failure to make this effort will make us last.' Success is never guaranteed, but failure to try will *always* guarantee failure.

Kennedy knew what needed to be done and everyone involved was under no illusions about the difficulties and expense of the road ahead. But making the commitment to the world so publicly was a stroke of political genius. He didn't tell the American people that they were going to the moon, he asked them. He laid out what the extra money would be used for and the burden it would inflict, adding, 'But in a very real sense, it will not be one man going to the moon—if we make this judgment affirmatively, it will be an entire nation. For all of us must work to put him there...'

'Let it be clear—and this is a judgment which the Members of the Congress must finally make—let it be clear that I am asking the Congress and the country to accept a firm commitment to a new course of action—a course which will last for many years and carry very heavy costs: $531 million dollars in fiscal '62—an estimated seven to nine billion dollars additional over the next five years. If we are to go only half way, or reduce our sights in the face of difficulty, in my judgment it would be better not to go at all... This decision demands a major national commitment of scientific and technical manpower, material and facilities, and the possibility of their diversion from other important activities where they are already thinly spread. It means a degree of dedication, organisation and discipline which have not always characterised our research and development efforts.'

By unveiling a bold vision and being honest about the hardship and sacrifice needed to accomplish it, and how each person must play his or her part, the President inspired a nation. All of those directly involved in the project, including the scientists, engineers and technicians, were asked to lay all else aside and arise, awake and stop not till the goal was reached. The American people were told plainly that if they agreed to the goal it would mean an all-out effort and there could be no turning back or compromising along the way. Kennedy acknowledged that despite all the money, effort and sacrifice, they might not win, but he encouraged the nation to appreciate that if they did not at least try their failure was guaranteed.

Some considered the dream to be crazy; others saw it as a strategic move in the Cold War between the United States and the Soviet Union. Kennedy was concerned about the 'march of Communism' and had recently been humiliated in the Bay of Pigs fiasco in Cuba. Whatever his motivation, the vision was dramatic. In today's money, he was petitioning Congress for some $3.2 billion with a further $64 billion over the coming five years, and that was just for the space program. But it was the boldness of the vision that made it so appealing. Kennedy often said in subsequent speeches, 'We choose to go to the moon in this decade, not because [it is] easy, but because [it is] hard'.

Kennedy did not live to see the fruition of his vision when, on 20 July 1969, Apollo 11 commander Neil Armstrong stepped off the Lunar Module onto the moon's surface and spoke the immortal words: 'That's one small step for man, one giant leap for mankind'.

Are great things ever done smoothly? Time, patience, and indomitable will must show.

What this principle means for you

The essence of this principle is relentless forward motion and productivity. There are few certainties in life, but one of them is that tomorrow the sun will rise on a new day and that new day will have exactly the same allocation of time as yesterday and tomorrow. Everyone can draw on 24 hours every day. Barring a global catastrophe, tomorrow will arrive on schedule and it's your responsibility to make the most of its possibilities.

This principle is a central element of Maha's approach to life. His appreciation of time emerged while he was at university, where he juggled classes with working to support himself. Every moment was precious and needed to be used productively. 'I remember I used to wear a shirt and jacket most of the time but to save time I'd only iron the front panel of the shirt that was visible under the jacket. There were a few times when it got warm that I wanted to take my jacket off but I couldn't because the rest of the shirt was crumpled! I knew one thing very clearly—a second gone is a second gone forever. There is no way of recovering it so I was always on the run. I placed great importance on what had to be done and never wasted a moment.'

You can't make the most of every opportunity lying in bed. You need to get into action early and pack as much as possible into your day, staying in motion until the goal is reached, whatever that goal might be! Now over 70 years old, Maha still has the energy of a man half his age. He's been an early riser all his life, getting up before 4.00 am most mornings, and has instilled the routine in his children. Interestingly, this habit was not something his parents drummed into him from an early age; it started out of necessity when he was at university, while living with other students who spent more time partying than studying. Maha didn't have that luxury, however, especially when he was also working as a taxi driver. He found that when he wanted to sleep he couldn't because his flatmates were coming in late and making too much noise, so he would have his dinner at about 8.00 pm and go to bed just as everyone else left to go out for the night. He would then get a good night's sleep and get up again in the early hours of the morning, as his fellow students stumbled home from their partying. That way he was able to get enough rest and enough quiet time to get through his work.

These days Maha uses the quiet time at the start of the day to collect his thoughts and it is this time, when most people are asleep, that he often finds the most productive. The peace and tranquillity allow him to turn his attention to critical decisions and prepare for what's ahead.

With no interruptions or distractions he is able to think creatively and strategise about how best to reach his goal.

Without preparation, time is always wasted and productivity drops. The power of this principle is fully realised only when you have taken one idea and made it your life. Without this focus to guide your activity it is too easy to fritter away your energies being busy but not necessarily productive. Without a clear purpose to guide your activity you will waste time, energy and resources.

Think of it as like digging a well in search of water. You could choose a promising location and start digging and you might be lucky enough to find water immediately, but it's unlikely. More probably you will dig for several hours, become disheartened and abandon the site to start digging somewhere else. Without the resolution to stay in one place and work diligently towards the goal, pretty soon you will have dug half a dozen holes and none of them will have struck water. You may be tired and others may assume you are busy, but the minute you jumped from one location to another you nullified all previous effort. If, on the other hand, you had stayed with your original choice and kept digging beyond the despondency, you probably *would* eventually have found water. In the end you've wasted your time, energy and resources looking for something that might have been reached with a little more perseverance.

This is why the first and second principles are so vital to success. Without a central focus it's too easy to get sidetracked and to find your day slipping away from you. At the end of the day you wonder what exactly you achieved.

There is a great old story about productivity and how the drive towards a single outcome can yield dividends for individuals and companies. In the 1920s the American steel magnate Charles Schwab was troubled by management productivity problems at Bethlehem Steel. In an attempt to find a solution he asked Ivy Lee to help. Lee, the man considered to be the father of modern public relations, offered to solve his problem on the spot and promised to give him the secret of time management. All Schwab had to do was implement the system for one week and then send him a cheque for what he felt the advice was worth.

The system was simple. At the end of every day all the managers had to make a list of their top six priorities. They were then to rank the list in order of importance. At the start of each new day the manager was to work on the number one priority until it was achieved or until no further action could be taken to advance the task at that time. Then and only then were they to move to priority number two and repeat the process.

The system was so successful that within a matter of weeks Charles Schwab voluntarily sent Lee a cheque for $25 000.

Relentlessly pursuing tasks towards a stated vision—day in, day out—will always yield results. So arise, awake and stop not till the goal is reached. It is the consistency of action together with the willingness to squeeze as much into the day as possible that can transform results.

This principle reminds us of the importance of *all* tasks—big and small, enjoyed and dreaded. Everything must be done in its own time without delay. Ivy Lee's advice focused the managers' attention on what needed to be done instead of what they wanted to do. The managers were no longer able to favour the easy tasks or the activities they most enjoyed or were most suited to. The priority of the work, not personal whim or preference, dictated when it was done. And productivity was transformed as a result.

Using time wisely and productively is critical to success. Time is your most valuable resource. As American management consultant Peter Drucker once said, 'One cannot buy, rent or hire more time. The supply of time is totally inelastic. No matter how high the demand, the supply will not go up. There is no price for it. Time is totally perishable and cannot be stored. Yesterday's time is gone forever, and will never come back. Time is always in short supply. There is no substitute for time. Everything requires time. All work takes place in and uses up time. Yet most people take for granted this unique, irreplaceable and necessary resource'.

If you are serious about creating success in your life, then use your time wisely, choose a target and get into action towards that target. That is the only sure-fire way to succeed.

Don't look back—forward, infinite energy, infinite enthusiasm, infinite daring, and infinite patience—then alone can great deeds be accomplished.

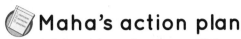Maha's action plan

Arise, awake and stop not till the goal is reached! In order to help you shift your thinking and incorporate this second principle into your life you will need to:

➤ create a bold vision

➤ rise early

➤ be productive.

Create a bold vision

The previous principle was about choosing an idea or area on which to focus your attention. Maha's central theme became real estate, land and development. But it was only when he developed the bold vision to create a new city that stellar success became possible.

What is it that you want to create? What grand vision do you have of the legacy you want to pass down? What will people say about you after you have gone? What will you most regret *not* doing? Use these questions to sculpt your bold vision, and make it known.

When Maha began Springfield he told everyone about it. He went about town telling everyone who would listen about the new city that was going to be built. Those who came to the site for the 'Springfield tour' would be taken up to the top of a purpose-built viewing tower in the middle of the dust bowl where a receptionist would serve scones! Maha would point enthusiastically to different areas and talk of the various facilities and features that would eventually embellish the land. This became known by his team as 'Maha's Disneyland Spiel'—an elaborate fantasy about schools and university, cutting-edge IT and state-of-the-art health facilities in the heart of Springfield. Yoga still remembers the looks of utter disbelief, pity and outright ridicule that would cross people's faces as they listened to Maha talk about Springfield. As the Roman poet Ovid once wrote, 'A new idea is delicate. It can be killed by a sneer or a yawn; it can be stabbed to death by a quip and worried to death by a frown on the right man's brow'. But for Maha it wasn't fantasy; it was prophecy. He knew in the early days there were very few true believers, but it didn't matter. Because the people who were making it happen *did* believe.

Bless people when they revile you. Think how much good they are doing by helping to stamp out the false ego. Hold fast to the real Self. Think only pure thoughts, and you will accomplish more than a regiment of mere preachers.

When John F. Kennedy announced his bold vision of landing a man on the moon he said, 'We take an additional risk by making it in full view of the world, this very risk enhances our stature when we are successful'. Kennedy knew that such a public declaration of intent massively raised the stakes and added a huge amount of pressure to the people who would make it possible. Once they had committed they would not want to lose face and would use that pressure to ensure they succeeded. Maha did the same thing through his constant proclamations of the new city. He was so sure that Springfield would happen, and that somehow he and his team would find a way past every obstacle, that he organised for Queensland's Deputy Premier to open Springfield before he and Bob even officially owned the land!

Good business leaders create a vision, articulate the vision, passionately own the vision, and relentlessly drive it to completion.

—Jack Welch (former CEO of GE)

This sort of audacity does add considerable pressure for Maha and his team, and certainly Bob would have preferred to work quietly and anonymously towards the goal instead of hearing it broadcast from the rooftops. But bold and confident was always Maha's way. The potential humiliation of defeat added extra juice to the tank and inspired greater effort. People mocked Maha openly, but he used that to propel him forward, as a spur to ensure that he and Bob would have the last laugh. And they did.

Throughout the centuries there were men who took first steps, down new roads, armed with nothing but their own vision.

—Ayn Rand (Russian–American novelist and philosopher)

Rise early

You have only a finite amount of time on the planet and you need to use that time constructively if you want to achieve success. Often the best place to 'recover' time is to get out of bed earlier.

Maha rises before 4.00 am most days, but the purpose of these 'action steps' is to encourage *you* to take action so you can build the muscles necessary for success and create positive new habits. If you aren't habitually an early riser, demanding that you start getting up before 4.00 am is a tall order. Instead, consider joining the six o'clock club. Set your alarm for 6.00 am and when it sounds arise, awake and stop not till the goal is reached. You won't be fully awake at first, but get up anyway and get on with your day. If you have a tendency to hit the snooze button, put the alarm clock out of reach so you have to get out of bed to turn it off! You will soon get used to rising earlier and those extra few hours you gain will feel like double their length.

Maha is not the only exponent of early rising. The Greek philosopher Aristotle wrote, 'It is well to be up before daybreak, for such habits contribute to health, wealth, and wisdom'. Benjamin Franklin, one of America's Founding Fathers, believed that only a few men live to old age and fewer still become successful who are not early risers! And billionaire American oil tycoon J. Paul Getty encapsulated his success in the dictum 'Rise early, work hard, strike oil'.

Success is not complicated. It requires sacrifices, including of a certain amount of leisure time. If you are serious about your future and about making an impact and creating something meaningful in your life, then you should turn off the TV and limit any activities that do not align with your purpose.

We must use time wisely and forever realise that the time is always ripe to do right.

—Nelson Mandela (former South African president)

If time be of all things the most precious, wasting time must be the greatest prodigality.

—Benjamin Franklin (one of America's Founding Fathers)

Be productive

Ever since Maha's university years he has sought to make every minute count and be as productive as humanly possible. Today his shirts, both the visible *and* non-visible parts, are properly ironed, but he still has a few productivity tricks up his sleeve. For example, he records the local and international news and fast forwards through the stories that are not relevant. He can read the local paper in six minutes and *The Australian Financial Review* in seven because he zeroes in on what matters to him and his goal.

Every major development around the world involves two things—people and money. Springfield began with neither. Nowhere else in the world is there a comparable example of a master-planned city or community being created by a small, privately owned company with very limited funds. Building a city from scratch is a massive undertaking. Just to bring roads, water, power and sewerage systems to the site demands the outlay of hundreds of millions of dollars. Every other master-planned community in the world has been built either by large, cash-rich public companies or with government backing. They were made possible by the collective efforts of hundreds of people. Springfield, on the other hand, was made a reality by the collective efforts of just seven extremely committed and productive individuals—Maha Sinnathamby, Bob Sharpless, David Henry, Barry Alexander, Malcolm Finlayson, Raynuha Sinnathamby and Ian Keilar. And what they have been able to achieve against unprecedented odds is nothing short of astonishing.

No matter how insignificant the thing you have to do, do it as well as you can, give it as much of your care and attention as you would give to the thing that you regard as most important.

—Mahatma Mohandas Gandhi (political leader)

You must learn to be productive. If you are unsure where to start, then try Ivy Lee's advice. Make a list of your most important outcomes and prioritise them from most to least important. Once you know what is the most important outcome, focus all your time and attention on completing the necessary tasks towards achieving it. Do everything humanly possible to progress it every day. Persist until it is complete or you reach a stage where you can't advance the outcome any further for the time being. Then, and only then, move on to priority number two.

Don't pick and choose tasks based on what you feel like doing. As Maha's ancient wisdom reminds us, 'Those who grumble at the little thing that has fallen to their lot to do will grumble at everything. Always grumbling they will lead a miserable life ... But those who do their duty putting their shoulder to the wheel will see the light, and higher and higher duties will fall to their share'. Do everything that is required according to outcome, not preference. And give everything you have to the task.

You've got to give great tools to small teams. Pick good people, use small teams and give them great tools so that they are very productive in terms of what they are doing.

— Bill Gates (founder of Microsoft)

Chapter 3
Work relentlessly

You have the right to work, but do not become so degenerate as to look for results. Work incessantly, but see something behind the work. Even good deeds can find a man in great bondage. Therefore be not bound by good deeds or by desire for name and fame.

The power of Maha's 10 principles is cumulative. Each fosters and facilitates the others, and they work together to generate forward positive motion, which creates a virtuous cycle. First you make one idea your life, then you arise, awake and stop not till the goal is reached, then you work relentlessly. But this principle also warns against becoming too attached to the goal. When all that matters is the goal, the way in which the goal is achieved can sometimes be lost sight of, and that is dangerous. Don't get so attached to the goal that you compromise the journey towards that goal.

Gandhi worked single-mindedly for 30 years to secure Indian Independence. He endured hardship and imprisonment. He never complained about the setbacks along the way but just did the work and kept going. And when the battle was finally won and India was returned to her people Gandhi didn't celebrate or gloat. He saw his role as to do the work to achieve the goal and that was all. With unrelenting work the outcome was assured and celebration wasn't needed. In an amazing example of principle, Gandhi refused to attend the handing-over ceremony and continued to work, demonstrating humility by cleaning toilets.

Your only task is to work relentlessly; forget about the reward. Success in any field is the result of consistent effort. When you reach your goal, don't dissipate the energy by gloating or endless celebration; instead just keep working still further. You should always enjoy your accomplishments and the wins along the journey, but don't ever take your foot off the accelerator or you will lose energy and momentum.

There are certain laws that govern the universe, and cause and effect is one of them. If you work relentlessly, monitoring your results to finetune your effort, then you *will* reach your goal. The measure of your success therefore depends on the scale of your ambition and your willingness to work. And the outcome is rarely instant.

Success or failure boils down to the price you are willing to pay and the exchange in time, effort and perseverance you are willing to make. People without talent, innovative ideas or ability who want to be famous may appear on a reality TV show or sell some scandal to a newspaper. People who want to be rich without effort may buy a lottery ticket—easy, but let's face it, the odds aren't good. Statistically speaking, you are three times more likely to be killed in a car accident while driving to buy your lottery ticket than you are of actually winning the jackpot. If you played golf with four people, the chances of two of you making a hole in one on the same hole are better than your chances of winning a lottery jackpot.

Some would argue that there are plenty of people in the world who work hard but have never experienced wealth or success. This is true, but not everyone aspires to wealth and success. For some the knowledge that they have made a contribution and taken care of their family is reward enough. The reward is the work itself. Nothing can be more debilitating for the soul than lack of work. The American actress Katharine Hepburn once said, 'I don't think that work ever really destroyed anybody. I think that lack of work destroys them a hell of a lot more'.

Perth, Australia 1971

When Maha returned to Malaysia on completing his engineering degree, he was restless. He soon secured a job and was doing well in a big international engineering firm. The company undertook major development assignments with clients such as the World Bank and the Asian Development Bank. It was interesting and challenging work, but Maha was still restless.

One of the things Maha loves most in the world is a deadline. He's an impatient man and his plans for the future were progressing a little more slowly than he had hoped. On a personal level he was 26 years old and it was about time he got married. Arranged marriages were still the norm and Maha learned of his match to Yoga, daughter of a Sri Lankan businessman.

A successful entrepreneur with significant real estate interests and a strong belief in the importance of education, Yoga's father had enthusiastically funded years of university study for four of his children. By the time Yoga and her older sister were ready for university, however, his health was failing and he was not in a position to send them overseas to be educated. Also weighing heavily on him was his responsibility as an Indian father to ensure his six daughters were securely married before he died. Not only were his two youngest daughters yet to complete their education but they were both still unmarried. Thankfully they were also very bright and both won nursing scholarships, which helped solve the financial challenge at least. Yoga and her sister travelled to the United Kingdom to study nursing, leaving their father to worry about his one remaining challenge.

Within three months of Yoga's sister's return from the UK she was married and soon after she became an expectant mother. Yoga knew it was only a matter of time before she would be expected to follow suit, and while she accepted the custom of an arranged marriage she was determined to delay any match for as long as possible. As a newly qualified nurse she wanted to work for a time first and use the new skills she had acquired in the UK. It just didn't make sense—all that hard work to win the scholarship, the study overseas and the professional qualification, only to marry and never use them. So when her father invited her to take a drive in his car, a very rare occurrence, Yoga was on high alert! Sri Lankan fathers are notoriously adept at emotional blackmail, especially when it comes to their daughters. Yoga's father reminded her of his two heart attacks and how essential it was that she be married before he died. He waxed lyrical about the respected Sinnathamby family and talked of Maha's 'solid grades' at university in Sydney. Yoga was unmoved. 'Leave me alone for a year', she insisted. 'I don't want to know about any of this and if you force it I will go back to the UK.'

These were strong words from daughter to father, but he appeared to drop the matter. Although she was taken to dinner at the Sinnathamby house, she didn't think too much about these evenings, especially as she was never formally introduced to Maha. She would dutifully stay for as short a time as she felt was polite before excusing herself.

One day her brother returned from Kuala Lumpur, where he worked as a doctor, and on seeing Yoga announced, 'So! I hear you're to be married'. Incensed, Yoga snapped, 'You're talking nonsense. I know nothing about marriage. Do you see a ring on my finger?' Her brother looked shocked and tried to calm her down. 'I'm sorry, I thought you must know. Father told me. Do you really not know? I understood he has been planning this since you returned.'

Yoga was livid. Evidently her father had been quietly planning the marriage ever since their first discussion and had even told other people about the arrangements. She was the last to know. This approach was not uncommon by fathers of unwilling daughters: the timing of the marriage was delayed a little, the groom was reassured, the arrangements were made quietly and the bride only told close to the day. Sure enough, soon afterwards Yoga's father invited her to take another drive in the car and Yoga knew it must be true.

She was told she would be marrying Mahalingam Sinnathamby, an upstanding engineer. A year had passed, her father's health had not improved and she dutifully accepted his wishes. They were married soon after—Maha was 28, Yoga was 22—and they welcomed their first child, Uma, into the world nine months later.

~

As he settled into married life, Maha became increasingly restless and spoke constantly of returning to Australia, to the increasing exasperation of his family. They had two daughters, a very comfortable lifestyle with a driver and two maids, and Maha had a wonderful job. Yet he felt unchallenged and understimulated. Finally his brother intervened: 'Stop mucking around. Make up your mind. Go. The number one thing your family wants is for you to be happy'.

Thirty days later Maha boarded a plane to Perth. He arrived in October 1971 with his life savings of $17 000. Maha had called himself Eddie at university, so he decided to keep the name Edward but adopt a more professional derivative and chose 'Ted'. It was agreed that Yoga, who was expecting their third child, would join Maha after the birth. This would give Maha time to establish himself and find a suitable home for his expanding family.

Maha's eldest brother already lived in Perth so initially he stayed in a small room at the rear of his brother's veterinary practice, but he was determined it would be only temporary. When he got to know the city, he would decide where it was best to live, but first he needed to secure a job. Having identified all the companies in the area who would need the services of a civil engineer, he wrote 42 letters to potential employers. He didn't receive a single reply. He put on his best suit and visited the Commonwealth Professional Employment Service (CPES) to register for work. The officer handling his application was not optimistic.

Maha had arrived in Australia towards the end of what was known as the 'long boom'. Perth was in economic downturn. From the start of the 1970s instability in the world economy and weakness in the home economy ended Australia's experience of the postwar boom and employment fell. There was no work for engineers, in fact no work for anyone. With the demise of the mining boom, the economy had collapsed.

On returning to the CPES a week later, he was advised to register for the dole. Reluctantly, Maha went to the dole office and was forced to accept that the employment services officer might be right, as it was by far the busiest place in the city. This must be a serious recession.

Dressed in his best suit and polished shoes Maha joined the long dole queue. As he inched forward, he thought about his predicament. A week ago the world wanted him. Before he resigned his post in Malaysia he'd been told by his boss that they had selected him to head their Indonesian office. But he'd turned his back on that opportunity. Now he was standing in a queue to register for unemployment benefits, his wife and children were thousands of miles away and now their very survival was threatened! This wasn't how it was supposed to be! Maha was devastated. Glancing up at the wall clock he realised he'd been in the queue only a few minutes yet it felt like a lifetime. Tears pricked his eyes and he stepped out of the line when he couldn't suppress his emotion any longer. Covering his eyes he pushed his way clear of the crowd. Outside Maha jumped into the first available taxi and broke down and cried, barely able to give the driver instructions.

Back home, Maha's brother apologised for encouraging him to come to Australia. He had not realised how bad the economic situation was; as a vet his business depended on sick and injured animals, not on market cycles. He felt guilty and responsible for Maha's distress and suggested he return to Malaysia—perhaps the job offer he'd turned down would still be open. This proposal was enough to jolt Maha out of his grief. 'No, I will rise again. I will make it here. The opportunity is out there somewhere. It is just a matter of finding it.' There was no going back; he must close the exits and push forward. He would find a way.

With no salaried positions available, Maha would go from business to business and just speak to the owners. He felt sure that if he kept his mind open and kept looking he would find the right person. Australia was still a predominantly white, monocultural country, so he had set himself a considerable challenge, but Maha didn't give his ethnicity a second thought. He spoke good English. He stayed focused on finding the right person.

Did Maha, a Sri Lankan migrant from Malaysia, experience racism and therefore find it especially hard in his adopted country? If you were to ask him he would immediately dismiss the question. Maha says quite simply, 'I've never, ever had in my mind that I'm any different from anyone else. To me racism is a man-made excuse not to perform'. He never expected to be treated differently and so he wasn't treated differently. Even when he was working as a taxi driver through university he would always be cheerful and friendly, and invariably people would be cheerful and friendly back.

Maha's approach has always been the same: stay upbeat and positive and expect the best from others. One day he entered a real estate office and struck up a conversation with the owner. The agent was really friendly and liked Maha's positive outlook and style. Maha had spent countless hours discussing real estate with his father-in-law and already knew some of the concepts and principles from years of talking business with him. The agent was clearly impressed, and Maha got his first job in Australia as a real estate salesman. It was unsalaried and he wouldn't get paid until he sold something, but he didn't care—he had a job! He had his start.

Maha worked tirelessly in his new profession and became *utterly* dedicated to learning the real estate trade. He rose before 4.00 am, bought the newspaper as soon as it was available and studied every property for sale in Perth from Applecross to Wanneroo. He called the agents and they would often drive Maha around to look at their properties. He walked the streets of Perth and asked questions. While the other agents hung around the office listlessly, he was on the move. He looked at every agent's window and physically inspected hundreds of properties. Maha was amazed at how much information and free advice was available. If he asked the right questions he could easily learn about the attributes and problems of the property and the reason it was on the market, and why it should sell for a certain amount. Agents loved talking property and Maha soaked it up. The agents answered his questions about council planning regulations and how to get houses extended or demolished, and ways of getting land rezoned. Within a few weeks of becoming a registered real estate salesman, Maha knew every suburb and street in Perth. He soon came to know *every* property type for sale and its relative worth.

Maha has always had the ability to make people feel comfortable. He is engaging and charismatic while also being very persuasive, which proved to be a powerful combination. As a result, he needed next to no training and was perfectly suited to sales. Maha was in his element.

With only a few months before Yoga and the children would arrive Maha found an old house on the esplanade, opposite the Swan River. The house was run-down and far from perfect but he bought it for $18000, financed by a $10000 loan from the bank and a further $8000 loan from his brother. Maha wrote proudly to Yoga that he was 'in business' and that the Sinnathambys officially had an Australian home opposite a beautiful, blue river. Now being a master salesman, he didn't feel it wise to mention the fact that he wasn't being paid or that the house was shabby and next to a petrol station! It was important to manage perceptions—something else Maha had learned through his real estate education. There was a different language in the industry and positive spin was essential.

In December 1971 Yoga telephoned Maha to tell him that she had given birth to another daughter. They agreed on the name Meera and that everyone would come to Australia in January.

He had come a long way. In three months he had suffered the humiliation of the dole queue and the reality of a depressed economy, but he had refused to give up on himself, refused to apply for the dole and continued to work relentlessly. He was now a registered real estate agent and a homeowner. Not bad for three months' work.

~

Yoga and the three children arrived in January 1972 and Yoga did her best to hide her disappointment when they drove up to their new home. For months she had been trying to determine what 'in business' actually meant and finally Maha relented: 'I don't have a proper job yet. There is no work for engineers so I have started in the real estate business. I have learned all about property, and I have made a few sales'. With a family to support Yoga was deeply concerned by this revelation.

For Yoga, arriving in Australia with three little girls was the absolute 'worst of times'. She had left behind a life of security and prosperity in Malaysia along with her family network and support system at the very time she needed it most. She had also left a good nursing job in the public hospital and a comfortable home. As was customary in Malaysia, Yoga had had a driver and maid who would take care of all the household chores including cooking. Now here she was in a strange country, in a dilapidated house filled with petrol fumes, with three small children, no cooking skills, no friends and a dreamer of a husband.

Although she never questioned Maha's commitment or faith in his ability to create a better life, she was grounded in the daily realities of finding enough money to feed the family and was constantly worried about where that money would come from. Yoga still remembers Maha heading off to work full of enthusiasm and excitement for what the day might bring while she sat quietly in the kitchen, sobbing for the life she had left behind.

For all that Yoga yearned for a better house and more stable income, she supported her husband and never showed her disappointment to him. She shopped at a discount grocery store. A retired farmer lived nearby and asked Maha and Yoga if he could use the garden behind their house to grow vegetables. They agreed and in return the farmer kept them well supplied with vegetables. But having the produce and knowing what to do with it were two different things! Yoga had always lived in a home with kitchen help so she had never learned how to cook. Now, thousands of kilometres from home, with three young children, she felt inadequate and upset that she couldn't prepare a basic meal for her family. Yoga recalls, 'I couldn't even boil rice. So I had to learn how to cook from scratch and my husband taught me. He'd learned how to cook in university and said you just throw everything in a pot and hit it heavy with the curry powder. In those early months in Perth my reading material every night was cookbooks.'

One of the family's favourite anecdotes, which still makes everyone laugh, is 'the spaghetti story'. When Yoga had been studying nursing in the UK, one of her friends used to make this spaghetti dish that was really tasty. 'She would put mince, carrots, cayenne pepper, cauliflower and tomato soup in a pan and boil it up. One day when I was in Perth I really fancied that spaghetti dish so I decided that it hadn't looked that complicated and I'd give it a try. The shops were just over the road so when the children were sleeping I raced over to the shops, grabbed what I needed and raced back. So I did what I remembered my friend doing back in the UK and dished it up. My husband took his first mouthful and I saw his face screw up and then he spat it out! In my rush to get the ingredients while the kids were sleeping, I'd bought kangaroo pet mince!'

Today Yoga is an excellent cook but she really struggled in those early months. So when a letter arrived from the Metropolitan Water Board just before Easter 1972 offering Maha a job, Yoga was thrilled. Finally the family would have a more solid financial footing and she felt the burden of worry and stress lift a little. But when she rushed to greet Maha with the welcome news as he arrived home from work it was clear he did not share her enthusiasm.

The job offer, made in response to one of the letters Maha had sent out some seven months before, offered an annual salary of $7500, but Maha was happy doing real estate. He felt free and exhilarated by the possibilities. The idea of taking a salaried job felt suddenly claustrophobic and he pleaded with Yoga: 'I don't want to live my life in captivity working for other blokes. I want to be in the wild'. But Yoga was firm: 'You cannot be a wild animal. You have been on your own for a few months but you have a family'. Yoga looked across at the children and the condition of the house. '*We* need you to take this position. *Please!*'

Maha commenced at the Water Board a week after Easter. He could have started earlier and been paid for the holiday but he was dragging his heels, much to his new boss's confusion. As always, he worked tenaciously, got his work completed and spent the rest of the time planning his escape. He lived a double life—as a water engineer by day and a real estate trader the rest of the time. Every Saturday while Yoga went to work as a part-time nurse, Maha would bundle his three children into their secondhand station wagon and drive for miles on 'sight-seeing' adventures. On his lap was the newspaper, with the 'sights' of interest already circled in red pen. For hours they would drive around the suburbs of Perth viewing property while he taught his children about real estate and land value. Needless to say the children, aged four, two and a half and one, were not always enthusiastic recipients of his property insights, but they could usually be bribed into acquiescence with an ice-cream.

When the Water Board hired two graduates, one of them, Ken Law-Davis, sat opposite Maha and over the course of two years was bombarded with his real estate ideas and plans. Over time Ken became more and more interested. If you have the opportunity to meet Maha you will realise Ken didn't have much choice. Maha is a very passionate and persuasive individual. So when he announced he was going to leave the Water Board and strike out on his own he asked Ken to join him. Still, it would be a bold and brave move for Ken, given that he was a strict nine-to-fiver and could be found most weekends riding a surfboard off one of Perth's beaches.

Having lined up a few development projects to kickstart the business, Maha resigned in 1976. His boss, surprised that anyone would willingly leave the public service, warned Maha of the dangers of his new business venture and sternly reminded him that 'those who live by the sword will die by the sword'. A few weeks later Ken also resigned and the two of them started Murdoch Constructions with combined seed funding of $17 000, Maha as the major shareholder owning 75 per cent of the business and Ken owning the remaining 25 per cent. By working relentlessly, planning for the future and refusing to be constrained by convention, Maha was back in the wild, where he belonged.

Your country requires heroes; be heroes; your duty is to go on working, and then everything will follow of itself.

One year to find $3 million

When it came to hard work and tenacity, Springfield was by far the most intense and complex challenge Maha and Bob had ever faced. Yoga still remembers when she first saw the land. She had of course heard Maha talk about the development at Opossum Creek but didn't visit the property until after they had bought it. Maha insisted they take a drive out to see the land and was obviously extremely excited. Yoga recalls, 'I expected to see rolling paddocks and a few cows grazing. So when he pulled up beside this desolate, rocky expanse I couldn't understand it. There was nothing there, no houses, I couldn't even see a green tree so I turned to my husband and asked, "So where is the land?" When he told me that this *was* the land I could have cried'.

It was also clear that Bob did not share Maha's early enthusiasm at being part owner of 2860 hectares. But Maha was undeterred; he had warned Bob and David that it meant all-out war, and all-out war it was. There was, and still is, nothing Maha loves more than an impossible deadline. Within one short year he and his team would have to secure development approvals on the most viable section of the land. And there was of course the small matter of finding $3 million so they could settle the sale and pay the first instalment in a year's time.

It was like no other project the team had ever attempted. Up to this point the biggest land parcel that Maha and Bob had ever owned or controlled was 15 hectares (37 acres). They were used to developments they could walk around in 10 minutes; at 9 kilometres by 4.5 kilometres, it would be impossible to walk the boundary of this monster in a whole day!

Once back in the office Bob insisted on a complete project strategy stretching far into the future so they could be confident of their position before they agreed to settle. They needed to workshop scenarios to establish what could be sold from day one and for how much. They needed to assess cash-flow requirements leading into the final payment, and exit contingencies should debt begin to spiral. And they were going to need some first-rate planning advice.

Enter Barry Alexander. Barry was a planning professional Maha had become aware of through previous projects. What Barry didn't know about planning and development could be written on the back of a postage stamp. He was a straight-talking, blunt and determined character—just the sort of person Maha needed and respected. It was Barry who took the photograph of David and Maha in the photo section of this book. The three of them had been visiting Opossum Creek to discuss options and Maha had told Barry enthusiastically, 'One day that will be a very famous photograph. A key day in the birth of a new city'. Barry thought Maha was insane and felt more than a little sorry for him.

The land was hilly, much of it forested, with no services, but Maha was talking about creating a fully integrated city for a hundred thousand people. Barry imagined the thousands of kilometres of pipes, wires and roads that would need to crisscross the land for it to even become habitable. Most major developments he was familiar with needed to lean on inherent features, such as scenery or beaches, or existing infrastructure or built features such as an industrial centre or major shopping precinct. But here there was *nothing*. There was a prison to the north, a big cemetery and a psychiatric hospital, which considering Maha's evident lunacy might come in handy, but these were hardly drawcards. Every major development needs access and transport, but Opossum Creek was accessible only in one corner via an average regional road. Barry shook his head. There were very good reasons why the land had been avoided by other major developers—it was impossible. He could think of no equivalent development *worldwide* that had succeeded without government subsidy and millions in private wealth. And to the best of his knowledge Maha and Bob had neither!

Barry cut to the chase: 'This will be *hard* work. My first impression is that it will take years of *hard grind*. You are going to have to deal with both the council and various state government departments on this. I can already think of a bunch of tough legislation you'll have to jump over. You really need to talk with the council and the state to see whether this thing has a chance of getting off the ground. You will need a firm steer from them before you sink any money into it'.

What Barry didn't realise at the time was that the prospect of years of hard work and headaches was not a deterrent, simply a fact that had to be negotiated!

It was clear, however, that the name needed to be changed. There were already rumblings from environmental groups about the sale of the AFH land to developers, and Opossum Creek gave the land environmental kudos that it simply didn't have. There may have been a creek but there were very few possums and the last thing this project needed was additional headaches caused by enthusiastic conservationists looking to save some cute fluffy critters that were not even there!

It was David Henry who came up with the name Springfield. One evening, as David and Bob shared a couple of beers after another long day at work, they were thinking about names. Looking at a large topographical map for inspiration, David noticed Spring Mountain just beyond the property and that the plain below the mountain looked like a field. The name Springfield suggested an inviting mix of land and water. Also, the distinguished US President Abraham Lincoln lived in Springfield, Illinois. Little could anyone have predicted then the rise in popularity of an animated TV sitcom featuring work-shy Homer Simpson and his family, who lived in the fictional US city of Springfield!

With the new name agreed and the action tasks distributed among the team, everyone swung into action to achieve their respective goals. Maha was to talk to his financiers about providing working capital to finance the operating period until the land was prepared for sale and look for a way to raise the $3 million. He was also responsible for building relationships with the decision makers and for rallying support from the politicians. Maha knew Barry was right about the crucial importance of involving council and state government departments, and he knew from past experience that getting to the decision makers early and presenting a strong case could mean the difference between success and failure. Bob was to focus on finance and legal. He too was concentrating on finding a solution to their $3 million problem and coming up with a financial model that would support the development and ensure they didn't end up broke. This required a new land valuation, which Bob was to arrange. He also needed to send a draft contract to the lawyers. Meanwhile David was to focus on town planning and surveying advice for the immediate development of the most viable section of land, and Barry was to push those through council. It was all-out war.

As Maha continued his campaign to meet and persuade decision makers, Barry pressed forward with the initial approvals. They were seeking approval to develop land they didn't own and didn't have the money to pay for. This was an aggressive and risky thing to do because if they couldn't raise the $3 million and couldn't therefore buy the land, all the money spent on rezoning and securing approvals would have been lost. The approvals were attached to the land, not the developer. If they couldn't settle, then AFH would be free to sell the land with approvals to the highest bidder, and Maha and Bob wouldn't have received a cent. By early 1992 they had submitted the rezoning and subdivision application and were expected to receive approval for 1100 residential lots. On one level at least the project was moving forward.

~

Over the course of several months the pieces in their giant chess game began to take shape. Maha and Bob had control of the land, Barry had pursued planning consent for the initial viable part of the property and approval was imminent. Maha had been able to build some political support, or at least he had not encountered any outright political opposition. Providing the initial approvals came through, there was a saleable residential land product with good planning and the salespeople were lined up. The remaining piece was the finance. And that would turn out to be a different game entirely.

The 2860-hectare land parcel at Springfield was divided into around a dozen titles, just as they were assembled by the AFH land agent in the mid 1950s. The plan was to sell one of those titles to pay AFH their $3 million. The beauty of using option contracts to control land is that options give you the right to sell something you don't actually own at a date in the future when you will own the asset.

Springfield was going to be possible only if they could start the project with minimal debt, hence Bob's desire to 'tread lightly', and that meant they had to find a way to buy the land without borrowing money. Operating costs and overheads would be significant through the approvals stage, and adding bank interest on $3 million to the mix would be fatal. Considering they didn't have the money to buy the land themselves, there was only one solution—find another purchaser.

What Maha and Bob needed was a buyer who would not be a competitor. There was no way they could sell one title, possibly 293 hectares (725 acres) of *raw* land for $3 million, but if the land also had development approval it *was* possible. According to the titles submitted to council, Maha and Bob would hold and develop 700 lots on one title with 400 lots available on another title. It was the smaller lot of 400 that they would sell to make the initial payment of $3 million to AFH. Maha had made this play many times: control the land with an option, get some council approvals and then sell it on to another developer and bank the profit from the increase in land value due to the approvals.

Only that wasn't going to work this time. Most buyers in this scenario will start building the moment their cheque is cashed. They want to build as fast as possible so they can sell and recoup their investment and bank *their* profit. What was to stop them selling the land cheaply and undermining the new city? And even if they did build great residential homes, two developments side by side would always depress sales. Maha and Bob needed to sell the title but they also needed to prevent the new owner from building, at least for a while, and that made the opportunity much less attractive.

Maha activated his property and real estate networks. He made presentation after presentation to potential investors. He beat the drum unceasingly and was sure that eventually the sound would reach an interested ear. But there was no-one listening. As the date for settlement drew nearer there was no solution in sight. Maha would rally his troops: 'This land *will settle* and we will be selling lots *this year*. Get on with it!'

But the final chess piece just wouldn't line up and optimism wasn't enough. Night after night he sat in his study, making calls and planning. They needed to settle by the middle of the year. The pressure was quickly mounting.

Apart from the obvious absence of a buyer there was additional pressure. First of all Maha and Bob were no longer the only horse in the race. All the noise that Maha had made beating his drum about Springfield had attracted developers back to the site for a second look. They knew that development approvals for part of the land were imminent and that if Sinnathamby failed they could expect better terms. They knew that Maha and Bob's option on the land was close to expiry and if they didn't exercise their right to buy the property, the Opossum Creek land parcel, complete with approvals, was now significantly more attractive than it had been the year before.

But that wasn't all. Sure, the team didn't have $3 million to pay the first instalment of the land, there was no capital partner in sight and other developers were circling the land like vultures, but the greatest pressure was personal, deep and of Maha's *own making*. He had whirled around Brisbane telling everyone he could find — ministers, political powerbrokers, mayors, councillors, investors, financiers and anyone else who would listen — that he was going to build a city. He had even been to the University of Queensland to try to get them to take some land to build a campus within the future city. He would face shame and ridicule if he didn't even make it past the first hurdle.

Right now finding that buyer was Maha's 'one idea'. He made it his life, and the entire team worked tirelessly to make it happen. Finally he met with an Asian business broker friend for coffee, and told him of his plans. As Maha reiterated his well-worn spiel his friend interrupted, 'Hey, I know someone this might suit'.

Within a week the broker introduced Maha to the potential investor he had been thinking of. The Taiwanese businessman was apparently interested in investing through his company Cherish Enterprises. He didn't appear to speak English very well, and the broker translated the proposition. Maha looked back and forth from the broker to the businessman, desperate to jump in and convey the full scale of this fantastic opportunity. After about 20 minutes the broker asked if he had any questions. The businessman looked at Maha and told them both, in surprisingly good English, that he had heard what he needed and would think about it.

What followed was an excruciating game of cat and mouse. Maha and Bob, both conscious of their impending deadline, worked on moving the deal forward. Cherish executives were in no hurry, however, and became distant and hard to reach. Maha continued beating the drum but with less than two months to go before settlement, Cherish was their only hope. After a few agonising weeks Maha organised another meeting with Cherish and delivered an ultimatum. He explained that there had been enough thinking time, that there were other interested parties but as the first investor to show serious interest it was only right that Maha extend the opportunity to Cherish first. At which point he produced a blank sheet of paper and said, 'Don't you think we should write down our terms, and settle what we are going to do?'

After an hour they agreed on some general terms. Maha and Bob would sell 293 hectares (725 acres) with development approvals. They would commence the development and bring services and a road to the other section. Cherish could not begin development until this was done, and when they did develop they could not seek approval for or build any retail. Maha insisted the deal be struck at no less than $3 million. There was some wrangling on the price and eventually they settled on $2.84 million. The meeting finished with the Cherish executive reiterating the need for more time to think about it. But Maha pressed on, telling the investor that he would organise a contract of sale to be drawn up and sent to his solicitors.

On 30 June 1992 Maha and Bob signed the land contract with AFH. It had been nine months since the start of the option agreement and AFH was keen to confirm contractual arrangements. There was a settlement period contingent on the final 'gazetting' of the land subdivision and the registering of the new titles with the government authority. With these formalities completed in July, settlement—the exchange of money and titles—was set for August.

~

On 19 August 1992 Bob waited in reception at the office of AFH's Brisbane lawyers. Although there had been almost constant communication through July, and Bob and Maha's solicitor had written to the Cherish representatives to explain the three-way contract exchange that would take place, the investor remained extremely elusive. Bob was tense. It all came down to this. Not long after Bob turned up AFH's legal representatives arrived. But would the third party turn up? All across town people knew of Maha's grand plans. The Deputy Premier had already announced that the project was 'on', and yet here he was in a solicitor's office, still wondering whether a cheque would arrive! If it didn't they wouldn't even own the land the Deputy Premier had just 'opened', and the media would have a field day.

After what seemed to Bob an eternity the lift doors opened and the Cherish representatives arrived. The large party proceeded to the boardroom and all the normal rules of ownership were suspended. Bob took the cheque from the investor for land he didn't yet own and couldn't therefore sell. Bob looked at the cheque. It was as per the instructions, $2.84 million made out to AFH. The vendor signed the contract; Bob handed over the cheque for $2.84 million and his cheque for the balance. He received the completed contract from AFH and signed a further contract with Cherish. After months of stress and sleepless nights, the exchange of papers took minutes. There were a few handshakes and everyone left.

Maha and Bob finally had clear ownership and control over the land but the deepest emotion Bob felt was one of relief. They were indeed 'treading lightly', entering the project with minimal debt.

And that has been the nature of the development of Springfield. The goals and targets have been so huge and numerous that what would under normal circumstances have been a moment of celebration was simply a box to be ticked and a prompt to move a little further towards reality. As for Cherish, they more than recouped their investment and eventually developed and sold the 400 lots.

> *This is the one central idea ... work incessantly, but be not attached to it ... Be unattached, let things work; let brain centres work; work incessantly but let not a ripple conquer the mind. Work as if you were a stranger in this land, a sojourner; work incessantly but do not bind yourselves; bondage is terrible.*

The principle in action

Dean Kamen invented the upright personal transporter called the Segway PT. He currently holds over 440 US and foreign patents and his inventions not only have expanded the frontier of worldwide medical care but have solved some impossible problems in unique and inspiring ways. Kamen is testament to what is possible through consistent effort and a refusal to accept anything as impossible.

While still at university in the 1970s Kamen invented the first wearable infusion pump, which rapidly gained acceptance in specialist medical areas such as chemotherapy, neonatology and endocrinology. The pump is now used by diabetics to administer insulin. He has also invented a portable dialysis machine.

The phenomenal success of these early inventions has given Kamen the resources to turn his formidable mind to some of the world's most pressing social and humanitarian problems, such as how to provide electricity and clean water to communities in the developing world.

Today more than a billion people, or nearly 20 per cent of the world's population, don't have access to clean drinking water, yet its supply could reduce illness by up to 75 per cent. Some 1.6 billion people don't have electricity. Building large, expensive, centralised supply systems is not always possible technologically, politically or financially. And even if they were possible, few businesses are interested in investing in infrastructure where there are no affluent customers to help recoup the investment and generate profit.

Kamen and his team of scientists set about trying to solve this challenge by creating a personalised distribution system for clean water and cheap electricity. The result was two black boxes, each about the size of a domestic front-loading washing machine.

'Slingshot' is an innovative vapor-compression water distiller that can take any water-based input, from sludge to sewage to sea water and purify it into drinkable water. Only 3 per cent of the world's water is fresh water so being able to convert the rest is not just an issue for developing countries; it is a global issue urgently needing a solution.

Kamen says, 'Our goal was to produce a small portable machine that could be placed anywhere and at the point of use create clean, reliable drinking water from any source'. Slingshot is a simple box with two hoses — one goes into anything wet, and pure drinking water comes out the other. Whatever goes in is boiled to the point of vaporisation. The output is pure distilled water, no matter how polluted the source water. Each unit can supply 1000 litres of drinking water a day, which is enough for a village of 100 people, and the units cost less than US$2000 each. And Slingshot requires less power than a handheld hair dryer.

About 1.6 billion people don't have access to power, even a tiny amount. So Kamen created another black box. The Sterling Generator runs on any type of natural fuel source. Kamen's generator has already been field tested in two villages in Bangladesh. The only available fuel was cow dung that was going through the natural process of decomposition in a pit next to each box, and yet they ran perfectly. The generators, which do not need extra maintenance or access to a power grid, gave these villages electricity using an environmentally friendly energy source.

Kamen says of his achievements, 'Life is so short, why waste a single day of it doing something that doesn't matter? Do something BIG'. He believes that when you look back on your life, you'll want to make sure you have put back more than you took out. There can be little doubt that Dean Kamen has achieved this objective in droves.

Work on with the intrepidity of a lion but at the same time with the tenderness of a flower.

What this principle means for you

There are several reasons that hard work is so vital to success. First is the matter of respect and dignity. Work is not solely about doing what needs to be done to get to an outcome; the act of working is of itself every bit as valuable as the outcome of that work. The ancient wisdom that has guided Maha urges us to 'work for work's sake' because work is good for the soul.

Too many people see work only as a means to make money. But work is far more important than that. In our society we now have three generations of families who have never worked. Instead many of them get up late and watch daytime TV. They develop a sense of entitlement that somehow the state owes them benefits for no effort. The welfare state is a necessary and vital part of any progressive economy but it is a safety net, not a way of life.

First, we have to bear in mind that we are all debtors to the world and the world does not owe us anything.

Maha could have accepted the dole when he arrived in Australia in 1971. But to Maha, doing this would have been an admission of defeat and that was not an option. Also even a little easy money would have dampened his hunger for success. He never gave up on himself and believed above all else that if he kept working, regardless of whether he was paid for the effort, he would find a solution. Eventually he did.

Nobody ever got anything by begging. We only get what we deserve. The first step to deserve is to desire; and we desire with success what we feel ourselves worthy to get.

Work develops character. There is nothing more liberating than self–reliance and the dignity that comes from hard work. Hard work is active, not passive. It allows you to take charge of your life and carve out your own future, and as a consequence it gives you the power to create whatever future you want. Maha deliberately turned his back on the dole because for him it was a matter of pride and self-respect. He didn't want to accept something for nothing and although he was down on his luck he never stopped believing in himself, and neither should you.

Hard work also leads to the development and extension of knowledge and the improvement of skills that perpetuate success. Persistent practice and disciplined effort is, after all, how mastery is created.

In 1992 researchers in England set out to determine whether 'musical talent' really existed. This form of talent was chosen because most people believe that either you're musically gifted or you're not.

Also, musical ability is very closely measured and graded in the UK, which means that recognising ability does not come down to personal opinion. The researchers studied 257 young people with varying musical ability. Some had played an instrument for six months and given up while others had been so good they had been accepted into music school after competitive auditions. The research study matched kids by age, instrument, gender and socioeconomic class and also interviewed parents at length. What they discovered was that there was no evidence of innate ability and no difference between the people in the lowest ability group and the musically 'gifted'. The only difference between the best and worst was that by age 12 the students in the top group were working much harder. The elite players were practising on average two hours a day compared with 15 minutes a day for the students in the lowest group.

Excellence in any field requires hard work and a certain number of hours to achieve. As one of the researchers, Professor John A Sloboda of the University of Keele, said, 'There is absolutely no evidence of a "fast track" for high achievers'. There is no short cut.

> *To succeed, you must have tremendous perseverance, tremendous will. 'I will drink the ocean', says the persevering soul. 'At my will mountains will crumble up'. Have that sort of energy, that sort of will, work hard and you will reach the goal.*

Maha's action plan

Work relentlessly! In order to help you shift your thinking and incorporate this principle into your life you will need to:

> ➤ chase success and money will follow
> ➤ recognise you can always do better
> ➤ say 'yes' and work out 'how' later.

Chase success and money will follow

Although Maha Sinnathamby has made and lost many millions in his lifetime, his motivation has never been based on the accumulation of wealth. Even today, when his net worth is estimated to be more than

$800 million, money is not what motivates him. He has lived in the same modest home for 24 years and is not interested in scaling up for the sake of show or extravagance. He drives a five-year-old Mercedes. Maha was inspired by the vision. Springfield was his opportunity to create a compelling legacy and to give back to a country that has offered him so much in opportunity. It is also a testament to what is possible if you chase success tenaciously. As the ancient wisdom that guides Maha teaches, 'Ask nothing; want nothing in return. Give what you have to give; it will come back to you—but do not think of that now, it will come back multiplied a thousandfold—but the attention must not be on that'.

Too often people set out on a particular course because they believe it will make them rich, but if your intention is only to accumulate personal wealth, then you simply won't have the stamina and inner resilience to battle through the inevitable obstacles that will stand in your way. If, on the other hand, you are inspired by something more personally meaningful to you, then the hard work and persistence necessary for success become a source of pride and enjoyment rather than a chore to be endured.

Maha and Bob have probably experienced more stress than most of us will in a lifetime. The pursuit of money alone will never keep you in the game long enough to bring about success, especially when every inch forward is a struggle and your blood pressure is through the roof. There has to be something more that drives you, otherwise you will quit at the first sign of trouble.

Both Maha and Bob are wealthy enough never to have to work another day in their lives, but they choose to continue full steam to bring the Springfield vision to fruition because they love it and are happy to continue chasing success in the creation of a world-class city.

The highest use of capital is not to make more money, but to make money do more for the betterment of life.

—Henry Ford (American industrialist)

Man must have an idol and the amassing of wealth is one of the worst species of idolatry! No idol is more debasing than the worship of money!

—Andrew Carnegie (Scottish-American industrialist)

Recognise you can always do better

Central to Maha's approach to life is the belief that he and everyone around him can always do better. No matter how hard you work, there is always room for constant improvement. As far as Maha is concerned, good is the enemy of great and that means never settling for good and always pushing for that little bit extra.

The constant drive for improvement, the ceaseless push for better or more, is an approach he finetuned early in his career. In the final minutes of negotiation with a major international hotel chain, after months of argument and discussion, Maha said he'd sign only if the hotel chain agreed to provide him with free accommodation at any of their hotels across the world for as long as he lived. The German negotiator was livid, but Maha secured the deal. Even when the deal is done Maha would always push for more. Although he never used the accommodation, it was a tactic he employs to this day.

This approach has also been influenced by various people along the way. Maha remembers hiring a salesman in Perth and showing him to his desk. Maha laughs at the memory. 'He just looked at me and said he'd need another phone. So we got a second phone for him and he would be talking on one while the other was ringing. It was a real reminder of always pushing for better and the willingness to break conventions.' Never settle. Seek constant improvement and little advantages.

There's a way to do better...find it.

—Thomas A. Edison (American inventor)

Part of this philosophy comes down to a willingness to train and retrain. Learning is not a process that ends once you leave school or university; it is a constant process. But education comes in many forms, and often the most potent is hands-on experience. All Maha's children recall how, when they were university students, their father encouraged them to offer to work for free so they could gain valuable hands-on work experience and perhaps a job on graduation. If you are already working in your chosen area, then always offer to do more than is asked of you, even if you will not be paid for it. Find the people in your business who have the most knowledge and invite them to lunch so you can tap into their knowledge and shortcut the learning process.

Formal education will make you a living; self-education will make you a fortune.

—**Jim Rohn (American businessman and author)**

Say 'yes' and work out 'how' later

This action step is about relentless forward motion. Maha has often facilitated that forward motion through his willingness to say 'yes' to whatever request comes his way and work out the 'how' later—or get Bob and the others to work out the 'how' later!

One of Springfield's major hurdles, explored more fully in chapter 7, was access. The council was in no hurry to provide the necessary road access to Springfield. Eventually, in an effort to discover how serious Maha was about the needed road, he and Bob were asked to pay half the costs of an Environmental Impact Statement. Maha knew it was another expense he could ill afford, and that the investigation and consultation would allow opportunities for public review and protest. It was also probably a stalling tactic by the government, but it was a watershed moment. For the first time the government was at least offering to start the process, so Maha agreed without hesitation. He knew if he said no it would give the government the excuse it was looking for to close the door. So he said yes and would work out how they were going to pay for it later.

Yes and no rule the world.

—**Italian proverb**

Many years later, when Springfield was a reality, the Queensland Premier told Maha, 'We put a number of hurdles along your path and you overcame them all'. He acknowledged that the government did not make it easy for them to get Springfield up and running; if anything they made it extremely difficult. From the government's perspective they wanted to test his resolve and were probably hoping he would refuse some of their requests so they had a legitimate reason to deny assistance. But the Springfield team never refused any requests. Maha's strategy has always been to enter all negotiations with an open hand, not a clenched fist.

> *Sooner or later you will have to give up. You come into life to accumulate. With clenched hands, you want to take. But nature puts a hand on your throat and makes your hands open. Whether you will it or not, you have to give. The moment you say, 'I will not', the blow comes; you are hurt.*

So say 'Yes' instead of 'No' if you want your goal to progress. It will show people you are serious and willing to put your own 'skin in the game' and are not sitting back waiting for someone else to provide all the solutions and take all the risks.

To say yes, you have to sweat and roll up your sleeves and plunge both hands into life up to the elbows. It is easy to say no, even if saying no means death.

—Jean Anouilh (French playwright)

Chapter 4

Be fearless — face the brutes!

'Face the brutes.' That is a lesson for all life—face the terrible, face it boldly. The hardships of life fall back when we cease to flee before them.

No-one likes confrontation. No-one enjoys facing opposition or telling people things they don't want to hear. It can be difficult and uncomfortable, but have you ever noticed that if you avoid the situation, or send a text or email instead of having a face-to-face conversation, problems just get worse? There is nothing to be gained by procrastination or avoidance. What we need is fearlessness. We need to have the courage to act well in uncertain and difficult times. We need to be fearless when we take a risk, strike out on our own to create a business, pursue a dream or face a challenge head on. Sometimes life is messy, unpredictable and painful. It is fearlessness that encourages us to stand firm, look squarely at what is before us and refuse to yield. Indian poet and playwright Rabindranath Tagore said, 'Let me not pray to be sheltered from dangers but to be fearless in facing them. Let me not beg for the stilling of my pain, but for the heart to conquer it. Let me not look for allies in life's battlefield but to my own strength. Let me not cave in...'. That is the spirit of this fourth principle.

Maha Sinnathamby is fearless, not just in his willingness to tackle the impossible but in his entire approach to life. When others looked at Opossum Creek, all they saw was an untameable brute! But Maha was not intimidated by the size of the land tract—he was inspired by it. He created the vision while Bob circled the brute to work out how to stop it turning on them and killing them all, and together they made it work! Maha says, 'When we were building a city from the ground up there were many brutes to deal with. The brutes were the planning approvals, the brutes were no cash, the brutes were a lack of roads and infrastructure, the brutes were all the other hurdles and trying to get the team revved up so they too believed in it. We all needed to be fearless'.

> If there is one word that you find coming out like a bomb from the Upanishads [Hindu philosophical texts], bursting like a bombshell upon masses of ignorance, it is the word 'fearlessness'.

Fearlessness is also required when things go wrong. In life, we can often be tempted to skirt around difficult issues or hide from our challenges rather than square up to them openly and honestly. No-one likes to admit they were wrong or they messed up. But the effort and stress caused by turning away from those challenges are infinitely more debilitating than the liberation that comes from courageous action. It is not easy but it is often the only way to really solve a problem. When we settle for compromise or implement bandaid solutions it never works for long, and invariably the challenge emerges bigger and stronger than ever. So be fearless—face the brutes!

The rise and fall in Perth

In 1977, a year after Maha and Ken Law-Davis had quit the Water Board to start Murdoch Constructions, Maha and Yoga's son, Naren, was born. As was customary after an Indian birth, they consulted an astrologer, who predicted five golden years ahead during which the family would achieve great prosperity. True to the prediction, over the next five years Murdoch Constructions' value rose from $17 000 in 1976 to $7 million, employing 48 people at its peak. Both Maha and Ken were multimillionaires and Maha bought a home in Peppermint Grove, one of the most prestigious suburbs in Perth.

In 1982 the company was on the crest of a wave. And then the wave broke and came crashing to shore.

Ken resigned from the partnership. He had married an American woman, who was keen to return home and persuaded Ken to try a new lifestyle. Maha was devastated. Although Ken had about $2 million of equity in the business, it was tied up in a host of assets and active development projects, so they agreed that Ken would get an immediate payment of $400 000 followed by progressive annual payments until the balance was paid. Ken knew that the immediate withdrawal of $2 million was inconceivable and had full confidence in Maha's capacity to pay.

Together they had been a tough and dynamic team. Maha sourced the deals and worked his connections and Ken managed the finer detail of the business, such as the contracts and finances. Without Ken, Maha had lost his sounding board and it took months to adjust.

Maha sought legal and financial advice on the structure of the business. Murdoch Constructions had grown very large, and as the sole owner of the business Maha was advised to restructure the company to create a public trust. For each new development project Maha needed to raise capital. A public trust would allow him to consolidate all the assets and attract investors to the trust rather than to individual investments. At the time, the public trust was a popular business structure for large, asset-rich private companies. It was suggested this approach could secure the company more investment funding and raise the overall value of the company. In principle the process was straightforward: nominate the assets that would enter the trust, appoint trustees, offer investment in the trust through an initial public offering (IPO), raise the necessary $14 million, finalise the trust documentation to transfer the assets to the trust, which would then be listed on the Australian Securities Exchange. Maha decided to take the advice on the understanding that the process would take three months to finalise.

When a trust is created the assets nominated for transfer are frozen until the trust is fully established. The assets needed to be stable and, once submitted, Maha could not change his mind, nor could he sell any assets or borrow against them. At the time this didn't especially worry Maha because the assets in question generated lease income and would be frozen for only three months. Only it didn't take three months. In the end it took nearly 12—all during a time when the economy had turned south and interest rates escalated to historic highs. Maha knew the signs of impending recession. He needed to reduce his exposure to the banks, but he couldn't liquidate the assets as they were frozen while the trust documentation was completed. It was a disaster.

As interest rates reached a peak the lease income on the underlying assets no longer serviced the debt; they depreciated in value and Maha was unable to do anything about it. He pleaded with the authorities to finalise the trust so he could sell some assets and avert disaster, but to no avail. He had provided everything they had asked for, including all the titles, ownership details, mortgages, valuation reports and list of trustees. But progress was slow and he was powerless to act. Maha was beside himself.

To add insult to injury there was talk of an early election and observers believed Prime Minister Malcolm Fraser was looking for ways to call a double dissolution of Parliament. Inflation was rising, there was a spike in industrial disputes, unemployment rose and drought ravaged much of the country. Maha was at the mercy of forces beyond his control and any power he had to take protective action was removed because of the bureaucracy surrounding the creation of the trust.

At last, on 14 December 1982 the authorities launched the trust, setting 14 March 1983 as the date for its establishment, by which time Maha needed to demonstrate he could raise the $14 million needed for the float to be successful. He worked for up to 20 hours a day, frantically seeking new investors and assistance. By early 1983 his efforts began to pay off and investors were pouring about $800 000 a week into the soon-to-be-established trust. Then Prime Minister Fraser called an election and by the first week of March, just days before the finalisation of the trust, Bob Hawke came to power. This represented a major shift in the political landscape. It was the start of a new, untested Labor government and investors and trustees alike became nervous.

Many of the trustees were ultra-conservative with no experience of a trust as big as Murdoch Pty Ltd. A clause in the documentation stated that the trustees had 30 days to buy the assets and transfer them into the new structure, and this clause proved fatal. One of the major shareholders insisted that the transaction occur within 24 hours so that the new entity would become active immediately. The trustees refused, largely because of the political uncertainty, and insisted on their 30 days. As a result, the main investor, who had committed $7 million, pulled out and on 14 April 1983 the trust collapsed. According to Chinese numerology, the number 14 is extremely unlucky and portends 'ultimate death'. Everything about the trust revolved around the number 14, even Maha's home address at the time was 14 View Street, Peppermint Grove. In the end it was indeed a prophecy of doom and would ultimately signal the end of their life in Perth.

Newspapers across the region carried the story of his decline, but Maha battled on. He now had access to his beleaguered assets and was being approached by financiers and liquidators. Everyone knew of his situation and bargain hunters were circling like vultures around the dying business, hoping to bargain over the carcass.

Yet for Maha bankruptcy was never an option. He would fight to the end to pay off his debts and maintain his ability to trade in the future. He was committed to doing what was right; he had arrived in Australia with nothing and had painstakingly built his reputation as a hard, shrewd but honest businessman. That reputation was priceless and he would do everything in his power to salvage it.

If the business went into administration, his assets would be sold off for considerably less than they were worth. He fought hard to avoid this situation and managed to persuade his financiers that an orderly disposal of his assets would make better financial sense for everyone involved. Across Perth, arrangements were made for partial, interim, staged and deferred payments, and he hoped there would be enough left over to start again.

Maha then owed $42 million to various institutions, financiers, contractors and suppliers. He was also liable for an $11 million debt in connection with a joint venture agreement after he had foolishly agreed to be guarantor for the joint venture partner. The bank in question realised they were not going to get their $11 million back from the partner, so they came after Maha. Although he was in financial difficulty he had a solid track record as a reputable and honourable businessman, and the bank believed he was their best bet for recovering their $11 million.

~

Maha battled creditors through 1983 and 1984. These were the darkest of days and the older children still remember hearing Maha sobbing late at night. And yet each morning he would get up early, dress well and face the day fearlessly. It would have been much easier to declare bankruptcy, walk away and find a loophole that would allow him to go into business again. But it wasn't ethical. He would find a way.

By 1985 Maha's business was at the point of complete financial collapse. Had the economy not been so depressed the debt might have been manageable, but interest rates were so high that Maha's remaining assets could not generate enough income. One day his brother, who had been watching his relentless battle to save the business, took him aside. They spoke of the three years of tireless effort and emotional pain, three years in which he barely saw his children and during which his health had deteriorated. He told Maha to face the brutes and have it out with his remaining creditors. 'Face all the people you owe money to. This must end.'

There comes a time in every life when we must face the brutes. These moments are not easy. Maha didn't want to face his creditors and tell them he could not pay them. He preferred to battle on, but it was an impossible situation and he accepted the wisdom of his brother's advice. There was nothing left to sell. Maha had already liquidated assets that were in Yoga's and the children's names. There were no offshore assets or hidden bank accounts.

Neither seek nor avoid; take what comes. It is liberty to be affected by nothing. Do not merely endure; be unattached.

At the first creditors' meeting no settlement was reached. Ironically the stumbling block was not Maha's own creditors but the finance company seeking to recover $11 million from Maha under his bank guarantee. Maha recalls, 'All my own financiers had agreed to release me, because they knew how hard I'd worked to repay the money, but this other finance company initially refused. I didn't personally owe them any money but I had acted as a loan guarantor for a joint-venture partner who then went bankrupt. The financier knew their only chance of getting their money back was to keep me on the hook. So they voted against the settlement'.

In an effort to resolve the situation, Maha immediately flew to Adelaide to meet the CEO of the finance company to convince him to release him from the obligation. Maha checked into a dark and dingy motel to keep his travel costs to an absolute minimum. 'I remember calling the office and speaking to one of the few people left, Digby Johnson, and he said, "Get the hell out of there, find some extra money and go somewhere decent".' Digby knew that Maha was fighting for his life, and that to be in such a depressing place, even for one night, was just going to make an already low moment even lower. He also knew that Maha would have to meet the CEO and really present a strong and emotive case so they would release him from the obligation. Maha was going to call on every scrap of his natural optimism, bravado and salesmanship to pull it off, and staying in a seedy motel room just to save a few dollars was completely counterproductive. Maha took the advice and moved.

The next morning he went to see the CEO and pleaded with him not to enforce the guarantee. It was clear the CEO had some sympathy for Maha; after all, it wasn't his debt and he too was fighting for his life. He knew Maha's own financiers had agreed to let him off, but he needed to be able to explain any decision he made to his board. The CEO asked for some time to consider the situation. Maha agreed but asked that he first speak to his administrator. The administrator told the financier of the lengths Maha had gone to in order to repay his debts and in the end the CEO decided to support him. Maha says, 'That was a turning point for me and I immediately went out and bought myself a big meal and got a haircut—neither of which I'd done in a long time'.

For the subsequent creditors' meeting 42 people crammed into a Perth CBD boardroom to decide Maha's fate. He had managed to pay off most of the debt. He had sold assets, and investors and his own financiers got almost all their principal investment back, although they did not always receive all of their outstanding interest.

The creditors knew the situation and knew Maha had worked hard, but it was little comfort when they were being asked to accept 10 cents for every dollar owed. Maha addressed the meeting. He explained the position, how it happened and what he tried to do to get everyone their money. But he now had little left to offer. He told the gathering,

'I have $170000 equity in my home in Peppermint Grove. I will sell it and you can share the $100000, but please leave me $70000. I have a wife and four children to support and I need to start again.'

Even the Australian Taxation Office (ATO) auditor voted to accept the deal. Normally the ATO delegate will only ever abstain from the vote as an indication of their acceptance. In this instance, they actively voted to accept the offer because their forensic accountants had painstakingly crawled through Maha's records and were satisfied there really wasn't anything hidden. They knew he had sold all the assets held in his wife's and children's names—something he was not legally bound to do—in an effort to pay off the debt.

Maha's creditors accepted the offer, albeit reluctantly, and he went around the room to apologise to everyone personally and thank them for agreeing to the terms. His solicitor, who was owed $70000, wished Maha well. 'I know you will leave Perth. I know you are going through hard times, and I know you have nothing. But what they can't take from you is what is between your ears. I know you will rise again.' Maha went home, emotionally and physically drained, and cried. There was no victory but at least he was a free man.

Maha's ancient wisdom counsels, '"Comfort" is no test of truth; on the contrary, truth is often far from being "comfortable".' Maha had been deeply uncomfortable over the preceding years as he tried to salvage his business and meet his debts. And yet he had faced the brutes as fearlessly as he could.

Local Government Springfield Rezoning Bill 1997

From the moment Maha and Bob bought Opossum Creek they knew they would have to be fearless. Nothing like this had ever been done in Queensland. If they were to get any approvals at all they needed to educate the decision makers as well as persuade them. In the initial approvals application the Springfield team sought the maximum number of lots possible—1100 residential properties split over two titles. The idea was simple: sell the 700 lots and use the money to fund the expansion of Springfield, and sell the title with approval for 400 lots to an external investor to fund the first payment to AFH.

But even 1100 homes was a shock to the area. Before Maha and Bob came along, the single biggest approval the council had granted was for 200 allotments. Even the first stage of development was a major departure from the norm, never mind a master-planned city of 46 000 homes! The only way to smooth fears and encourage others to share his vision was to get officials involved. So David, Barry and Maha ran bus trips for local council decision makers, on which they would take them to view similar large-scale residential developments, local and interstate, so they could appreciate exactly what they were trying to do.

Maha sought to educate local and state government officials, to explain his vision and ensure they would give the development a fair go. At the very start he enlisted the support of Brisbane's much-loved former Lord Mayor Clem Jones. Together with planning and approvals expert Barry Alexander, the three of them took a light aircraft flight over the property as Maha enthusiastically sold the dream, pointing out where the residential community would be, the schools, the shopping centre and even the university.

Maha's speech must have sounded crazy, especially when all you could actually see were trees and parched vegetation, but the former mayor was a shrewd man. When Clem had been in office most of Brisbane's suburbs didn't have sewers or footpaths. There was no such thing as peak-hour traffic and everyone was in bed by 9.00 pm, including on weekends. Only a few dozen police were needed for the whole city, and most of them had nothing to do. But things were changing. Back on the ground Clem turned to Maha and said, 'If I didn't have a few years under my belt and a bit of experience I would tell you to come to your senses and walk away. I would say that as a friend, not a cynic. But it is inevitable that development *will* come out this far. It has to. The issue for you is not if, but when'. Maha was thrilled — a true believer!

Clem Jones could see the merit of what Maha was proposing and agreed to introduce him to the Deputy Premier and Minister for Housing and Local Government. To add to the headaches, however, Maha's push for a new city happened to coincide with a very difficult political climate. The new state government had been in power only a couple of years. The previous administration had been tossed out, largely because of corruption. Government dealings with developers and business had been heavily criticised and the new Labor government was on a campaign to clean up the system, purge some past practices and improve the quality of planning.

The Australian people were stunned by the breadth and depth of the corruption scandal that ended Joh Bjelke-Petersen's 19-year reign as Premier of Queensland, and many government officials felt they needed to demonstrate excessive caution and restraint when dealing with business—especially developers. From extremes of corruption the government swung to extreme conservatism. Developers faced widespread mistrust or open hostility, and all government officials were keen to keep them at arm's length to avoid being tarnished with any hint of wrongdoing. All of which meant there couldn't have been a worse time to seek political support for development, never mind the largest development Queensland had ever seen!

Clem Jones agreed to attend the meeting with the Deputy Premier, Maha and Barry Alexander but warned Maha to stick to the facts and present his case without razzle-dazzle or hard sell! Maha unrolled his map and made his presentation, working hard to restrain his natural exuberance. The Deputy Premier told the delegation he liked the idea of a planned city but explained the climate in government and how his constituents were demanding more transparency and more say over what was being developed. Above all else the government wanted good-quality, well-positioned housing. He added, 'For this specific rezoning and subdivision application with Moreton shire [the 1100 approvals], I don't see how that will be a problem. As for the plans for the broader city, well, it is fair warning that if the plan for a large satellite city out there arrived in government, it will be pushing against the grain'.

And push against the grain it did. But Maha and his team worked to stay one step ahead. They took advice, anticipated problems and faced them head on before they could grow. For example, word of the development had reached the ear of local environmentalists and there were already complaints and protests. By this time Maha was meeting regularly with Moreton Shire Mayor John Nugent. Initially John wasn't interested in meeting, but Maha is nothing if not persistent. Eventually he came to realise that Maha was not asking for favours or special treatment but for an opportunity to explain the project and his long-term commitment to the area.

More than anything John respected the fact that Maha could have taken the easy, fast money route and carved Opossum Creek into smaller land parcels. This was, after all, the advice he received at the start of the project — a course that would have easily generated $8 million in profit with minimal stress. John recognised that Maha was a man trying to do something different, something that could radically improve the area and create a stronger, more affluent community. As mayor of an economically depressed region, John was very interested in the new jobs that would be created by such an ambitious project, not to mention the increase in rates income. It was John who encouraged Maha and his team to face the potential challenges head on and seek the advice of local environmental guru Lloyd Bird and meet with the land's traditional Aboriginal owners — the local Jagera clan — to establish the history of the land and discover whether it contained any sacred sites.

But initial approvals were just an interim step. A constant round of challenges and obstacles had to be anticipated, managed or eradicated on the way to the main prize — full approval for the master-planned city. Fearlessness became a way of life for everyone involved.

~

In mid 1993 the new Planning Minister, Terry Mackenroth, accepted Maha's invitation to visit Springfield. The 1100 lots had been approved and sales of the 700 lots they had retained were well underway, but Maha remained focused on securing full planning approval for the new city. The project first needed to be supported by local council, but ultimately state government approval was required. Maha knew that the Planning Minister would have a strong say in whether the city went ahead.

The day of the meeting Minister Mackenroth lost his way in his four-wheel drive, so it took him longer than expected to find Springfield. In truth there wasn't much to see! Maha rolled out his maps and enthusiastically launched into his pitch, but was soon interrupted.

The minister already knew that Maha was in almost daily contact with his planners seeking information, advice and support for the new city and they in turn had briefed him before the meeting. He explained to Maha that as far as his experts were concerned Springfield was 'an out of sequence development', meaning the proposal was not within the plans for urban expansion. And while the planners accepted that there would probably come a time when development did move west in the direction of Springfield, in their opinion it wouldn't be necessary for at least 20 years. If the proposal was backed earlier than that, the government would inevitably be dragged into funding infrastructure and services before they were needed. The official line, then, was that the proposal needed to be firmly and swiftly turned down.

Maha tried hard to maintain his composure as the minister explained that his experts in government believed they needed to support logical development north and south of Brisbane towards the popular coastal settlements, and concentrate on urban infill, or using up capacity already within the urban footprint such as redeveloping the old industrial sites and wool storage warehouses in the inner city.

Maha argued his cause passionately and logically, reminding the minister that he could have easily subdivided, taken the money and ruined the land for any meaningful future planned development. If he was prepared to take the hardest possible path to do something right, that would lift the whole region, bringing much-needed income, investment and jobs to a depressed economy, then surely the government wouldn't stand in his way.

Mackenroth listened. He knew that what his planners said was true, but what Maha was saying also made a lot of sense. Brisbane was already expanding; he'd been to LA and Western Sydney and knew the blight of urban sprawl. The need for greater government control was on the agenda and a master-planned city was a bold solution. There was also something unusual about Sinnathamby. As Planning Minister Mackenroth had met hundreds of developers, and they all had their shiny plans and high-rolling speeches, but Terry was surprised at the depth of thinking and breadth of real substance of this one. They had already visited 15 master-planned communities around the world to isolate the best features and incorporate them into the Springfield plans. And Terry saw something different in Maha's eyes. It was grit. He respected grit.

Finally he turned to address Maha again: 'I reckon there can be development on the edges and in the middle. I don't see that it has to be one or the other. I am also interested in how a whole new urban community can be fully planned and delivered from scratch, but if you think I am softening I'm not. Government will not be dragged into premature development and paying for roads to nowhere. If you want this, you will have to make this work, brick by brick. If you want a road, if you want a school, if you want a police station, whatever you might want from government, *you* are going to have to pay your way. If you are mad enough to try, you must recognise this proposal is not within the government's forward planning and budget and that remains a cold, hard fact. We won't spend a dollar of government money unnecessarily on this'.

Terry concluded by saying, 'My attitude is that if you are mad enough to try, government should not unduly stand in your way'.

By late 1993 the council would not approve any further development on the Springfield land without looking at the infrastructure and how the development could be supported. The Planning Department agreed to consider a land use plan for the entire parcel, called a Development Control Plan (DCP), *if* it was prepared and supported by the council. The draft DCP would need to observe the planning legislation and would require final sign-off by the state government. What followed was years of wrangling and negotiations.

As Barry pushed forward with the approvals, obstacle after obstacle was put in their way. There were fresh waves of environmental protest. There was a merger between Morton Shire Council and Ipswich Council. Although John Nugent, who supported the development, was re-elected as mayor of the new council, there was a lot of bitterness. But in true Springfield fashion they had already anticipated the likely shift in government and had taken the time to introduce themselves to new prospective council members. One of the biggest risks in development projects of any kind is a change of council or government. Regardless of how valid or worthwhile a project is, the incoming power often feels bound to sweep previous projects aside. It's a political norm that can kill a development stone dead. Maha knew this from past experience and was determined it would not happen again. Springfield was not 'political', in that its merit bore no relation to the political ruling party. His job was to make sure that message reached the ears of the right people so that any transition that did occur did not automatically alienate Springfield. His vision would not become collateral damage in political turf wars if he had anything to do with it.

On top of the political challenges that engulfed the project there were road problems, army problems and mining problems, all of which are discussed in chapters 7 and 9. For every solution a new problem emerged, but the team kept working. Finally, in April 1995 the DCP was passed at council nine votes to four. It had been a long, often contentious battle. Barry had done an outstanding job to get the DCP this far, but it was not over yet.

The next milestone involved state government review and agreements with council and the government on infrastructure funding. There was still a long way to go, but Maha and Bob had already created history, with the biggest ever community master plan decision by an Australian local government.

The proposed master-planned city was so large that an Act of Parliament was required to ensure the DCP could be included in the Ipswich City town plan. The legislation would allow the council to enter into an Infrastructure Agreement that would formalise the necessary investment and who was responsible for what. Finally the day arrived on which Parliament would decide whether to pass the Local Government Springfield Rezoning Bill 1997.

On 24 January 1997 Barry and Maha entered Parliament House and climbed the stairs to the horseshoe-shaped public gallery. Everything came down to this moment. Years of hardship, struggling to meet and convince the right people, political upheaval when no sooner had one key politician been convinced of the merits of the project than he or she was replaced by a new one, who without fail would resist it so that the process of education and persuasion would have to start again. Mountains of paperwork, hundreds of thousands of hours of planning, meetings, discussions, arguments, highs and lows. Now here they were, perched above the legislative chamber, waiting for the politicians below them to seal their fate.

Springfield was just one of countless discussion points during a normal day in Parliament. Whatever the outcome, each of those politicians would go home and sleep soundly. Their life's work was not under scrutiny, they had not put their reputation or money on the line, and it was not their lives that were hanging in the balance. As the proceedings below rumbled on Maha tried to empty his mind. He knew they had done all they could, he knew Springfield was an important project based on the highest possible standards and ideals, but for now he just had to wait.

Eventually Maha caught the familiar word, 'Springfield', through the din and leant over the railing to hear more. The Bill was put to a vote. There were 89 politicians from both sides of the political divide in the chamber that day, and in an unprecedented outcome 89 politicians supported the Bill. The Local Government Springfield Rezoning Bill 1997 was passed into law unanimously. Maha quietly let out the breath he was unaware he'd been holding and turned to Barry and smiled — they'd made history!

~

What made this part of the Springfield story so extraordinary was that Barry had sought and achieved approvals for the *entire* master-planned city. Widely viewed as visionary by the town planning community, the plan has withstood the test of time and will continue to guide the development for decades to come. While the Springfield team had to keep council apprised of their progress, and there were restrictions on the total number of homes that could ultimately be built, they did not have to go back to council or state government for additional approvals as the development rolled out. The residential area was locked in, as were the areas for the CBD, Health City, Education City, parklands and protected areas. Barry had also successfully imposed 'deemed approvals', whereby the council had a finite number of days to review future Springfield applications and provide development conditions, otherwise the opportunity expired and the approval was considered granted. Time is the biggest killer of major development projects and these deemed approvals removed that future threat. Without Barry Alexander, Springfield would not be what it is today and it would certainly not be what it will be in 60 years' time. It was his drive and meticulous attention to the detail in the DCP that resulted in a planning protocol that set a new benchmark for planning in Australia.

Maha had first met Barry when he was the chief planner for Brisbane City Council. Maha recalls, 'I was trying to set up an appointment with him about a project I was considering, but he was too busy to see me. Eventually I managed to get in with the help of a mutual connection and then Barry dismissed my project instantly'. Maha laughs at the memory. 'I wasn't very happy.'

A few years later Barry left the council to start his own planning consultancy and contacted Maha to drum up some business. Barry began working on a few of Maha's projects before being persuaded to join the Springfield team full time.

Barry was an exceptional individual. Not only was he capable, credible and well connected, but he had an unusual work ethic. Raynuha recalls when she and Barry were negotiating a major Springfield deal. As each new draft was prepared, the Springfield team would go through the document page by page. In one of the debriefing sessions Maha told Barry he wanted the other party to pay for a section of road that was required as part of the deal. But the negotiations had already progressed significantly and this issue had never been raised before. Barry was adamant that he wasn't going to raise it so late in the negotiations. He believed that introducing extra points in the middle of a negotiation could lose you ground, and Barry certainly didn't want to lose any ground—especially as this particular deal was critical to the survival of the project. He was no yes-man and he fought tooth and nail with Maha against it. Eventually, after 10 minutes of very heated debate, Maha put his foot down and told him to 'do it!' Next day Barry and Raynuha went to the meeting. Raynuha remembers, 'I was dreading the discussion, wondering what was going to happen. Within minutes Barry had raised the issue and had launched himself into an aggressive and unflinching argument as to why they should pay for the road. I was in shock, remembering how forcefully he had argued the exact opposite less than 24 hours earlier. I just couldn't believe the turnaround. And they agreed to pay for the road! Barry was amazing like that'.

It would have been so easy for Barry to go into that meeting and say, 'Hey look fellas, Maha wants you to pay for the road', but if he had there is no way he would have got the same outcome. He was a brilliant negotiator, strategist and true professional.

 ## The principle in action

One of the most significant events during Gandhi's struggle for Indian Independence was the Salt March or Salt Satyagraha.

Gandhi's decision to protest over the salt tax was initially met with British incredulity and amusement. But Gandhi had chosen this hugely unpopular tax because of its relevance to all Indians regardless of wealth or status. Salt was an essential daily item and the tax represented 8.2 per cent of the British Raj tax revenue. Gandhi said, 'Next to air and water, salt is perhaps the greatest necessity of life.'

At the time the British administration ran an absolute monopoly on salt production. Since everyone, rich and poor, needed salt for health, cooking and food preservation, Indians were forced to buy it from the British at extortionate prices rather than making their own from seawater for free. There was no escaping the tax. As Gandhi foresaw, the salt protest would be deeply symbolic. And as an unfair impost that affected everyone equally he believed it would also unite Muslims and Hindus. As the protest gathered momentum the British began to realise how strategic Gandhi had been in his choice.

Gandhi marched for 24 days over 388 kilometres from his base near Ahmedabad to the coast near the village of Dandi. Every day more and more people joined the march, until the procession was at least two miles long. By the time they reached Dandi more than 50 000 people were gathered. Near the end of the march, Gandhi declared, 'I want world sympathy in this battle of Right against Might'. Gandhi had given interviews and written articles along the way, and foreign journalists made him a household name in Europe and America, drawing much-needed worldwide attention to the independence struggle. At 6.30 am on 6 April 1930 Gandhi publicly broke the salt laws by boiling down seawater to produce his own salt, thus sparking large-scale acts of civil disobedience by millions across the country.

Gandhi then continued down the coast, producing salt and addressing meeting after meeting along the way. Just days before a planned protest action at the Dharasana Salt Works, 40 kilometres south of Dandi, Gandhi was arrested.

The Dharasana protest went ahead in Gandhi's absence, first under the leadership of Abbas Tyabji, a retired judge, and Gandhi's wife, Kasturbai, and then, when they too were arrested, under Sarojini Naidu, a female poet and freedom fighter. She warned those marching, 'You must not use any violence under any circumstances. You will be beaten, but you must not resist: you must not even raise a hand to ward off blows'.

The growing number of women in the fight for independence was considered to be a 'new and serious feature'. A government report stated that 'thousands of them emerged... from the seclusion of their homes... in order to join Congress demonstrations and assist in picketing: and their presence on these occasions made the work the police were required to perform particularly unpleasant'.

At Dharasana the protesters were required to face the brutes! Wave after wave of unresisting demonstrators approached the salt works where soldiers beat them to the ground with steel-tipped clubs, whereupon other protesters would simply pull the wounded aside as the next wave of marchers approached the works. United Press correspondent Webb Miller reported: 'Not one of the marchers even raised an arm to fend off the blows. They went down like ten-pins. From where I stood I heard the sickening whacks of the clubs on unprotected skulls. The waiting crowd of watchers groaned and sucked in their breath in sympathetic pain at every blow. Those struck down fell sprawling, unconscious or writhing in pain with fractured skulls or broken shoulders. In two or three minutes the ground was quilted with bodies. Great patches of blood widened on their white clothes. The survivors without breaking ranks silently and doggedly marched on until struck down...'.

The story of what happened at Dharasana appeared in 1350 newspapers around the world and was read into the official record of the United States Senate. Although it didn't bring about immediate change, the Salt March contributed to a shift in Indian, British and world opinion over the legitimacy of British rule in India. It forced the British to recognise that their control of India depended entirely on the consent of the local people and that the events at Dharasana represented a significant step in removing that consent.

Gandhi was fearless and spent his life facing the brutes, whether in the form of inequality in South Africa or Imperial injustice in India. He never shirked from taking responsibility, even when he was personally blameless. In March 1922 Gandhi was tried before Mr Broomfield, ICS, District and Sessions Judge of Ahmedabad, for sedition. In his trial Gandhi took responsibility for riots that had occurred as a result of his writings and famously stated that he was 'here to submit not to a light penalty but to the highest penalty. The only course open to you, Mr Judge, is, as I am just going to say in my statement, either to resign your post or inflict on me the severest penalty'.

Equally famously the judge replied, 'Mr Gandhi, you have made my task easy in one way by pleading guilty to the charge. Nevertheless, what remains, namely the determination of a just sentence, is perhaps as difficult a proposition as a Judge in this country could have to face. The law is no respecter of persons. Nevertheless, it would be impossible to ignore the fact that you are in a different category from any person I have ever tried or am likely ever to try. It would be impossible to ignore the fact that in the eyes of millions of your countrymen you are a great patriot and a great leader; even all those who differ from you in politics look up to you as a man of high ideals and of noble and even saintly life'. After, apparently reluctantly, sentencing Gandhi to six years' imprisonment, the judge added, 'If the course of events in India should make it possible for the Government to reduce the period and release you, nobody would be better pleased than I'.

Gandhi taught, 'True mortality consists not in following the well-beaten track, but in finding out the true path for ourselves and in fearlessly following it'.

What this principle means for you

Everyone has to face life as it comes. On the way to achieving our goals there will always be tasks that are hard or unpleasant. Nothing worth having has ever been achieved without hard work and sacrifice. Nothing worth having has ever been achieved without fearlessness.

No-one is born fearless. We become fearless by our willingness to accept the fear and continue to do what needs to be done. Maxwell Maltz, a famous plastic surgeon and the author of *Psycho-Cybernetics*, writes, 'It is an old psychological axiom that constant exposure to the objects of fear immunises against the fear'. In the same vein, the American poet Ralph Waldo Emerson, who led the Transcendentalist movement of the mid 19th century, said, 'Do the thing we fear, and the death of fear is certain'.

Developing fearlessness begins with choosing not to let the inevitable ups and downs of life stand in the way of your dreams. It is strengthened through continual action, the determination to do all the things that need to be done in their due order whether or not you want to do them. Fearlessness is the consequence of continuously facing the brutes—large and small, real or imagined—so you can develop the self-confidence, self-belief and resilience you need to finish the job at hand.

When we allow our children to do what they want without discipline, or allow them to give up on a task because they are not immediately good at it, we rob them of the opportunity to develop fearlessness. When we continually allow our children to break their commitments to others and to themselves, we rob them of self-reliance and self-belief.

> *If you think that you are bound, you remain bound; you make your own bondage. If you know that you are free, you are free this moment. This is knowledge, knowledge of freedom. Freedom is the goal of all nature.*

Maha had what most people would consider an incredibly tough early life, but that hardship is what made him the man he is today. He learned fearlessness at his mother's knee during a time when the family's only goal was survival. That type of hardship breeds character and, whether consciously or not, he did whatever he could to breed the same character into his own children, because he knew that toughness and resilience were essential life skills. To meet his children is to recognise that he and Yoga have imbued their children with those same qualities through encouragement and a level of discipline that is almost unheard of in the modern world. Yet all his children are grateful for it; none admits to enjoying the process as children, but as adults they all appreciate the benefits.

Most of us, at least most readers of this book, live in a world of abundance. Most parents want to give their children everything, and every generation is more spoilt and pampered than the last. Children are encouraged to do what they want rather than what needs to be done. As a result they lose the ability to be fearless and face the brutes, and that in turn will make life increasingly difficult for them as adults.

Failure and disappointment are part of life. What doesn't kill us makes us stronger. Difficulty is not an invitation to go to bed for a fortnight and wallow. It is an invitation to dig deeper, to plumb your inner reserves, to find a higher gear of operation so you discover more about yourself and your capabilities. It is an invitation to foster fearlessness, face the brutes and do what needs to be done to achieve your dream. As British writer Charles Caleb Colton reminds us, 'Times of great calamity and confusion have been productive for the greatest minds. The purest ore is produced from the hottest furnace. The brightest thunder-bolt is elicited from the darkest storm'.

Besides, actually facing our fears and taking action is *never* as bad as the torture you endure imagining what will happen. Do it! Stop thinking about it, stop procrastinating or avoiding — just do it and move on. Failure is always preferable to never having tried at all, and you will only ever truly fail when you quit.

> *Be brave! Be strong! Be fearless! Fight as long as there is any life in you. Even though you know you are going to be killed, fight till you 'are killed'. Don't die of fright. Die fighting. Don't go down till you are knocked down.*

 ## Maha's action plan

Be fearless — face the brutes! To help you shift your thinking and incorporate this principle into your life you will need to:

> ➤ burn the boats
> ➤ learn to detach
> ➤ relentlessly seek solutions.

Burn the boats

Fearlessness is fostered through commitment to one course of action. If there are options for retreat or an opportunity to change direction, then when the going gets tough you will take one of those options rather than battle on. This is often a mistake. Once you have committed to something you need to burn the boats so that you can't retreat or change your mind. Maha is fond of telling the story of Hernán Cortés who led a coalition army of Spanish conquistadors and Tlaxcalan warriors against the Aztec Empire. Although not a fan of his brutal actions towards the Aztecs, Maha acknowledges that Cortés was strategically brilliant when it came to closing exits!

Cortés landed on the coast of the modern-day Mexican state of Veracruz in 1519. Hearing of a conspiracy among some of his men to seize the ships and escape, Cortés swiftly quashed their plans by scuttling all his ships except one, which would be used to take communications back and forth to Spain. In destroying the fleet, Cortés made retreat impossible and failure unthinkable. The only way the men would get to go home alive would be through the success of their mission.

It is a tactic also discussed in the classic Chinese treatise on war *The Art of War*, in which Sun Tzu advised, 'Throw your soldiers into positions whence there is no escape, and they will prefer death to flight. If they will face death, there is nothing they may not achieve. Officers and men alike will put forth their uttermost strength'. He also recommended the burning of boats and breaking of cooking-pots as a way of focusing the army's efforts on victory.

This is the Sinnathamby way. Burn the boats behind you so retreat is impossible. Tell people of your goal to increase the internal pressure you feel to achieve your goal. Use the prospect of ridicule associated with failure as fuel to power forward, and never back down. Close your exits so the only way to go is forward.

Every person who wins in any undertaking must be willing to cut all sources of retreat. Only by doing so can one be sure of maintaining that state of mind known as a burning desire to win — essential to success.

—Napoleon Hill (American author of *Think and Grow Rich*)

> *No retreat. No retreat. They must conquer or die*
> *who've no retreat.*
>
> **— John Gay (British playwright and poet)**

Learn to detach

Fearlessness is not the absence of fear. Rather it is the willingness to ignore the fear and push onward to do what needs to be done regardless. It's not easy and by definition you will be called upon to be fearless in the most pressing and challenging times.

For both Maha and Bob the Springfield journey has been phenomenally stressful at times. There have been moments when they were hanging on by a thread, when they have had to take actions that neither enjoyed but that were necessary for survival, yet through it all their own close families remained largely oblivious to the precariousness of the situation.

Yoga knew of the challenges. During the dark times in Perth she was aware of the conversations with creditors. And she frequently consoled her husband as he wept, but the children were protected from just how bad (or good) things really were. The older girls would occasionally hear their father upset, but they had no real idea what was happening — and this was true during the up times as well as the down. This consistency allowed them to feel secure even when they were not. Uma remembers learning of her father's success and wealth through her school friends, who had overheard their parents talking. She had had no idea.

Maha has a very strong mind and he has learned to detach from his worries and rest. Naren talks of his father's ability to sleep anywhere, under any circumstances. He can board a plane and within moments he has worked out how long he has before landing, has settled himself and is asleep. He detaches and gets the rest he needs. This ability has almost certainly been honed over many years and been assisted by regular meditation. As his ancient wisdom advises, 'We must learn not only to attach the mind to one thing exclusively, but also to detach it at a moment's notice and place it upon something else. These two should be developed together to make it safe'.

If something is wrong, fix it if you can. But train yourself not to worry. Worry never fixes anything.

— Mary Hemingway (journalist)

Although Bob was never into meditation, he did believe in keeping problems close to his chest. As far as Bob Sharpless is concerned, a problem shared is a problem doubled. In the early days in Brisbane he did occasionally talk of some of the challenges with Belinda, but he invariably regretted it because it would upset and worry her. This was doubly futile because Belinda would then become very anxious about something over which she had no control, and then Bob would have to divert some of his energy and attention away from solving the problem in an effort to reassure her. A problem shared is halved only when the person you are sharing the problem with is in a position to help find a solution. When that person is powerless, it's unfair to burden them and Bob did all he could to protect Belinda and his family from the dark times. He never brought work home, and while Belinda would ask about the business he kept her away from most of his business struggles and pressures. Wherever possible the weekends were for Belinda and his children. Bob would leave his business troubles—of which there were always many—behind and enjoy the time with his family.

There is nothing that wastes the body like worry, and one who has any faith in God should be ashamed to worry about anything whatsoever.

— Mahatma Mohandas Gandhi (political leader)

Relentlessly seek solutions

To be fearless you have to push forward. Never back down, never back away or hide from your challenges. Instead keep focused on the future and finding solutions.

Maha has faced more than his fair share of dark times. When he first arrived in Perth he could have registered for the dole and waited for the economy to recover. There was genuinely no work for which he was trained, and he could have been justified in blaming the economy and taking the benefit, but he refused to take the easy way and give up on himself. Instead he threw himself into becoming a real estate agent even though he made very little income. While working as an agent Maha met another migrant, Bo from Sweden, and together they would cook up businesses ideas. At that time Australia had recently converted from imperial to metric measurement and Bo remembered seeing rulers in Sweden that had both systems, one on each side. The two believed it was a great opportunity and ordered 2000 wooden rulers from Sweden. Maha still has one of those original rulers in his office as a constant reminder to pursue opportunities and relentlessly seek out solutions — no matter what the challenge.

In his darkest times in Perth following the collapse of his business, he never took his foot off the accelerator. He never hid himself away even though his fall from the top was well documented in the local papers. He just kept moving forward seeking out opportunities.

Things didn't improve much when Maha and Bob first set up in Brisbane. They had no track record and virtually no money, and sourcing finance was next to impossible. Although Maha didn't go bankrupt in Perth, this background made potential financiers very edgy. While on a trip to Sydney in search of a solution to their financial problems, Maha noticed an advertisement for a mortgage brokerage firm. It was a long shot but he called the broker. Within a few hours Maha was in the office of John Genner explaining that he needed money to fund some projects. Then he said, 'Before I describe the projects and what I would like to do, I have a story to tell you first. After you hear that story, you can then decide whether you want to work with me'. Maha then told him everything about what had happened in Perth, adding, 'John, I have experienced a financial failure. I want to be straightforward with you before we start. You have been kind enough to see me, but I don't want to waste your time'.

Maha's honesty and sincerity were so unusual that John decided to try to help him secure the funding he needed. Back in Brisbane John eventually called to deliver the news: 'The banks won't touch you on your own, but they will if you have a guarantor'. In an act of faith that Maha and Bob are immensely grateful for to this day, John then added, 'I don't know what has got into me, and I haven't done this for someone, like you, who is a virtual stranger to me, but I will act as your guarantor'. And so began a very positive and productive business relationship between them.

Believe it can be done. When you believe something can be done, really believe, your mind will find the ways to do it. Believing in a solution paves the way to the solution.

— David J. Schwartz (American trainer and author)

When Maha sought the land at Opossum Creek John was instrumental in convincing the AFH board that Maha and his offer were bone fide. You can't help but warm to Maha, and his honesty and passion have allowed him to develop positive relationships with people, like John Genner, who have been critical to Springfield's success.

No obstacle is insurmountable if you are willing to stay vigilant to opportunities. If you don't believe there is a solution you won't search for or find one. If you believe there is a solution out there somewhere you'll endeavour to find it. There are always opportunities and solutions to every problem—you just have to be committed to finding them.

To every problem there is already a solution whether you know it or not.

— Grenville Kleiser (American author)

Chapter 5

The darkest night brings the brightest dawn

Never mind failures; they are quite natural, they are the beauty of life, these failures. What would life be without them? It would not be worth having if it were not for struggles. Where would be the poetry of life? Never mind the struggles, the mistakes. Never mind these failures, these little backslidings; hold the ideal a thousand times, and if you fail a thousand times, make the attempt once more.

If you've ever been hooked up to an ECG machine you've had the opportunity to see your life depicted on a fuzzy green monitor that beeps at you to remind you that you are still alive. What's interesting is that every pulse is represented by a line that travels across the screen in a series of peaks and troughs. That is life. Literally, figuratively and biologically, life is a series of peaks and troughs. The day you have no peaks and troughs will be the day your life is over.

Every life is a series of highs, lows and average times. Everyone will experience pain and suffering in some way, whether connected to their health, their finances, their business or their relationships. No life is untouched by these things. You may feel that the world hates you or that you are overstressed or have too many problems, but whatever those difficulties are you must accept them as part of being alive. Or as Maha says, 'Every human being goes through problems in life. Every human being will suffer and you have to recognise that you are not going to be any different and withstand those challenges. No human being is ever going to escape this—somewhere, somehow, something or someone is going to get you and when that happens you just have to tell yourself it's going to be all right, tomorrow will be better, and keep moving forward'.

Many qualities characterise Maha Sinnathamby, but one of the most pronounced is his resilience in the face of steep and complex adversity. Time and time again he has faced serious challenges and persistent failure. He failed twice at university before finally graduating, but in failing he realised the power of resilience and the possibilities that are inherent in persistence. If Maha had not failed to find work when he first arrived in Australia, he probably would never have entered the real estate world that sowed the seeds of his greatest achievement. In Perth he lost everything, all the wealth he had accumulated over many years of dedicated hard work, his home in Peppermint Grove and his business, but he never lost his dignity or his resilience. Although devastated by the situation he never gave up.

It is not failure but how we respond to failure that defines us. Failure is nothing but a necessary stepping stone towards success. Maha's life has been packed with disappointments, failures and struggle, but when those challenges are viewed in the context of a whole life, it is easier to see the purpose or learning inherent in each situation. Each challenge, no matter how painful or difficult, took him one step closer to his destiny. Real failure happens only when we stop trying.

So welcome failure, embrace it and use it to propel yourself forward, finetune your approach and try again. When you are weary and despondent, pull yourself up, dust yourself off and try again. If you do you *will* succeed. If you quit and stay quit you will *always* fail. The height of your successes is directly correlated to the depth of your failures. If you want to succeed in a spectacular way, you must accept that you will almost certainly need to fail first—in a spectacular way!

The success sometimes may come immediately, but we must be ready to wait patiently even for what may look like an infinite length of time. The student who sets out with such a spirit of perseverance will surely find success.

Rising from the ashes

In 1984, still reeling from the trust debacle and the economic down-turn, Maha looked for solutions outside Perth. He was determined to rise from the ashes of disaster. He continued to maintain his real estate connections, and heard about a possible shopping centre site in Adelaide. Maha had been very successful in retail development and knew how to make a profit. He was advised that the land was owned by two Greek businessmen. Although the site was not officially for sale, the rumours were that the men were losing interest and might be persuaded to sell for the right price. Maha was warned that they were formidable negotiators and striking a deal would not be easy, but he asked his contact to set up a meeting.

When he met them in Adelaide the businessmen were sullen and unwelcoming. Although very wealthy developers, their office was small and disorganised with stacks of files piled on the floor. Gruff, uncompromising men, they bluntly explained their situation to Maha: they had taken three other inexperienced property investors into the land purchase, which had turned into a major headache as they couldn't agree on the best strategy. The Greek businessmen were losing patience. They indicated to Maha that they would be happy to sell, but only if the terms were right. They were not desperate to sell, however, so didn't want to engage in any games.

Maha could sense an opportunity. Unhappy owners were always easier to deal with, regardless of what they told you! The Tamil warrior within stirred, and Maha spoke slowly and warmly. He sympathised with their challenges and diplomatically concurred that the way things stood, it was a mess. The businessmen were interested in what Maha had to say and, as he spoke further about his plans, were reassured that he clearly knew a thing or two about shopping centres. What they didn't know, however, was that he had no money.

But Maha did have an idea. He knew they wanted a solution and he agreed without any argument to the price they suggested — $1 million. The contract was drawn up and the commitment was to be confirmed with a 10 per cent deposit. As discussions progressed the businessmen softened as Maha told them about the numerous shopping centres he'd successfully developed. He also knew that sooner or later they would ask for their deposit.

When they did, Maha confronted them head on. With considerable force and passion he demanded, 'Do you want the $1 million, or are you more interested in getting $100 000 right now? I have got a lot of work to do here. I have to draw up the plans, get them approved by council and entice a major tenant. Do you want to strangle me before I begin?'

The Greeks were silent for a few moments and then exploded. Maha rose quickly to his feet, never losing eye contact, reached into his pocket and pulled out a shiny new $1 coin and placed it on the table between them. The $1 coin had only just been released in Australia.

The developers fell silent again and stared incredulously at the coin, each other then Maha.

He met their stare and explained with sincere authority, 'Take that coin. You will get your $1 million. I will make this shopping centre work, but I have a lot of work to do before then. I will shake your hands on it. Look into my eyes, and I will look into yours. Now tell me, what is it that you want?'

Two minutes later he was on the street with the signed contract. He had just secured a shopping centre site valued at $1 million in an Australian capital city for one shiny new $1 coin.

Maha presented the contract to a financier who paid the full deposit to the businessmen and Maha received $7500 a month to help finance his resurrection.

Thinking back on the situation Maha smiles: 'All this was going on as I was fighting for survival in Perth. So I was in discussions with the Greek businessman to buy their shopping centre site with the bravado of a man at the top of his game while at the same time I was battling creditors in another city. When I flew to Adelaide to plead with the CEO of the finance company to release me from my bank guarantee for $11 million I was on high alert looking out for the two Greek businessmen. I had managed to convince them that I was some sort of property wizard and was going to get them out of their problems. The last thing they needed to discover was that I was desperately trying to get out of my own far more serious problems!' Maha chuckles at the memory. 'I was looking around me all the time, cautiously turning corners and just praying I wouldn't bump into them. I think if I'd seen them I'd have jumped into the bushes.'

Maha was deeply distressed about his situation and the strain it had put on his family, but he never backed away from finding a solution. His fearless resolve was sustained by his abiding belief that the darkest nights bring the brightest dawns.

His business days in Perth were over, however. Although his creditors had accepted the settlement and he was a free man, Maha was keen to make a new start in a new place. As he hunted for opportunities like the Adelaide shopping centre he was away from home more and more, and Yoga and the children were missing him. When he returned from Brisbane one evening, Yoga told him that although she was reluctant to uproot the children, who were happy in school, it was time for the family to be together again, and if that meant all of them moving interstate then so be it. Yoga had never liked their Peppermint Grove house—it was too big and never felt like a real home. They had moved there to be close to the children's schools but never really enjoyed the area. Like many exclusive suburbs it had its cliques and it was just a little too pretentious for the Sinnathambys. Maha already had some contacts in Brisbane and it had been a happy hunting ground for him in the past. So together they agreed to make a fresh start in Brisbane.

Murdoch Constructions did not need much winding up. The peak staff of 48 had dwindled to just two—Digby Johnson, who had fought alongside Maha tirelessly on the creditors deal, and another unpaid recruit, Bob Sharpless. Bob had originally written to Maha looking for work while he was completing his MBA. He already had qualifications and experience as a civil engineer. After graduating he worked for the government for a few years but was frustrated by the slow pace of the work. Everyone had their defined roles and he was rarely instrumental in decision making or leadership. So Bob struck out, starting his own engineering consultancy while also studying for his MBA. When he found that even a consultant engineer did not have the financial opportunities he was seeking he decided to pursue property development.

At the time, property development was not a subject you could study at university and the only means he saw of learning the ropes was to work for someone who had been successful in the area. Around Perth in the late 1970s early 1980s there were few more successful than Maha Sinnathamby. Murdoch Constructions offered Bob an opportunity to use what he had learned and to build his knowledge about property development in a small, fast-moving business. As there were no vacancies at the firm, Bob was sent the standard letter wishing him well and inviting him to reapply in a year. Twelve months on, Maha invited him to join the business, on the understanding that there was no money and he would be paid only when projects he worked on were successful. Bob had heard they were in trouble, although he readily admits now he didn't realise quite how bad things were. There was certainly no indication from Maha's demeanour; he still radiated optimism and energy and Bob felt sure that if there was a collapse this was a man who would fight back. Bob had heard good things about Maha and decided to accept the terms, despite having a far more stable opportunity to work for one of Australia's construction giants, Multiplex.

For Bob, it was a chance to work in the dynamic, opportunistic environment he was searching for. He knew that at Multiplex he would have been a small cog in a massive wheel, confined to specific duties, in much the same way as he was when working for government. With Maha, there was no army to appoint tasks to — he was just thrown in at the deep end to sink or swim. This really was a place to learn the ropes, where he would be free to make decisions and act on them without being bogged down in bureaucracy. He felt sure he could learn a great deal from Maha, and he wanted to *use* his newly acquired MBA instead of mounting it on some stuffy office wall. Besides, Bob liked Maha — he couldn't quite put his finger on why, but he liked him.

Both Bob and Digby were invited to join the caravan heading east. Digby was older and wanted to stay in Perth but wished Maha and his family every success. Bob and Belinda decided to take the leap of faith and join the Sinnathamby family in Brisbane.

Bob had been at the creditors' meeting with Maha both as a member of the Murdoch Constructions team *and* as a creditor (he'd done some engineering work for Maha as a contractor). He recognised how hard it must have been for him. But Maha's head never dropped; he maintained his self-belief. This was a man with steely determination, courage and grit; he had faced his challenges head on and fought tooth and nail to salvage the situation. That type of tenacity was rare and he admired it. If he was to partner with anyone in business, this was the sort of individual who could create something really significant. After speaking to Belinda, Bob agreed to join Maha in the partnership if he would agree to the same deal he had had with Ken Law-Davis. Maha agreed immediately. They would establish a partnership in which Maha owned 75 per cent and Bob owned the remaining 25 per cent.

Many would be amazed that Bob, having two good degrees and strong career prospects, should actively choose such a risky path, but perhaps even more amazing is that his wife would support him. At least Bob had met Maha, had seen him in action and had a sense of his mettle. Belinda did not have that advantage. She first met Maha and Yoga when she and Bob were invited out to dinner. Maha spoke almost constantly of land and property. He thanked Bob for joining him, adding, 'Bob, right now I am a negative millionaire. You are a future millionaire. In the near future we will be millionaires together!'

Belinda Sharpless must have thought both Maha and her husband were insane. And yet, despite her misgivings, she agreed to give up her life and travel to the other side of the country to support Bob, a decision that would affect her life in many significant ways. Belinda is the only child of a successful Perth surgeon. Her upbringing had been financially secure. This move made no logical sense and was riddled with risks. She would have to leave her parents, a burden of guilt compounded by the fact she had no siblings. Finally, Belinda had to leave a job she loved at a private ladies college in Perth. There were no guarantees that she would find a position she enjoyed so much in Brisbane. The move to Brisbane was not an easy or logical choice, especially considering that Bob would make very little income while he established a partnership with a man who had just narrowly avoided financial oblivion in her home town! Despite all these considerations, Belinda too chose to leap into the unknown.

On 15 September 1985 the Sinnathamby family flew to Brisbane to start a new life. After living in an inner-city apartment for a time they rented a small house in Kenmore—a far cry from the mansion in Peppermint Grove. The name Murdoch Constructions was dropped in favour of the MUR Group, which was an earlier business name and drew on the initials of Maha's three daughters. At the start Bob flew to Brisbane alone and the two went to work. The plan was simple—rebuild.

> *'The earth is enjoyed by heroes'—this is the unfailing truth. Be a hero. Always say, 'I have no fear'.*

The ultimatum and the new dawn

By 1998 much had been achieved at Springfield. No-one had believed it possible and yet Maha and Bob had defied the odds. They had bought the land with very little money of their own and had secured initial council approvals for residential lots. The first land and home package sold in Springfield in March 1993 and a new residential community was taking shape. They had survived a council merger and secured DCP approval for a fully master-planned city in 1995. They had successfully neutralised multiple threats, including an extremely damaging story on the ABC's *The 7.30 Report* and subsequent Criminal Justice Commission inquiry, which will be examined in the next chapter. Their proposed development was so large and comprehensive that local and state government did not have a planning instrument to deal with it, so that a special Act of Parliament was required. Astonishingly, the Local Government Springfield Rezoning Bill 1997 was passed by an unprecedented unanimous vote. They had paid AFH in full for the land and the first Springfield state school had opened. Every achievement was a battle, requiring a phenomenal amount of work, and the stress eventually took its toll on Maha, who underwent heart bypass surgery in December 1997.

But despite the huge strides that had been made, by 1998 sales were drying up, costs were mounting and the bank was getting nervous. Everyone scrambled to reduce overheads to appease the bank. By mid year rumours that Springfield was in trouble began to circulate and by December the only people calling were irate creditors looking for money. It was a terrible time for the business. Some of the worst tasks fell to Bob, as the money man.

In the run-up to Christmas Bob was tipped off about an impending lawsuit. At a Christmas party the previous evening his informant had heard someone complaining about Springfield and how they were going to sue for overdue payment. Bob went in search of their accountant, Malcolm Finlayson. Malcolm was, and still is, a true believer in Springfield and was passionate about what Maha and Bob were trying to do, which was just as well because he was also the person who copped a great deal of the flak from angry suppliers — and occasionally from Maha himself. Malcolm knew better than most how dark the night really was for the Springfield team, yet he remained loyal and committed to the project despite the difficulties.

Together, he and Bob went through the history of invoices and payments and pored over the contract conditions and terms. Bob scanned the contract, addendums and all letters of agreement between them in search of something he could use. He spoke with Malcolm about performance and delivery. Had this company fulfilled its part of the bargain? There were only a few minor matters that Malcolm could point to that could potentially be related to the faltering payments. Technically the company was in breach of contract. It was enough. Bob drafted a brief letter and went to find Maha.

In his office, Maha put aside the Christmas cards he was signing. He looked over the letter then set it down. They needed to make a pre-emptive strike and issue a writ for underperformance before the supplier's writ for non-payment reached them. The plan was simple: sue first. The matter would then be referred to mediation, which would buy them some time until the new year. If they didn't stop this in its tracks it could set off a chain reaction that would bring everything crashing down. Although the tactic was distasteful to both men, they felt they had no choice. Business has its ugly moments and this was one of them. They were in a terrible position. They needed time. Bob walked back to his office, feeling like Ebenezer Scrooge's more miserable brother and instructed their lawyers.

In January 1999 the bank sought a meeting with both Maha and Bob. As their partnership had progressed Bob had taken increasing responsibility for the financial side of the business, and had proven to be a genius at solving problems. Known around the office as Black Hat Bob (in reference to Edward de Bono's 'Six Thinking Hats'), he was the person who tempered Maha's enthusiastic plans, grounding them in financial reality. It was his role to look at all the negatives, assess the risks and establish contingencies for possible problems. Although never considered as 'sexy' as the entrepreneurial 'seat of your pants' approach, this type of thinking is fundamental to successful business because it forces logic, rigour and resilience in decision making and planning. There can be little doubt that without Bob's influence Springfield would not exist, as they navigated their way through financial minefield after financial minefield.

Bob knew the bank was losing patience and was keen to reduce its risk. And he was pretty sure Maha's razzle-dazzle presentation on the future of Springfield and how the Act of Parliament gave them a licence to build a city was not, in this instance, going to cut much ice.

And he was right…

~

As Maha unfurled his maps, the account manager stopped him in his tracks. 'This meeting is not about future plans. It's about the here and now.' Maha pressed on to emphasise the opportunities and reiterate the fact that the project had full approvals and the unanimous backing of 89 state Parliamentarians. But the account manager was not interested. After a brief exchange he came abruptly to the point of the visit: 'The bank wants its money back. We have lost patience. Will you pay?'

Both Maha and Bob sat in stunned silence for a few moments. The blow felt almost physical. When calculating all of the debts, loan exit fees and general charges they owed nearly $10 million and the bank wanted it back in 30 days! They were both already taking a minimal salary from the business, cutting costs wherever they could, and had even asked staff to accept half pay. Suppliers were calling daily to be paid and they were pleading with them to 'hang in there'. It was impossible as it was, yet the woes of 1999 had just got a whole lot darker.

In the face of ruin, Maha told the account manager they would pay and they left the meeting. Maha had just applied their time-honoured technique—say yes and work out how it could be done later.

Perhaps one day they would look back and laugh, but right now they had 30 days to find $10 million, and there wasn't even enough in kitty to pay their suppliers. Yet despite the news there was no talk of caution or consolidation—their immediate concern was to finalise a multimillion-dollar golf course and road deal. They both knew that nothing is ever so bad that you give up.

The pressure following the bank meeting was at an all-time high. Tempers were frayed and everyone did all they could to find a solution. It seemed so unfair. After years of solid and relentless effort the full approvals were finally in place, and now the bank had 'lost patience', just as Springfield was due to take flight. An aircraft will consume most of its fuel during takeoff, and it is the same with large-scale developments. Most of the heavy investment is needed up-front—surely the bank knew this? Indeed Springfield, as a fully planned city, went far beyond a 'large-scale development'. A project of this size and vision did not happen in a few years. Surely patience was part of the deal?

A couple of weeks after the bank meeting a call came in from Delfin CEO Chris Banks. Delfin (now known as Delfin Lend Lease) was Springfield's immediate rival and the developer of a very popular residential community called Forest Lake, which had set the benchmark for land sales in the local area. Delfin was a public company, which meant they had access to huge cash reserves. Specialists in large-scale residential developments, they would source large sites and bankroll the entire infrastructure requirements, landscaping and amenities *before* they sold the land and home packages. People could visit, walk around and get a real sense of what the community was like and what it would provide.

This was a far cry from what Maha and Bob had to offer. When Springfield first sold their land and home packages there was nothing to see but open space, dust and the occasional wild horse. There were no landscaped parks, sweeping boulevards, mature Moreton Bay fig trees or even roads! They were putting in infrastructure as it was needed, funded by the sale of the plots. The only way Springfield could successfully compete with Forest Lake in the early days was through a very strong sales team led by Peter Sissons. Peter had worked with Maha and Bob before and together they created a winning strategy: offer larger blocks for less money. It was a strategy that worked, but Forest Lake was by far the more polished of the two residential communities.

Word was out that Springfield was in trouble and while there was a fair amount of interest from potential capital partners, they were all bargain hunters who could smell blood and were circling the land waiting to get what they wanted at rock-bottom prices. Initially Maha assumed that Delfin would be another such bargain hunter, but he returned their call and a meeting was scheduled.

Maha and Barry met with Chris Banks at the Heritage Hotel in the Brisbane CBD. Chris asked about Springfield and Maha gave him the usual spiel. Chris didn't look convinced and after a few moments he leant forward and almost whispered, 'Let's not beat around the bush. You need someone who can actually drive this development, sell land and build homes. I suggest Delfin should be your residential partner'.

That olive branch represented a potential lifeline, but there was no way Maha was going to let it show. Besides, there were things that immediately concerned him. What if Delfin only wanted to control the land to prevent any building, remove competition and drive prices higher at Forest Lake? Even if he was sincere, how much would he want? It was imperative that the vision to build an integrated city be retained. He didn't want little boxes all over his land. He wanted the city centre, the shopping centre and all the components.

As the conversation progressed Chris assured Maha that he was only interested in the land to develop immediately. Forest Lake was nearing the end of its journey, and Delfin believed Springfield represented a good opportunity to branch into another large development. People had come to associate Delfin with the region and it had been lucrative for the company. Chris acknowledged how hard it was to secure large parcels of land and acknowledged that Springfield had a large parcel with good agreements with council.

Leaning forward again he added, 'Look, I can see that you have done a good job up to this point. The plans and approvals, the start of the road are all very impressive but I think you guys could use a hand'. Chris went on to explain that they didn't just want the residential areas—they wanted to develop the entire Springfield site. Immediately Maha replied, 'No. Absolutely not!'

In a matter of weeks the bank was going to foreclose and shut Springfield down for good, shore up the assets and sell them to the highest bidder. The bank didn't care about a master-planned city or full DCP approvals; they would rip the land apart and recover their money any way they could. The dream and the vision were weeks from collapse and yet Maha Sinnathamby still played hardball. The proposition offered an opportunity for him and Bob to save their own skins and walk away from the grinding, unending pressure very rich men, but still Maha refused.

It was obvious from the conversation that Chris didn't believe that all that was planned for Springfield was feasible and expected the city would eventually be scaled back. The Springfield CBD, for example, was bigger than the CBD in Brisbane or Sydney, and a business centre of that size would need a massive population base to support it. Chris deemed it unrealistic to assume that Springfield would ever have such a population base. Again Maha was adamant: 'This is the city that will be delivered. Nothing less. The residential portion is available, if you are serious'. Chris could develop the residential areas but the rest was not available, and that was non-negotiable.

Maha ran over the meeting in his mind all night. As Delfin was a public company, he felt sure that Chris would just want to control the land, not own it. They would develop the residential site, sell the homes and pay Springfield a royalty. He also knew that if Chris got control, Springfield would never fulfil its potential. He had already admitted they would scale back the development. Maha couldn't decide if Chris was throwing out a lifebuoy or waiting for him to drown. Was this a sign of salvation or the beginning of the end?

A number of further meetings followed. From Maha's point of view the city in the plans was going to happen. From Chris's perspective the shopping centre and university were possible with a sufficient population base, and he was best placed to create that population base. It was a solid and logical argument, but Maha would not move. For seven years Maha, Bob and the team had eaten, slept and dreamt Springfield. It wasn't about the money—it was about building a city, pushing the boundaries of what was possible and creating a meaningful legacy. Springfield could become a showcase for what planning could achieve, a living, breathing model of what James Rouse had dreamed of back in 1963. A city that would 'provide new communities sensitively designed to meet the real needs of people; shaped to be in scale with people—communities in which people feel important and uplifted—where there is some hope of matching growth in numbers with growth in human personality, character, and creativity'. Maha was not going to compromise on that vision.

Finally Chris agreed to focus on the residential section only in the hope that they would come to some other agreement later. The plan was to structure a simple agreement between them outlining the terms under which they would negotiate a deal and develop a contract. As expected, Delfin didn't want to own the land. They would design residential estates and sell land and pay Springfield a royalty on every plot sold. It made sense: the money they would have had to spend buying the land could instead be injected into developing the infrastructure such as parks, landscaping and water features, all of which would make the plots more attractive and easier to sell.

A residential partner was essential not just to get Maha and Bob out of the immediate danger with the bank but to build the population base that would make the rest of Springfield possible. A large population would bring certainty to Maha's plans for the city centre. Without people, the shopping centre and other parts would remain a colour on a plan. Maha knew it was extremely difficult, if not impossible, to entice commercial business to an area lacking a significant population. But the bank remained a threat. If Delfin invested in the infrastructure up-front, then Springfield would have to wait for royalties for what could be years, and they didn't have years. There needed to be a significant up-front payment to pacify the bank. An advance royalty payment would ensure that Delfin had skin in the game and that they would get on with the development.

On their third meeting Barry accompanied Maha and they were back at the Heritage. Less than 10 minutes later they were back at their car. Chris had come back with an offer: an advance of $1 million as opposed to the $8 million Maha had asked for. The negotiations ended abruptly. Maha was furious, and Barry was adamant that they needed to forget Delfin and look elsewhere—but where else was there? Bob had told the bank of the Delfin negotiations, which had bought them some more time, but if the deal collapsed then Springfield would probably follow suit.

For the next few days Maha was despondent. He could feel the banker's noose closing around his neck but he remained active, chewing over potential alternative solutions or reasonable counter-offers. He was desperate, and there was little doubt Chris Banks knew of Springfield's precarious position. But Maha couldn't go back to Chris. This would signal capitulation and he would know that whatever they offered, no matter how measly, Maha would have to accept.

Three days later Maha received a call at the office. His secretary tapped on the window and pointed to the phone. She had her hand covering the mouthpiece. 'Chris Banks', she whispered.

Maha shook his head. 'Tell him I'm not in.'

Chris was phoning from Cairns. He had been to Maha's office, so he knew it was tiny and that there was no need to check whether someone was there or not. Refusing to take his call was a bold move, considering Maha's position. Chris said he'd try again in a few minutes. He did and was told that Maha was unavailable.

Chris said he was coming to Brisbane that afternoon and would call again when he arrived. Two hours later Maha took his call and they agreed to meet. Things moved quickly and then they had a basic agreement in place: there would be an advance royalty of $4 million, Delfin would be the only residential partner in the development and they would need to settle some royalty ratios. It was time to bring in the lawyers.

In the Springfield corner was Maha's daughter Raynuha, now a fully qualified corporate lawyer, Barry and Andrew Erikson. Andrew had moved to Brisbane to build his legal firm's property practice in Queensland and approached Springfield as a potential large new client. He had been warned that the Springfield crew didn't pay that well, but he met with Maha and Barry anyway. As always, Maha was theatrical and expansive about his vision of the city then Barry grounded the hyperbole with a description of the robust planning and government review and approvals. Maha cut to the chase: 'Andrew, you have been introduced to me as someone who can do a good job. Now I need to introduce myself to you as someone who doesn't have any money'. Maha went on to describe how they would only pay on results: if he managed the Delfin deal through to success, he would be paid; if he did not, then he would not. It was an unusual arrangement and Andrew's partners disagreed with the terms and asked him to refuse, but he resisted. If this deal came together, Springfield represented a huge opportunity for his fledgling practice and he was willing to take the risk.

In the Delfin corner were Chris Banks, Delfin's chief financial officer and their lawyer. Over the next few weeks draft agreements, financial documentation, sales forecasts and royalty models were traded between Springfield and Delfin. Come April, after another batch of revisions was sent to Delfin and many were accepted or modified only slightly, Bob decided they were close enough in general terms to conclude the negotiations in person.

Delfin's CFO and lawyer flew to Brisbane for the meeting, to be held in a neutral venue. The draft documents were completed for final review. It was now over to Barry, Raynuha and Andrew to finalise settlement and close the deal. Because of their busy meeting schedules, the negotiation teams agreed to meet on a Friday and if necessary continue discussions over the long weekend.

The principles were set: Springfield would own the land and Delfin would be granted a licence to develop and sell residential plots. The deal revolved around land sales and royalties. Barry stated that they wanted an outline of the sales program and a guarantee of sales. This was instantly rejected by the CFO. 'No! How can we know what the market is going to do? We'll do our best, but we will not guarantee sales.'

The negotiations had begun. The arguments had started, and with both sides unwilling to concede on major sticking points the atmosphere soon became combative and hostile. After hours of wrangling with little agreement to show for it, Delfin's CFO suggested they break for lunch.

The Springfield team returned after lunch around 1.30 pm and waited in the boardroom. By 2.00 pm the Delfin team had not arrived; another hour went by with still no sign of them. Perhaps they were calling Chris. It wasn't uncommon in negotiations for parties to break and work separately for periods. By 4.00 pm the Springfield team were bored, by 4.30 pm they were impatient and by 5.00 pm they were just pissed off. Barry called Maha—perhaps it was time to call Chris and find out where they were.

When Maha heard the news he was apoplectic and couldn't decide who to be more angry with—his team or Delfin's! It was now late afternoon on Friday of a long weekend. What if he couldn't reach Chris? Maha hunted for his number. He only had the Delfin headquarters details, but the offices were already closed for the long weekend. He looked through his business cards ... No, it couldn't be! How was it possible he didn't have Chris's business card? He checked his wallet, his mobile phone, his diary. He scanned the message pad on his desk—perhaps there was an old message from Chris? By now frantic, Maha drove home quickly, his mind racing. There was a chance that the number was among some old messages in his study. Again he came up empty. He looked through the Brisbane phone book and systematically called every 'C Banks', but of course his number wasn't listed. He'd hit a dead end.

Meanwhile Yoga walked through the house to find him. Their bags were packed for the long weekend. Maha had suggested they take off to the Gold Coast for a break. He was sure the Delfin deal would be wrapped up and it had been an extremely stressful few months. Yoga was thrilled. The last year had been grinding—maybe not quite as stressful as the trust situation in Perth, but bad enough. But as soon as she saw her husband, head in hands, looking desperately deflated, she had an inkling that this was going to be the longest of long weekends.

Maha and Yoga drove to the Gold Coast, the silence punctuated periodically by Maha's thumping of the steering wheel and incoherent grumblings. After two torturous days on 'holiday' with her sullen and despondent husband, Yoga called home after breakfast on Sunday. Raynuha passed on some messages and told her mother she had provided the telephone number of the apartment to a couple of people—including Chris Banks! Yoga immediately told Maha, whose eyes lifted from the newspaper he was pretending to read and lit up. His people walked out of the negotiations and now he is calling. Was it a blessing in disguise that he hadn't been able to find his number? To have called in such a desperate state would surely have been a tactical error. Was it possible that he had inadvertently outwaited him? Maha was instantly revived and within moments the phone rang. It was Chris. 'Hey Maha, what happened?' Maha replied, 'Ask your blokes. They were the ones who walked out!' They spoke for a few minutes and agreed to meet in the Chairman's Lounge at Melbourne Airport the following morning. Maha got off the phone and immediately called Andrew and Barry—'It's back on!'

Chris and Maha duly met and formulated a way forward: Delfin would pay $4 million up-front, with the remaining $8 million a year later once the new road to Springfield was complete. They both knew the road was pivotal to the development. With the final $8 million tied to the completion of the road, Delfin had their guarantee. They would also include a sales objective and as firm a number as they thought fair. Maha had his guarantee of sales.

Delfin also wanted to change the name from Springfield. There were now too many negative connotations to the name because of the rise in popularity of *The Simpsons*. But Maha was adamant that Springfield should stay. After a few minutes' discussion they agreed on Springfield Lakes as the name for the residential parcel that Delfin would develop. Again documents were traded and a few weeks later the negotiation teams reconvened, with the addition of Bob. After three days of tough negotiations a deal was agreed and documents signed in June 1999.

A couple of fortuitous events helped secure the transaction for Springfield despite their very poor hand. Maha and Bob needed to pay back the bank, and the last-resort solution was to sell a chunk of land with some approvals to another developer. They instructed their sales agent to find a possible buyer and by a stroke of luck the agent contacted Delfin. The last thing Delfin wanted was another developer in the area undercutting or undermining their existing development. That acted as a spur to Delfin. The second stroke of luck, which had been an unmitigated disaster only a few months earlier, was that everyone thought Maha and Bob were going to go broke.

In the same way that Christopher Columbus was able to negotiate a 10 per cent cut of all the riches from his expeditions because the Spanish thought he wouldn't survive the voyage, Springfield were able to negotiate a strong deal because Delfin probably didn't think they would survive either! It was common knowledge that Maha and Bob were in trouble, so while they were pushing for first right of refusal on certain parts of the development Springfield was pushing for escalating royalties for properties that were sold over a certain price. Delfin didn't argue too fiercely over this because (a) Springfield were probably going broke so it was a moot point and (b) even if they didn't go broke, Delfin didn't believe property in the area would ever reach the price that would trigger the higher royalty. But Springfield did survive, and property did reach new highs in the area.

Springfield had escaped the hangman's noose ... for now.

> *In studying the great characters the world has produced, I dare say, in the vast majority of cases, it would be found that it was misery that taught more than happiness, it was poverty that taught more than wealth, it was blows that brought out their inner fire more than praise.*

The principle in action

Maha's father had often reminded him of this principle during difficult times, such as when Maha was failing his university exams. The darkest night brings the brightest dawn: the truth in those words can be seen in action in all walks of life and throughout history.

A famous exemplar of perseverance in the face of failure was Thomas Edison. Edison was one of the most prolific inventors in history, holding 1093 US patents in his name as well as many in the UK, France and Germany. In relation to his invention of the light bulb he once said, 'If I find 10 000 ways something won't work, I haven't failed. I am not discouraged, because every wrong attempt discarded is another step forward'.

More recently, inventor Sir James Dyson's focus was the humble vacuum cleaner and his goal was to create a bagless model, which at the time was considered impossible. Also, the industry was against him because the disposable bags represented a significant additional revenue stream for the major manufacturers.

Dyson did eventually create a bagless vacuum cleaner, but it took him 15 years, most of his life savings and 5127 prototypes before he succeeded. He refers to his persistence as a process of 'purposeful failures'. In other words, he tried things he expected to fail in order to rule them out and get closer to the solution. Dyson believes in trying things that conventional wisdom says won't work. When working on his now famous vacuum cleaner, he initially used a conventionally shaped cyclone, the kind you see in textbooks. But the device didn't work. So he purposefully tried the 'wrong shape', which was the opposite of conical. And it worked. Dyson says, 'It was wrong-doing rather than wrong-thinking. That's not easy, because we're all taught to do things the right way'.

Dyson believes that the only reason people fail in any endeavour is because they give up too easily, especially when the world seems to be against them. For Dyson it is exactly at this point, when it's tough and seems hopeless, that you must push harder. 'I use the analogy of running a race. It seems as though you can't carry on, but if you just get through the pain barrier, you'll see the end and be okay. Often, just around the corner is where the solution will happen.' Dyson had always felt success was just around the corner, and at corner 5126 it was. Knighted in 2006, Sir James is now one of the richest men in the UK, with an estimated net worth of more than £1 billion.

Everything worth achieving takes time, effort and patience. The journey towards success is never linear or easy. Sophocles acknowledged this fact two and a half thousand years ago when he said, 'There is no success without hardship'. Hardship and discomfort are part of the process. If they were not, then everyone would be successful and success wouldn't be exceptional.

Dark times are part of life; it is what we do about those dark times that defines our life. There are people who have experienced unimaginable horror. Some have been broken by those experiences, while others have used the pain to help others and find constructive and powerful reasons to survive.

Even at the gate of death, in the greatest danger, in the thick of the battlefield, at the bottom of the ocean, on the tops of the highest mountains, in the thickest of the forest, tell yourself, 'I am He, I am He'.

What this principle means for you

Life is good or evil according to the state of mind in which we look at it, it is neither by itself. Fire, by itself, is neither good nor evil. When it keeps us warm we say, 'How beautiful is fire!' When it burns our fingers, we blame it.

Instead of looking at the events of your life as good or bad, success or failure — just do the work. Remain true to your dreams and aspirations and never stop. Failure is the end only when you choose to give up. The ancient wisdom that guides Maha's life reminds us, 'We must learn that nothing can happen to us, unless we make ourselves susceptible to it... We get only that for which we are fitted. Let us give up our pride and understand this, that never is misery undeserved. There never has been a blow undeserved: there never has been an evil for which I did not pave the way with my own hands. We ought to know that. Analyse yourself and you will find that every blow you have received came to you because you prepared yourself for it. You did half, and the external world did the other half: that is how the blow came. That will sober us down. At the same time, from this very analysis will come a note of hope, and the note of hope is: "I have no control of the external world, but that which is in me and nearer unto me, my own world, is in my control. If the two together are required to make a failure, if the two together are necessary to give me a blow, I will not contribute the one which is in my keeping; and how then can the blow come? If I get real control of myself, the blow will never come"'.

In other words, sometimes life is extremely difficult. This is true for everyone. These challenges and dark times represent the first blow. And very often we have no control over these events. But although we may not always be in control of what happens to us in life we are *always* in control of what we decide those events mean and what we decide to do about them. If we choose to interpret failure as evidence of our personal weakness or that we are not worthy of success or don't deserve to achieve our dreams, then we provide the second fatal blow to our own success. If we decide that the odd failure is the end and stop trying, then it is the end.

If, on the other hand, we decide that failure is a temporary and necessary step towards success, that we are merely engaging in 'purposeful failure', then it is not a personal indictment on our abilities or character. If we can remember that no matter how bad something seems in the moment, no matter how useless and how desperate the situation may appear the sun *will* still rise tomorrow and with it a new day and a new opportunity.

Nothing in life means anything until we ascribe meaning to it. And it is that meaning that either propels us forward or holds us back.

> *You are the makers of your own fortunes. You make yourselves suffer, you make good and evil, and it is you who put your hands before your eyes and weep that it is dark. Take your hands away and see the light.*

When you remember that the darkest night brings the brightest day or, as Richard Nixon once said, 'the finest steel has to go through the hottest fire', then you are reminded that you can end your dreams only by giving up. Just keep going. Just keep putting one foot in front of the other and you will reach the top. Give up and you're finished.

> *I fervently wish no misery ever came near anyone; yet it is that alone that gives us an insight into the depths of our lives, does it not? In our moments of anguish, gates barred forever seem to open and let in many a flood of light.*

Maha's action plan

The darkest night brings the brightest dawn! In order to help you shift your thinking and incorporate this principle into your life you will need to:

➤ turn every stone
➤ manage perception
➤ never, never, never give up.

Turn every stone

When you are in a tight spot, turn every stone. Too often in life we pre-assess outcomes before taking the action, so we come up with potential solutions and immediately discount most of them because 'they won't work'. But it is not for you to decide if those potential solutions will work or not.

Success or failure is a two-part equation—what you do and what the universe does. Both must align for success or failure. If you do nothing and sit around waiting for a solution, then you will be waiting a long time. Your job is therefore to turn every stone and fulfil your side of the bargain. Don't pre-assess the likelihood of success—just try everything, and keep trying until you succeed.

When Maha was looking for a capital partner to fund the first payment of $3 million to AFH he contacted everyone in his network. He even asked the agent responsible for selling the land to him in the first place if he knew anyone else who would like a part of it. At a time when Maha and Bob didn't even own the land! This is not an approach Maha uses only at work. Naren remembers one time when he was at school and one of his teachers had really upset him. He went home that evening and must have been unusually quiet. Maha kept asking him what was wrong and eventually, after hours of cajoling, Naren told him what had happened. Quietly, Maha left Naren's room and called every person in the phone book with the same surname and initials until he found the teacher and calmly requested a meeting with him the following day. Naren remembers, 'I thought he'd give up after about a dozen calls but he just kept calling until he found him'.

Raynuha has a similar story. She had failed an exam at school and was so distraught about it that she locked herself in her room and refused to let either her mum or her dad into the room. Maha could hear her crying on the other side of the door and gently coaxed her to open the door but she refused, telling him to 'go away'. After several minutes of this it went quiet and Raynuha thought he'd given up. But Maha returned with a screwdriver and took the door off its hinges so he could get in to comfort his daughter.

Determine that the thing can and shall be done, and then we shall find the way.

—Abraham Lincoln (16th US President)

Maha's approach has always been a little unorthodox. There have been many times in the Springfield journey when problems seemed insurmountable but the team continued to turn every stone. Neither Maha nor Bob enjoyed issuing writs at Christmas but it was a necessary evil to survive and continue to take one more step. As predicted, the matter went to mediation and the supplier was eventually paid in full in the new year, although they never did business with Springfield again. It wasn't pretty and the incident represented a low moment for both Bob and Maha, but they needed to stave off a lawsuit that could have signalled the end for Springfield.

Be careful what you water your dreams with. Water them with worry and fear and you will produce weeds that choke the life from your dream. Water them with optimism and solutions and you will cultivate success. Always be on the lookout for ways to turn a problem into an opportunity for success. Always be on the lookout for ways to nurture your dream.

—Lao Tzu (Chinese Taoist philosopher)

Manage perception

Success is built largely on confidence. People want to do business with people who are successful or who can demonstrate ability and a track record. That is not always possible, so managing the perception in any venture is vital.

When Maha arrived in Perth in 1971 he walked the streets in his best suit looking for work, regardless of the weather. When Murdoch Constructions was in trouble he was advised not to downgrade his car because that would send the wrong signal to the market.

When Springfield was in serious trouble in 1998 Maha remembered the advice. Offers were being made from possible capital partners but they were ridiculously low and Maha and Bob knew that if they sold land below its worth, industry confidence would evaporate. It would be a clear sign of serious problems, so regardless of how hard it was inside the business they needed to manage perception and maintain their standards. Credibility was critical, so the BMWs were not replaced by Holdens.

Men in general judge more from appearance than from reality.

—Niccolo Machiavelli (Italian writer and statesman)

One of the saddest moments in Maha's life was when he and Bob had to ask senior staff to accept half wages, and they are both eternally grateful for the loyalty and support that all the staff showed during that dark time. All pretence of success was managed externally, while inside the business everyone focused tenaciously on reducing costs and overheads. Staff were making notepads from scrap paper and volunteering to do the office cleaning, but from the outside it was business as usual. Whatever you do and whatever challenges you face, keep them to yourself. Maintain appearances or confidence will crumble and your problems will escalate.

Confidence is contagious and so is lack of confidence, and a customer will recognise both.

—Vince Lombardi (American football coach)

Never, never, never give up

If there is one secret to success, then this is it. If you refuse to give up regardless of the obstacles and hurdles thrown in your path, then you will eventually succeed.

Maha has instilled the same dogged determination in his own children, just as his father had taught him. When Raynuha and Meera were studying at Australian National University (ANU) in Canberra they would ring home every Sunday night. One particular Sunday when they were speaking to their parents Meera became very upset. She'd recently sat an exam and was convinced she had done poorly. Raynuha remembers, 'The next day we were in the library as usual and it was about 9 o'clock at night and in walks Papa. He'd flown to Sydney for meetings and then on to Canberra to see us. He'd asked someone where we would be, been told the library and came and tracked us down'. Maha stayed overnight in their student accommodation and then left the next day. Nothing was ever too much effort for his children. He wanted to make sure that Meera felt safe and supported and to reassure her that with hard work it would all work out, which of course it did.

Never give in! Never give in! Never, never, never, never — in nothing great or small, large or petty. Never give in except to convictions of honour and good sense. Never yield to force. Never yield to the apparently overwhelming might of the enemy.

— Winston Churchill (British politician)

It is this trait perhaps more than any other that defines Maha Sinnathamby and all successful people. His levels of resilience and persistence are extremely unusual. It is not that he is unaffected by the failures and the challenges he meets; he certainly is. His life has been strewn with difficulties, many of his own making. He has sought out unusual projects and been willing to take on risks that others simply would not contemplate. And with his infectious enthusiasm he has managed to enrol other willing risk-takers, each as determined in their own right to see the vision to fruition.

If someone somewhere has achieved their dream, then it is possible. Hold on to that thought and persevere no matter what difficulties arise. Nothing that can happen is ever bad enough to warrant throwing in the towel. Not if you want it badly enough.

The greatest glory in living lies not in never falling, but in rising every time we fall.

— Nelson Mandela (former South African president)

Chapter 6

Pure in thought, word and deed

The infinite future is before you, and you must always remember that each word, thought, and deed, lays up a store for you and that as the bad thoughts and bad works are ready to spring upon you like tigers, so also there is the inspiring hope that the good thoughts and good deeds are ready with the power of a hundred thousand angels to defend you always and forever.

Purity in thought, word and deed are the three essential ingredients for success. This powerful trilogy represents the internal, the external and the bridge between the two. Everything begins as a thought. The chair you are sitting on, the book your are reading, the house you live in and the car you drive—everything began life as a thought in someone's head. It was invisible and intangible but it began a process. That idea was then expressed through words to other people and finally the cycle of creation was completed by deed or action. An idea without expression and ultimately action will remain invisible and intangible. It is only when you do something with it that it comes to life.

Each element on its own has inherent power. The power of thought is well documented, as is the power of the written or spoken word. The outcome of action is equally well known, but action alone is as futile as thought on its own. If you do not take the time to think something through and express the vision accurately, the action is uncoordinated and ineffective. People can easily look busy without achieving anything meaningful if action is initiated without thought or effective expression. Bring these things together, however, and something magical happens.

When there is congruence between thought, word and deed a purity of purpose emerges from infinite possibility, and it is that congruence and unity that brings bold visions to life. When the trilogy is active, a goal can often take on a sense of divine providence. When there is alignment between what you think, say and do, a sincerity is created that generates a huge amount of energy and momentum towards your goal. As Ralph Waldo Emerson said, 'Once you make a decision, the universe conspires to make it happen'.

> *Purity, patience, and perseverance are the three essentials to success and, above all, love. All time is yours, there is no indecent haste. Everything will come right if you are pure and sincere.*

Brookwater — the Greg Norman-designed golf course

After the bank delivered its bombshell Maha and Bob spent several minutes in stunned silence. The bank had just 'lost patience' and effectively demanded that they repay $10 million in 30 days. It was a severe blow and they needed time to digest the information. As Maha says, 'In life there will always be moments when you will be at your lowest level. When you reach that point, you have to believe that tomorrow will be a better day. The belief that the darkest night brings the brightest dawn will revive your spirits and help you to surge forward towards a brighter tomorrow. For us, in that moment we thought, "OK, we've just heard the worst possible news, but we're going to find a solution and tomorrow will be a better day"'.

Once the initial shock wore off, Maha and Bob soon rallied. Neither man is a quitter and there was never any question of capitulation. Part of Bob's role has always been to cover contingencies. They had a plan in place in the event that the worst really did come to pass, but the focus was almost entirely on the future, and business as usual. In this case it involved finalising a very important addition to the Springfield landscape — a golf course and residential development.

The only way to move forward with Springfield was to continually add value to the land and attract more people to the area. Increasing demand would naturally increase land value and increase interest from other parties who could add even more value to the area. Much of the overall master plan relied on staged development. First they needed to bring people in, to build the population base, and this was given a boost by the deal with Delfin. Without the people it was difficult to attract a commercial partner to develop a shopping centre; any entertainment facilities also largely depended on an expanding population.

Although the team had already considered a golf course development, it wasn't until mid 1999 that the idea really began to take shape. David Henry had a relative who worked for Macquarie Group and he'd been told that the company was moving into golf course development. They had raised capital through AMP and had linked up with Greg Norman and his golf course design team to create Medallist Developments. This was very interesting news because Maha and Bob didn't just want a world-class golf course; the course also had to be the centrepiece of a premium residential community. Having such a recognised name as Greg Norman associated with it would be a huge drawcard, especially once the course was capable of hosting a major international golf tournament.

The challenge, as always, was that they had no money. Added to that, they had no experience of building golf courses or premium golf residential communities, and they were proposing a world-class golf course in a less than world-class location.

The Macquarie Group/Medallist solution offered them both a Greg Norman design and a finance solution, but there *was* a sting in the tail. The interest rate on the finance was as extravagant as the golf course, and the design fees didn't come cheap either. Yes, a Greg Norman-designed golf course could add significant value to the land and surrounding area and really lift the whole region, but they needed to make sure that what was invested in the project could be extracted as return and profit. Above all they absolutely needed to control the debt, and with the interest rates that Macquarie was charging that wasn't going to be easy.

The name Brookwater was chosen for the golf course and the residential development that would rise up around it. Maha, Bob and David had spent time overseas looking at the very best golf course communities and had learned valuable lessons about the right and wrong way to proceed. Nothing could be left to chance. They would need to keep control of the golf course until the development was complete to ensure that it remained as stunning as it was on opening day. Ongoing maintenance was also crucial; there was no point creating a world-class course only to let it and the surrounding area go to rack and ruin within a few years. In the US they successfully managed this challenge by means of a homeowners' association or body corporate through which all residents contributed an additional annual charge for maintenance over and above what could reasonably be expected of the council.

The team commissioned research into local golfing facilities and were buoyed by the evident demand. There had not been a new tournament-standard course in the Brisbane region for 30 years, and memberships of existing clubs were high and queues to play long. All good signs! Less favourable, however, were the results of the marketing analysis, which concluded that there was absolutely no support for building a Greg Norman-designed golf course in the City of Ipswich. Without such support how would they be able to sell the premium land and house packages that would make the project viable and keep a lid on escalating debt?

In August 1999 all these issues were swirling around Bob's head when Maha appeared. 'So, what do think we should do?' Bob was concerned about the body corporate charges, unsure how they would affect sales. Would people baulk at the charges or welcome them as a guarantee that what they bought today would still look as good in 10, 20 or 50 years' time?

Maha was unusually reticent about the decision, admitting to Bob that he was probably blinded by the opportunity and his characteristic impatience. They were both aware of the potential dangers of the Medallist deal, but the upside was also significant. After more deliberation Bob finally said, 'Let's do it. Medallist. Greg Norman. The corporate charges. The lot. It's a package. We need to stay guided by our principles: we pursue quality and we keep raising expectations and perceptions of Springfield'.

Maha pulled out his pen. 'Excellent! That's the spirit. Now where are those contracts? This looks like a tough project. We just have to fight to make it work, right? If we get into it and find that the market is weak or that the land is seen as too expensive, whatever! We don't look back and wish we had listened to cautious advisers and critics. We just *make it work!*'

And, as always, they did.

Nine months later the earthmovers were on site and Brookwater residential plots were being prepared for sale, roads were going in and the Brookwater Country Club was underway.

In June 2000 David Henry and consultant surveyor Ian Keilar were waiting on site for Greg Norman. As the helicopter touched down Greg and two other men jumped out. Following the introductions, David handed Greg a clipboard and began: 'We're at the base of the first hole? So the clubhouse will be where you have just landed?'

What followed was nothing short of a master-class in golf course design.

The men followed the plastic tape fixed to the trees that indicated the approximate configuration of holes. After a few minutes, and deep in the bush, Greg stopped. 'What we've got here is the perfect condition for a classic par four, with a slight dogleg—got a nice little valley through here.' He pointed to the left. 'Good trees there to line the hole. Now we need to allow people to warm up the shoulders with a nice smack of a low iron or a wood to start their round. Let them think they should be playing at Augusta next year.' On he marched. 'But then, we bring them back to earth. Show 'em who's boss.' He pointed up a slight hill. 'I am thinking a devilish two-tiered elevated green guarded by a couple of deep bunkers. Most players will chip up there and either see their ball roll back past them or have it swallowed by a deep bunker.' Greg laughed.

Ian and David looked ahead. There was nothing but trees and a sketch to guide them. Greg clearly had a good imagination and must have studied the contour map. They marched on all morning, Ian, David and the Medallist contingent marking their maps and taking down

Greg's instructions. There was genius and even a little devilry in his suggestions. Fairways were narrowed. Greens were elevated and located awkwardly or on angles. He identified obstructions, mature trees, creek beds and small cliffs that were not to be touched. 'I don't want anyone to have a round here without cursing me!' he chuckled. Clearly, golf course design was something Greg Norman loved and was extremely good at. Hole after hole Greg wrote on trees and marked the tees, bunkers, general green area and approximate pins. Greg was confident that the design would suit the shape of the land. He enthused, 'The place was made for a golf course and the tall gum trees are going to be a real feature'.

The end product certainly bears out that prediction. Brookwater is designed in a butterfly configuration, following the natural topography of the land. This has maximised the course front land but also allowed retention of the natural watercourses. It has also assisted with the rejuvenation of the creek that travels through the Springfield project, ensuring that native wildlife and habitats did not have to be relocated.

Today Brookwater is a world-class, 6505-metre, par 72 golf course that meanders through naturally undulating Australian bushland. Each fairway is lined on either side with towering eucalypts. It was delivered in less than 14 months at a total cost of $21 million. In 2011 Brookwater was named Queensland's best public access golf course for the sixth time running by *Golf Australia* magazine. It is regularly placed in the top 30 courses in Australia.

The Brookwater Golf and Country Club is now a beautifully positioned clubhouse and function venue and also home to the Brookwater Drift restaurant. This award-winning eatery used to be located over the Brisbane River, where Maha and Yoga were frequent diners. During the devastating Queensland floods of January 2011 iconic news footage beamed around the world showed the floating café attached to the main restaurant torn from its mooring and hurled down the river before its white awnings were crushed against the bridge downriver. Springfield was completely unaffected by the flooding and Maha immediately approached the owner to offer him the opportunity to relocate to Brookwater, an offer he gratefully accepted.

As planned, Brookwater is the jewel in the crown of a highly successful residential community. Although the research indicated that lots would be saleable for no more than $60 000, the first lots were successfully introduced at $90 000.

When the first nine holes were completed, Maha invited local politicians, councillors and dignitaries to a breakfast to be held in a demountable clubhouse overlooking the 17th green. Maha was excited to share progress and to advise on the launch of the final nine holes and the residential community that would be built around the course. When one of the councillors asked how much they would sell lots for, Maha suggested a price of between $90 000 and $150 000. *Everyone* in the room burst out laughing. At the time the average house *and* land package in Ipswich was $80 000. One of the councillors often tells the story of how he laughed all the way back to his car, and yet two years later he himself bought a Brookwater lot for $250 000!

Before the global financial crisis land in Brookwater sold for up to $600 000 and there are countless multimillion-dollar homes in the area. The first display homes were intentionally developed on some of the steepest sloping blocks to showcase how beautiful, unusual homes could be created to conform to the natural topography. It was another bold step that paid off, as buyers embraced the individuality of the development and immediately appreciated the benefits of working *with* the natural environment rather than flattening it to create unimaginative boxes. The result was homes that enjoyed improved natural light and airflow, which in turn reduced dependency on artificial temperature control. Brookwater has even retained an in-house architect, who provides a free service to builders so that each individual house enjoys maximum environmental sustainability according to its site. There is also a strict design covenant in Brookwater to ensure the exclusive golf community retains high levels of architectural design and quality. The development is further testament to what can be achieved with purity of thought, word and deed.

Criminal Justice Commission investigation

Maha has always relied on his ability to reach the right people to explain the full extent of the Springfield vision. To Maha, Springfield was never just a 'development'. It was the creation of a completely new city based on the most innovative and forward-thinking planning and building practices in the world. He knew that the only way to get the approvals he needed was to educate the decision makers ahead of time so that when the documentation crossed their desk they would understand what was at stake. This education process has always been an essential part of Springfield's success.

He learned fairly early on in his career that if you don't educate the decision makers and build connections, you massively reduce the project's chance of success. When in doubt, those in government will always find it easier and safer to say no, and that is especially true when, as with Springfield, the proposal in front of them is untested.

To be successful in this education process you need certain characteristics: you need to be likeable and well connected in the community, and it helps if you are part of the establishment. While he is likeable, charismatic and engaging, as a Sri Lankan immigrant from Malaysia Maha was certainly not part of the establishment. In fact, for years he was known in some circles as 'Black Ted'. What Maha did have, however, was an incredibly thick skin and a willingness to go the extra mile in order to connect to an influential decision maker. He would donate to political parties, both in power and in opposition, in order to get invited to political functions. Night after night Yoga would be dragged along to political functions and presentations at which she would listen to her husband talk enthusiastically about his vision.

Maha would even book plane tickets to places he wasn't interested in visiting just because key people he needed to speak to were also on that flight. This was an especially effective tactic because once the plane was airborne it was impossible for his prey to escape! Maha Sinnathamby was and always will be a master in disseminating information. He was constantly tuned in to opportunities to present his case to influential figures and was ever on the lookout to lift and extend Springfield's profile. So when the ABC contacted him Maha was delighted. He understood they wanted to ask him about Springfield and the developer's relationship with council, although the details were sketchy. But overall he saw the opportunity of national coverage for Springfield as an absolute coup.

After the interview Maha called Bob, who was sceptical, especially when he heard that it was for the well-known current affairs program *The 7.30 Report*. An infrequent TV viewer, Maha was not alert to the potential minefield he was walking into. As soon as Bob heard Maha's voice he knew his worst fears were realised. It was a hatchet job!

The reporter had targeted his close relationship with the council and asked whether he had provided donations to any Ipswich councillors. Someone, probably a councillor, had gone to the media with the suggestion of impropriety. It was clearly being suggested that Maha and Bob had paid money to key councillors to garner favour and thereby win planning approvals and other support.

This was bad. It didn't matter that it wasn't true. Every mum and dad in the area would see the story and think that Springfield had bought political favours, and yet nothing could have been further from the truth. Across town the Mayor of Ipswich, John Nugent, was also being targeted by reporters.

Maha had not been prepared for the line of questioning and he didn't deny having financially helped some political campaigns. But how would this come across? He knew the power of editing and packaging, and he was deeply worried. The night the program was due to air Maha sat in his lounge at home. It wasn't a room he spent much time in. Yoga sat quietly beside him, holding his hand. Together they watched the weather report marking the end of the news bulletin, then abruptly *The 7.30 Report* was introduced. There were brief film clips of the stories to be featured to accompany the opening music and an overlay of commentary. In that two-second flash he saw all that was to come: an image of his face looking unsteady and guilty, words he vaguely caught — 'developer ... donations ... cash for favours ... calls for a formal investigation'.

The program was a PR disaster and Maha watched in horror as the anchor, looking especially austere, presented the 'story'. Sound bites from Maha just seemed to confirm the implications. Maha was devastated.

Through the ups and downs of his life he had always maintained his integrity. Even in Perth when he could so easily have kept the assets in his wife and children's names and walked away from his responsibilities, he didn't—because his own sense of right and wrong and honour wouldn't allow it. Maha came from a culture in which the standing and worth of the family name was of paramount importance. A man's reputation was hard earned by those who went before him, and his every action and utterance was considered in terms of how it would reflect on the family. Anything that could bring disgrace was absolutely avoided. All of his achievements were meaningless without a positive reputation, the most precious thing a person owned. Now, in the space of 30 minutes, Maha had been accused, tried and convicted and his reputation thrown into question. The irony might have been amusing, but at that moment no-one was laughing.

The run-up to this TV roasting had begun two years earlier in January 1994, when Maha and Bob were told that Moreton Shire Council and Ipswich Council were to merge. At the time this was bad news. A great deal of effort had already been spent on educating local and state politicians about the merits of a master-planned city. So when Maha and Bob discovered that the councils were to merge, they were deeply concerned. One of the most challenging aspects of political life for businesses and developers is that it doesn't matter what political side of the fence you support or how valid a project is, the new will almost always brush aside the old. It's not fair, smart or efficient but it remains a political reality.

If the councils merged, then new faces would enter the new amalgamated body, new decision makers could easily pull the pin on the project just to make their mark or because they didn't like someone involved in the project. It was a precarious time. To try to circumvent this possibility, Maha set out to identify those likely new faces and to meet with as many as he could. Some were genuinely interested and broadly supportive of the project, and others were not. Most alarming was the promise by the politician running for mayor against John Nugent that if he won office he would push to have 50 per cent of the land set aside as green space.

Initially Maha had been disturbed by the mixed responses he received from the councillors-in-waiting. Springfield was caught between a rock and a hard place. The DCP for the new city had yet to be passed by council. If they pushed it through before the merger, Springfield would almost certainly become a political issue, and although that might be safe on one level it could also create a great deal of animosity, which could prove fatal in the long run. If, on the other hand, they delayed the vote, then people who did not understand the vision could dismiss it as untried—and they could lose everything. What was more, John Nugent was already getting a lot of heat over the project.

Although both courses of action were risky, Barry managed to persuade Maha that the lesser of the two evils was to delay the DCP vote until after the new council had been elected. Of course, if there really was corruption in the approval process, there is no way that Maha or Barry would have postponed the decision. They would have pressed hard to get the DCP through *before* the election. Yet here they were being accused of corruption anyway. In the end the DCP took place after the merger, everyone involved in the decision had fair warning of the agenda item and it was passed by a clear majority of 9 votes to 4. The four who voted against evidently believed that the vote had been needlessly rushed. They may not have known that the Springfield team had deliberately waited until after the council merger precisely to avoid this impression.

The day after *The 7.30 Report* aired, Maha and Bob met with Con Galtos. At the time Con was vice president of the Liberal Party and had considerable experience with the media. He and Maha had become friends several years earlier. Con agreed to help Maha and Bob navigate through the situation on condition that they could successfully convince him that the allegations were totally false. For the next few hours Bob brought Con up to speed about their limited political donation history. The donations, always the smallest possible, made to both sides of the political divide were to ensure that Maha would be invited to political events and functions. Maha needed to make contact with political decision makers. But the official channels for arranging meetings were controlled by numerous experienced gatekeepers often intent on preventing those meetings. Donating to all political parties got him into the evening functions, where the officials were usually more relaxed and key people had more time to hear about Springfield and its future, not just in three to five years but in 30 to 50 years!

It was normal practice for business people to attend these functions when seeking to promote a proposal to various stakeholders. A project of the scale of Springfield needs the understanding and cooperation of countless people inside and outside government. What made the media allegations unreasonable was that there is always separation in the decision-making process. Premiers, mayors and ministers are always accompanied at these events by their departmental planning specialists, from whom they receive impartial assessment and advice, so the decision is never made by one person but collectively.

Maha simply presented the case for Springfield and encouraged the decision makers to make up their own minds. 'The council planners', Bob insisted, 'provide recommendations as per policy and legislation, and we are not aware of the mayor or councillors ignoring the reports or changing any process for us'. 'Far from it', Maha added. 'We have been subject to every test, study and process. All the council reports are public and the meetings and debates are public. Besides, this is a council of Independents. Only a couple of them are in a political party. It is not like state and federal politics where the elected reps have to think and act as a block and follow the party line. How could we possibly corrupt the majority of the individual Independent councillors and hope to get away with it? It doesn't make sense.' What's more, Bob explained, in most cases Springfield was approached to make a donation, not the other way around.

It was enough for Con, who was by then convinced of their innocence, and together they formulated an action plan. They would come out strong. They would welcome a full investigation into the matter and would cooperate fully in order to clear both Maha and John Nugent, who was also implicated in the story. In the meantime lawyers were instructed to issue defamation of character writs. For the sake of his health, Maha was encouraged to take a break and he and Yoga went to New Zealand for a few days.

When they returned to Brisbane, Maha was reconciled and calm. While there had been further media coverage the story was fragmenting, now focusing on the adequacy of the regulations requiring disclosure about political donations. John Nugent had asked the Criminal Justice Commission (CJC) to investigate any claims of wrongdoing and their investigation was underway.

When Maha spoke with John, he found he was strangely unaffected by the matter. Maha had always been impressed by John, whom he described as one of the most honourable and down-to-earth men he had ever met. John knew he had done nothing wrong; his only concern was that the council would be tarnished by the accusation. What made him such an effective and popular mayor was that he genuinely didn't care about what people said about *him*. All he was interested in was doing what was right for the people of Ipswich, and he knew that Springfield would bring work and opportunity to the economically depressed region. It was the right thing to do and he would not stand in its way unnecessarily.

After several weeks of intense scrutiny by the CJC investigators, Maha and John were totally exonerated of all accusations. Sadly, reports of their innocence were not widely reported. The outcome of the investigation ran to a few paragraphs buried deep in the local paper.

Pure in thought, deed and action, so honest that a bag of gold left in a public place would be found unharmed twenty years after.

What matters in life is purity of intention. On Springfield, Maha's purity of intention cut through all opposition and slander. When you are honest and truthful, when your thoughts, words and deeds align and you refuse to compromise, then right prevails. When you say one thing and do another, your efforts are diminished. You must stay true to your goal. Every great idea has its opponents. Sometimes these opponents will be hostile and bitter, but it's hard to derail the sort of integrity reflected by unity of purpose and congruence between thought, word and deed. Gandhi once said, 'The main purpose of life is to live rightly, think rightly, act rightly'. Maha and Bob acted 'rightly' and the commission vindicated their actions.

The goal of all nature is freedom, and freedom is to be attained only by perfect unselfishness; every thought, word, or deed that is unselfish takes us towards the goal, and, as such, is called moral. That definition, you will find, holds good in every religion and every system of ethics.

The principle in action

Purity of thought, word and deed. Each element of the trilogy is potent in its own right. But truly exceptional accomplishments are possible when you combine the three.

It takes courage and audacity to hold fast to a bold vision when that vision seems unattainable. William James acknowledged this challenge when he said, 'A new idea is first condemned as ridiculous and then dismissed as trivial, until finally, it becomes what everyone knows'. In a similar vein, Mark Twain said, 'The man with a new idea is a crank until the idea succeeds'. Over the years the opposition to Springfield has been immense and Maha's journey from crank to visionary has been a long and difficult one. But Maha and Bob have always held fast to their vision, staying true to it in thought, word and deed.

And that takes courage.

When Sir Richard Attenborough was approached to make a film about Gandhi he was curious but not immediately smitten by the idea. One of the main attractions was that Attenborough had inherited the same mantra from his father, whom he affectionately called the Governor, that Maha had from his: education, education, education. The Governor had wanted his sons to go into academia. None of them did. Although Attenborough won the only scholarship to the Royal Academy of Dramatic Art in London, he suspected that his father was still disappointed. But here was an opportunity to make a film that had something important to say about a man the Governor held in very high esteem, a film that could reach out and educate a huge number of people.

So he agreed to read Gandhi's biography, and he became hooked. One particular story made a significant impact. As a newly qualified lawyer practising in South Africa, Gandhi had been walking along the footpath with a friend. As was expected in those days, when two white South Africans approached his friend had pulled Gandhi into the gutter to let them pass. Gandhi thought for a moment and said to his companion, 'You know, it has always been a mystery to me that men should feel themselves honoured by the humiliation of their fellow human beings'.

Attenborough was astonished when he read this. Gandhi was then in his early twenties and this comment demonstrated a perception far beyond his years. From that moment on Attenborough's thoughts, words and deeds were single-mindedly focused on making the film. He didn't have the money. He didn't have the contacts to make it possible, and to make it especially difficult he was British. The idea of an Englishman making a film about the man who, it might be argued, had effectively brought down the British Empire was unthinkable. Not surprisingly, it was a struggle that would take 20 years to bring to fruition. Realising his vision brought Attenborough close to bankruptcy and made him a laughing stock in the film industry. One studio boss encapsulated an industry-wide attitude when he spat, 'Who the fuck wants to see a movie about a little brown guy dressed in a sheet carrying a beanpole?'

Diana Hawkins, co-author of Attenborough's biography, *Entirely Up to You, Darling*, wrote, 'Part of the incredible tenacity that made Dick persevere with the film even when all seemed lost, is his own ability to soldier on, no matter what. Setback, exhaustion, illness... none are good enough reason to give in or give up'.

Attenborough made the movie *Gandhi* against all the odds. In 1983, against strong competition including Steven Spielberg's much loved *E.T.* and Sydney Pollack's *Tootsie*, the film was nominated for eleven Oscars. *Gandhi* won eight, including the much-coveted Best Film award. Critics praised Best Actor winner Ben Kingsley's on-screen portrayal of the lead as 'the most astonishing biographical performance in screen history'. *Gandhi* still holds the record for the most Oscars awarded to a British film.

Sir Richard Attenborough became obsessed with completing that movie. All his thoughts, words and deeds were aligned with that goal, and that sort of force is hard to resist. Even when the whole world thinks you're crazy.

There are many parallels between the making of *Gandhi* and the creation of the city of Springfield. In both cases the creative authors experienced wave after wave of obstacles, including indifference, ridicule, disappointments, broken promises and near financial ruin. As with Attenborough, even illness couldn't stop Maha. After his heart bypass in 1997 he kept working, his office shifting to his hospital room and eventually his home. The individual and collective commitment never waned.

What this principle means for you

We don't always realise the power of our thoughts and the words we use and how those two elements determine what actions we take (or don't take).

Everything is created twice. When Maha saw the land at Opossum Creek, the idea of Springfield formed in his mind. That vision was expressed to the outside world and brought to life through the relentless hard work of many people who believed in it. Everything in life has been through the same process of creation: thought–word–deed. An idea is brought to life through external action, and words act as the bridge between the two.

As the name of his famous book *Think and Grow Rich* suggests, Napoleon Hill was convinced of the overarching significance of the great asset of the mind. Hill believed that 'an intangible impulse of thought can be transmuted into its physical counterpart by the application of known principles'. Ancient spiritual texts are littered with references to the power of thought and now modern science is demonstrating just how accurate this notion may be.

For many years classical Newtonian physics was believed to offer the only valid explanation of the world around us. It was and still is very useful in predicting the behaviour of things like falling apples and orbiting planets. But when science focused on what was *inside* falling apples and orbiting planets, Newtonian physics came up short.

The closer we look at the smallest components of life, the less solid we find everything is. Matter mainly comprises empty space, which is populated by particles, but they aren't solid either. Philosopher and theologian Dr Miceal Ledwith explains that 'Reality is not solid, it's mostly empty space and whatever solidity it has seems more to resemble a hologram picture rather than solid harsh reality. It's a shimmering reality that seems to be very susceptible to the power of thought'.

Thought—especially focused, emotion-fuelled thought—somehow makes an impression on reality to create a manifestation of that thought. When thoughts are consistent and constant, and there is

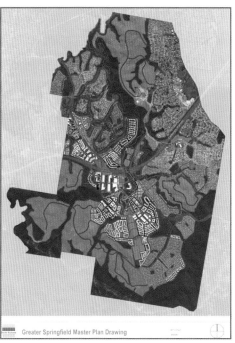

Springfield Masterplan.

Greater Springfield Master Plan Drawing

Maha Sinnathamby with a model
of his vision of the Springfield
CBD on completion, 2011.

Maha's parents, Valipuram and Pavalaratnam, circa 1950.

Maha with fellow University of New South Wales students, mid 1960s.

First sales office at Springfield, 1992.

Springfield Land Corporation photograph showing the team. Top left to right: Barry Alexander and David Henry. Front left to right: Bob Sharpless and Maha and Raynuha Sinnathamby, 2001.

Springfield archive

Sod turning, Education City, 2005. Left to right: Councillor David Morrison, Councillor Paul Tully, Maha Sinnathamby, Gary Hardgrave MP, Mayor Paul Pisasale, Bernie Rippoll MP, Don Livingstone.

Springfield archive

Springfield campus of the University of Southern Queensland (USQ) in Education City, June 2006.

Maha Sinnathamby and then Prime Minister John Howard in the Springfield Land Corporation boardroom on the occasion of the official opening of Education City, 2006.

Birdseye view of Education City, Orion, Robelle Domain (under construction) and Parkside, 2010.

Maha and Bob in front of Springfield Tower (under construction), 2008.

Valipuram and Pavalaratnam (centre) on the night of their 60th wedding anniversary with their eight children and their sons' wives, 1987.

The Sinnathamby family. Left to right: Meera, Uma, Maha, Yoga, Raynuha and Naren, March, 2008.

Maha with the FIABCI Prix d'Excellence Award for World's Best Master Planned Community—Bali, 2010.

Springfield archive

Maha in his office at home with his guiding mantra in the background, 2010.

Bode Photography

congruence between thought, word and deed, then the impression is deeper and stronger and speeds up the process of manifestation.

Think of reality like a radio. If you are angry and negative, then your thoughts, words and deeds will converge and you will tune into 'Angry & Negative FM', with the result that your experience of reality will be angry and negative. If, on the other hand, your thoughts, words and deeds are focused on positive solutions, then the stuff of life will vibrate at a different frequency and you will tune into a very different channel and experience a very different reality. Everything is possible. So what you choose to tune into through your thoughts, words and deeds will determine your outcome.

Mind becomes matter, and matter in its turn becomes mind, it is simply a question of vibration.

Think of the power of words! They are a great force in higher philosophy as well as in common life. Day and night we manipulate this force without thought and without inquiry.

Thoughts are powerful seeds for change: we have a greater capacity to change things in our lives than we realise simply by changing our mindset. Often we don't appreciate just how transformational that simple truth is. Instead of managing our thoughts, choosing those that help us weather the storms, we are buffeted about and smashed against the rocks of our own making! If you are on holiday and it's raining, it may not be what you'd hoped for but you can't change that external event. What you *can* change is your own interpretation of that event. As a result, whether or not the rain ruins your holiday is entirely up to you.

At Brookwater building covenants were imposed for residential lots that obligated builders to follow strict design guidelines to ensure a high standard for all homes. This practice is not uncommon in larger residential developments, yet an interstate roofing manufacturer threatened to sue Springfield unless they relaxed the covenant. No-one likes to be sued, but with a little help from their head of sales Maha and Bob chose to interpret this event as a positive sign. After all, why would a roofing company located in a different state bother to sue if it didn't feel Springfield was a growth area and represented a huge opportunity? Every event is open to interpretation, so choose an interpretation that supports your goal.

The greatest truths have been forgotten because of their very simplicity. Great truths are simple because they are of universal application. Truth itself is always simple. Complexity is due to man's ignorance.

Words too have immense power. The language you use, to others and yourself, has a profound influence on your life and your results. If you constantly tell yourself that you can't do something or that you are not good enough, then you shouldn't be surprised to find out you are right. The Tamil priest Valluvar cautions us, 'Guard your tongue, for it is highly dangerous; unguarded words can cause terrible distress. A single bad word can destroy a vast quantity of good. A wound caused by fire will eventually heal; but a wound caused by the tongue leaves a scar that never heals'.

Words give direct access to the mind and have a powerful influence over the body. If you were scared of snakes, for example, you would have the same biological and neurological response whether you saw a real snake or someone simply said the word.

At university Maha found he didn't really like engineering much, but he would tell himself that he loved it. Driving around Sydney in his taxi he would tell himself over and over again that he was one of the greatest engineers in the world. By constantly reiterating the same positive message he started to believe it and he actually began to love his studies.

And finally deeds complete the cycle of creation. To achieve anything in life it is vital to take action. Purity of thought and word will take you only so far; relentless action is what brings ideas to life.

Whatever you think you will be, that you will be. If you think yourself weak, weak you will be. If you think yourself strong, strong you will be.

It's important to appreciate the flipside of this idea. If science is now proving that intense, focused, emotion-fuelled thought has a measurable impact on reality, then what are we creating? The intense, focused, emotion-fuelled thoughts that many of us engage in most often are negative. The modern world is awash with stress. Millions start their day reading the newspapers, which are almost entirely devoted to doom and gloom. We fill our minds with inane drivel from the TV and worry about our credit card bill. And by doing so, by focusing on the negative, we are helping to bring about the very situations we most fear. What you think about today is creating your tomorrow. So think about something positive that uplifts your spirit.

> *Let us calmly go to work, instead of dissipating our energy in unnecessary fretting and fuming. Fill the brain with high thoughts, highest ideals, place them day and night before you, and out of that will come great work.*

Maha's action plan

Pure in thought, word and deed. In order to help you shift your thinking and incorporate this principle into your life you will need to:

➤ dismiss all negativity
➤ act with integrity
➤ be accountable.

Dismiss all negativity

Once you have chosen your path then dismiss all negativity in thought, word and deed. Negativity is like rust on a car—it might start as a little speck on the bonnet but unless you get rid of it quickly it will radiate out and consume the whole car. We are the same—if we don't rid ourselves of negativity quickly, it will radiate out and consume us, until we can barely get out of bed in the morning. Maha says, 'Once you start on a negative thought pattern it's like you're applying all the brakes to yourself and you immobilise yourself before you've even got out of the blocks. Don't limit yourself. As soon as a negative thought arises, wipe it out and stay away from negative people!' Misery loves company. Negative people usually hang around with other negative people, and they create negative clubs that just makes everyone in the club feel helpless and depressed.

You need to dismiss all negativity. Nothing can be achieved if all you feel is gloom and uncertainty. Science has found that your brain doesn't know the difference between something real and something vividly imagined. If you are gloomy, the chemicals released by your brain will make it very easy for you to spiral downward and very difficult to 'pull yourself together'. In that frame of mind it is easy for you to think of reasons why you shouldn't do something or can't find a solution, and it is hard to think constructively. But if you close your mind to negativity and stay positive, your brain will release positive chemicals that will encourage you to into action and root out solutions. Staying positive in the face of doom and gloom is the only viable option. Even if you have to pretend to be positive to start with (your brain won't know the difference), do it and you will kick-start a physiological and psychological chain reaction that will positively alter your brain chemistry. That in turn will give you access to solutions and ideas you simply wouldn't have access to if you had remained gloomy and uncertain.

Ask Maha about negativity and he will tell you, 'The mind is like a pure white sheet of paper. Negativity stains it. It dilutes creativity, dulls imagination and your capacity to solve problems'. Over time, through meditation, Maha has mastered the ability to dismiss negativity and gain extraordinary control over his mind and thoughts. Consequently he is solely focused on the positive; he hears only the positive and engages only in a positive mindset.

Be vigilant; guard your mind against negative thoughts.

—Buddha (spiritual teacher)

If you were in conversation with Maha and you decided to tell him a little of your troubles or talk about something that was meaningless or irrelevant, then he wouldn't listen for long. Depending on how well he knew you, either he would subtly change the topic to something more constructive or he would simply disengage. If he knew you really well he would quietly psych you up until you were running out the discussion desperately seeking a solution. Or, if you'd been sulking for too long, you might get a swift verbal kick up the backside!

You need to guard your mind against negativity. Never indulge in negative conversation and do your best always to direct such conversations towards the positive. Surround yourself with positive people and remember you are the sum total of the company you keep. Or, as Oprah Winfrey suggests, 'Surround yourself with only people who are going to lift you higher'.

Staying positive is not always easy and even Maha becomes negative occasionally. 'No-one can be positive 100 per cent of the time, but I get over it quickly. Lift yourself by yourself.' And for the record, guarding your mind against the toxicity of negativity and doubt does not mean you should be delusional and stick your head in the sand when things get tough. It means that you face it honestly, define the problem clearly and move immediately into finding solutions instead of dwelling on the problem.

Leaders need to be optimistic. Their vision is beyond the present.

—Rudy Giuliani (former mayor of New York)

Act with integrity

Once you have chosen your one idea, then don't change or compromise your vision. When you think one thing and say and do another, you dilute the energy and power of that vision. Gandhi fought for Indian Independence for 30 years, and during that time there was complete congruence between what he thought, said and did in pursuit of that outcome. He spoke and behaved consistently and acted with integrity.

When there is congruence between thought, word and deed amazing things will happen. In his book *The Scottish Himalaya Expedition*, written in 1951, writer and mountaineer W. H. Murray reported on this effect: 'Until one is committed, there is hesitancy, the chance to draw back, always ineffectiveness. Concerning all acts of initiative (and creation), there is one elementary truth the ignorance of which kills countless ideas and splendid plans: that the moment one definitely commits oneself, the providence moves too. A whole stream of events issues from the decision, raising in one's favour all manner of unforeseen incidents, meetings and material assistance, which no man could have dreamt would have come his way. I learned a deep respect for one of Goethe's couplets: Whatever you can do or dream you can, begin it. Boldness has genius, power and magic in it!'

Integrity is the essence of everything successful.

— R. Buckminster Fuller (American inventor and futurist)

Murray discovered what everyone who has ever relentlessly pursued a goal discovers. The Greek poet Euripides said, 'For to the worker God himself lends aid'. Whether or not you have religious faith, it holds true that when you truly commit to a goal, work tirelessly towards it and refuse to yield, then the universe conspires to assist you in strange ways — chance meetings with key people who can help your cause, access to capital that you had never considered and innovative solutions brought forward by unknown or unexpected sources. Act with integrity at all times and make sure what you think, say and do fully align with your goal.

Become a principled human being. Become an authentic human being. When you say that you are going to do something, do it. Don't say you will do something and then not do it. That's not what a principled human being is like. Thought, word and deed must come together. These are actually the holy trinity within the human being: thought, word and deed. When thought, word and deed are in alignment at a very high level, then you are living a principled life. You are living an authentic life. This takes you to living a divine life.

— Swami Prematmananda

Be accountable

Life, like your heartbeat, rises and falls constantly in a series of greater or lesser breakthroughs and disappointments. We can't always control everything that happens in life, but we can control what we decide those events mean and what we choose to do about them. And that means taking personal responsibility and being accountable for what happens. It may not always be your fault, but it is always your responsibility.

When officials and decision makers were opposed or scorned the Springfield idea, Maha was accountable. He didn't blame them. As far as Maha was concerned, if people were against Springfield they simply didn't understand what they were trying to create there, and it was his and his team's responsibility to fix that. One of his solutions was to take delegations to visit other master-planned communities in Australia and around the world so as to allow decision makers to see the scale and possibilities of the vision.

When Maha was seeking a commercial partner to create the shopping centre, there was at first minimal interest because the population base wasn't large enough; and the only people who were interested wanted to build a standard box with strip shops and several levels of above-ground parking. The Springfield team, headed by David Henry, wanted something different. They had seen the 'main street shopping' concept in the US, where shopping centres were created around a traditional main street. People could park on the street to collect a few groceries or use designated parking areas and stay longer. So when Greg Paramor, CEO of the James Fielding Group (now Mirvac), expressed an interest in developing the shopping centre, David Henry took him to see an example of a 'main street shopping' development in the US. Greg loved it and could see for himself how the design helped to create a community. As a result of that initiative, Springfield's Orion Shopping Centre is one of the most innovative and environmentally friendly shopping centres in Australia and the first retail development to be awarded a 6-star Green Star rating. All because Maha and his team constantly took personal responsibility.

I believe we are solely responsible for our choices, and we have to accept the consequences of every deed, word and thought throughout our lifetime.

—Elisabeth Kübler-Ross (Swiss–American psychiatrist)

Maha's ancient wisdom counsels us, 'We only get what we deserve. It is a lie when we say the world is bad and we are good. It can never be so. It is a terrible lie we tell ourselves. This is the first lesson to learn: be determined not to curse anything outside, not to lay the blame upon any one outside, but be a man, stand up, lay the blame on yourself. You will find that is always true. Get hold of yourself'.

Wherever you are right now, start by getting hold of yourself. Pull in your energy, forget blame, excuses and recriminations—all they do is diminish *your* power. They do not affect the other person at all. Whatever you want to achieve in life is possible when you take personal responsibility for making it happen. 'Stand up, be bold, and take the blame on your shoulders. Do not go about throwing mud at others; for all the faults you suffer from, you are the sole and only cause.'

Man must cease attributing his problems to his environment, and learn again to exercise his will—his personal responsibility.

—Albert Schweitzer (German theologian and philosopher)

Chapter 7

Character is established through a thousand stumbles

Great work requires great and persistent effort for a long time...
Character has to be established through a thousand stumbles.

Goethe once said, 'Character develops itself in the stream of life'. It is forged not by the events of life but by our reaction to those events and what we choose to make those events and circumstances mean. Character is therefore the result of the decisions we make.

Just as our external results are influenced by the impressions of our thoughts, words and deeds, so too is our character. Or as Maha's ancient wisdom suggests, 'Every work that we do, every movement of the body every thought that we think leaves such an impression on the mind-stuff and even when such impressions are not obvious on the surface, they are sufficiently strong to work beneath the surface, subconsciously. What we are every moment is determined by the sum total of these impressions on the mind... Each man's character is the sum total of these impressions. If good impressions prevail, the character becomes good; if bad it becomes bad'.

There is good and bad in all things. Difficulty and failure may appear in the moment frustrating and upsetting, but when viewed in the context of a life they are the necessary building blocks of character. All bad can eventually lead to good if you use it properly, just as all good can eventually lead to bad if you don't. If it had not been for the challenges of Maha's life, which at the time seemed hard and painful, he would not have forged the character necessary to create his legacy.

Stumbles are inevitable in every life; how you deal with those setbacks and disappointments is what really matters. Doing what is right, even when it's hard—that is what creates character and delivers success. As US Republican politician J. C. Watts said, 'Character is doing the right thing when nobody's looking'. Character is therefore as much about what you don't do as what you do. Maha could have walked away from all his troubles in Perth but he didn't. Maha and Bob could have parcelled up the land at Opossum Creek once the first round of approvals was in place and taken the money but they didn't. The Springfield team could have pushed through the DCP before the council merger but they didn't.

> *What you want is character, strengthening of the will … Build up your character, and manifest your real nature.*

Stumbles, spiders and Queen Street Down Under

American actress Anne Baxter once said, 'It's best to have failure happen early in life. It wakes up the phoenix bird in you so you rise from the ashes'. By the time Maha arrived in Brisbane in September 1985 the phoenix bird was already stirring. He had secured the Adelaide shopping centre site for $1 and had negotiated monthly payments with his financier of $7500 to cover basic operating costs in Brisbane, where Bob had joined him and together they had started to rebuild. But it wasn't easy. They had developed excellent business contacts, a trusted set of town planners, surveyors, leading real estate agents and a sound knowledge of the market. But the lucrative start they had banked on didn't materialise. It was a stressful time and their relationship was at times tense. When they broke for Christmas and Bob flew back to Perth to spend the holidays with Belinda and his family, Maha wasn't even that sure if he would return.

It had been agreed that Bob would come round for lunch when he arrived back from Perth, and as the day arrived Maha became increasingly anxious. He had pushed Bob hard and they were still not making any money. He knew that back in Perth his trust situation would still be a hot topic of conversation. Belinda had yet to join Bob in Brisbane and the couple were still obviously living off her income. Perhaps she would encourage Bob to do something less risky. Maha knew that western women had a great deal more say in such matters than was common in his culture.

Maha looked at his watch: 12.30 had come and gone. Lunch was prepared and sat in the kitchen. Yoga knew of her husband's concerns but assured him, 'If Bob said he will come, he will come'.

Every few minutes Maha would peer out the window. Every second man walking in the street came to look like Bob. As another lookalike approached Maha ran to the door for a closer look. It was Bob. 'Yoga, Bob's coming! He's coming!' As Bob reached the door Maha rushed towards him. Bob's arm was almost shaken out of its shoulder socket, tears welled up in Maha's eyes and his face split into a wide grin. Bob was surprised, 'Bloody hell Maha, what's the matter with you? Sorry I'm late but I had a brush with a nasty little Australian!'

What Maha had yet to realise was that he was not the only one with rock-solid determination and grit. Bob and Belinda were made of much stronger stuff than Maha had given them credit for. If Bob wanted to go to Brisbane and pursue this partnership, then Belinda was with him 100 per cent. Maha has always been deeply grateful to Belinda for her willingness to support her husband in much the same way Yoga has supported him. That itself requires commitment, loyalty and its own brand of resourcefulness.

But the trip from Perth to Brisbane had not been easy. Belinda's parents were naturally upset they would no longer see their only child so frequently. But Belinda's mother had done the same thing to *her* mother many years before, when she met her Australian husband in London in the 1950s and left England to be with him. And at least their daughter was only going to the other side of the country, not the other side of the world!

So they had dismantled their home, selling or giving away most of the contents, packing the rest of their possessions in the back of a 1970s Subaru ready for their drive to Brisbane. The plants in the house were to go to Belinda's parents and as Bob moved one he was bitten by a redback, one of the most dangerous spiders in Australia. Although there is an anti-venom, Bob's father-in-law, a respected local surgeon, advised him not to take it. The effects of the 'cure' can often be as bad or worse than the bite itself, and as Bob was fit and healthy he was in no mortal danger. He just needed to wait for the toxins to flush out of his system and for the symptoms to subside. The problem was, in a matter of days Bob and Belinda were due to drive thousands of miles across Australia. Bob endured two days of sweating, aching and insomnia. By the third day he was exhausted and desperate to get some sleep so he'd be capable of making the long drive the following morning. Bob took a sleeping tablet and was out like a light. The morning of their departure Belinda couldn't wake him and had to endure an emotional departure from her parents' home without his support. At 6.00 am she had bundled Bob into the passenger seat and taken the wheel herself. For six straight hours she drove, tears streaming down her face as her husband slumped in a semi-conscious state in the passenger seat beside her.

The drive to Brisbane took a week. They crossed the Nullarbor Plain then headed to Canberra and Sydney, where they spent New Year's Eve with friends. By the time they reached Brisbane Bob and Belinda had travelled more than 7000 kilometres. To this day Bob is quietly grateful to that redback spider because he missed the tearful farewells in Perth and slept through Belinda's tearful trip. Knowing it was his decision that had caused her grief would have made it difficult to bear if he'd been awake.

~

We must struggle, and through struggle growth will come. We shall make mistakes, but they may be angels unawares.

Maha had always been aggressive in his pursuit of deals and profit, but his experiences in Perth had taught him that they needed 'a sword and a shield'. They needed to make money aggressively but also to defend themselves more rigorously against risk and failure. As the business began to gather momentum he would talk of the need for a bold new project, something that would really announce their arrival in Brisbane.

One day while walking through the central business district, Maha found such a project. He was standing in the Queen Street Mall, the premier shopping precinct in the heart of downtown Brisbane. Looking in all directions, Maha stepped into the street at the base of the mall. Thoughts formed wildly as he stood on the busy city road looking at the buildings. It was clear that the Brisbane CBD had greater capacity for retail, and a different form of shopping experience. Observations from his travels to Sydney, Melbourne, Singapore and other international cities returned to him. Brisbane should have underground shopping. And in that moment Queen Street Down Under was born — at least as a thought.

Over the following few weeks, Maha transferred the idea into words and met with planners and architects, showing them his sketches. He described his vision of an underground retail arcade and once the planners stopped blinking in disbelief they began to formulate workable plans. Maha sought specific surveying and architectural advice that pointed to the viability of the idea, and the team commissioned the architect Robin Gibson, who had designed the Queen Street Mall.

Brisbane was to host the World Expo in 1988 and Maha felt optimistic that they could tap into the city's urgent desire to upgrade in preparation for the influx of visitors and increased international attention. The city wanted more sophistication and Maha positioned the project accordingly. For months he strode around town with his plans and drawings under his arm. He visited politicians and business leaders and enthused about how Queen Street Down Under would herald the rebirth of CBD retail in Brisbane.

In the end, though, Queen Street Down Under failed to see the light of day. Although there was a lot of support for the project, including the Premier and Deputy Premier, nothing was formalised in writing, so when the leadership, and eventually the government, changed Queen Street Down Under became collateral damage. After two years of solid work and more than $200 000 in expenses the project was terminated by the state government.

But it wasn't just politics that killed the project. Maha will readily admit he did not go about it in the right way. If the civil engineering itself was complex, it wasn't a patch on the complexity above ground with politicians and business interests vying for position.

Maha learned that some long-established Queensland businesses felt the project was too audacious, and it almost smacked of sacrilege for an outsider to be allowed to develop under the main street. Other businesses complained about possible disruption to trading, the probable weakening of building foundations, and security threats from the underground work. Maha sought out these people to counter their criticisms and forcefully defended the plan.

The project became a political hand grenade and controversy was inevitable. In addition, Maha had not sold the vision and fostered positive relationships well enough. He had tried to drag people round to his way of thinking rather than educating them to bring them on-side. And he had wrongly assumed that political support, especially at the top, was enough. It wasn't. It was just part of the overall picture. To make the project successful, everyone needed to buy into it—the public, the business community, politicians and the people pushing it through. He had underestimated the individual and collective power of the different stakeholders. It was a mistake he would never make again.

Maha learned many valuable lessons from Queen Street Down Under and, while painful and expensive, those lessons helped him accumulate experience and insight that would prove of great value when applied to the most important project of his career. Maha's ancient wisdom reminds us, 'There are certain works which are, as it were, the aggregate, the sum total, of a large number of smaller works.' Springfield would become the aggregate of all Maha's previous, smaller enterprises. His successes and failures, the highs and the lows, came together to provide a breadth and depth of experience that ultimately created a temperament equal to the challenges of Springfield. The same was true for Bob and in many ways each key member of the team—Springfield was and is the culmination of a lifetime of previous smaller works.

Onward! Upon ages of struggle a character is built. Be not discouraged.

All roads lead to Springfield

One of Springfield's most significant character-building hurdles was a lack of adequate access to the site. There was only a standard regional road along one edge of the property, and even that was in very poor condition.

Roads are notoriously expensive to build and developers are always keen to minimise this expense by tapping into existing council infrastructure. Traditionally they would pay for the immediate vehicle access around the development and for those branching into their land from other routes, but major road works are always funded by government. As far as the government was concerned, however, Springfield was an 'out of sequence' development. They had no solid plans to build a highway to Springfield in the foreseeable future. The government has an obligation to spend taxpayers' money responsibly based on need. When there were already areas in the constituency that badly needed road upgrades and investment, it was political suicide to siphon off those finite funds to build a road to a development that at the time had only a few thousand residents. At the same time, Springfield offered council a unique and exciting opportunity to massively increase rates income, raise land values and boost the reputation and socioeconomic conditions of the entire region. It was a delicate balancing act, but the fact that Maha had managed to locate an obscure old map that indicated the possibility of council interest in putting a road in didn't cut much ice with council officials.

When Maha had originally looked at the site he, like all other interested parties, was immediately struck by the access challenges. The agent had assured him there were plans for a new road in council, but he checked it out for himself. To his amazement he tracked down a regional planning document from Moreton Shire Council that showed the dotted line of a possible future 'Camira Bypass'. Although the plan was clearly marked 'draft' and 'not government policy', Maha chose to interpret the existence of the map as proof that the road they needed for Springfield would be built and government would build it. Besides, if Maha and Bob didn't have the money to buy the land they sure as hell didn't have the money to build millions of dollars' worth of road. And yet bringing it to Springfield was always going to be critical to the success of the development.

The road not only made the land more valuable but it made their overall plans much more practical, and approval would provide immense leverage with other government departments and capital partners they needed to get on-side.

The road was needed to support the development but it also had to make sense to the whole region, otherwise it would never get the backing it required. They could bring a road through the southern section of the land but this would only connect two rural areas. Without close association to the large existing population base in Brisbane, people would still face a long commute and would not be attracted to Springfield. Connections to the existing highways, however, would bring the economic centres of Brisbane, Ipswich and the Gold Coast within range. Until industry and business relocated to Springfield it was inevitable that the population would, at least in the short term, empty out of Springfield through the day as residents went to work. If access to those jobs was too remote, it would stifle population growth.

The only logical action, which roughly tallied with the draft government plan, was to extend the Centenary Highway towards their land from the north. This would join the highway to another major link, the Logan Motorway, and from this junction they could lay a road towards the heart of the development site. This would also connect to Ipswich to the west via the Ipswich Motorway, thus opening up the whole western corridor for future development. It was that fact that was going to be most appealing to local government.

But there were significant character-building problems to navigate. The route of the new road would pass through land managed by Brisbane City Council as well as a live ammunition testing and training facility for the Army!

Maha went to see the Minister for Main Roads, who was pleasant but non-committal. A new city sounded like an interesting proposition but any extension to the Centenary Highway would have to be assessed by his department and Treasury and considered within the overall mix of state funding demands and priorities. Maha produced his 'draft plan', but it was immediately dismissed—it simply represented someone's line on a map. And it would not translate into a plan of action until the business case for the new road could be thoroughly justified.

In 1993 the Planning Minister, Terry Mackenroth, had told Maha that if he was mad enough to try to get Springfield up and running, then government would not unduly stand in his way. But it was clear they were not going to roll out the red carpet either! Now the Roads Minister told him to speak to the official in charge of regional roads — Steve Golding.

The following day Steve Golding was listening, largely unmoved, as an evangelical Maha explained the new city and the benefits it would bring to the region. Steve was used to enthusiastic developers, but he had existing construction plans and a finite budget. When Barry and David, also in the meeting, unrolled the plans, however, he realised these guys were not your average developers. Most of the plans he heard about were conceptual: the developers would come cap in hand wanting a new road to somewhere, and when they learned of the due process involved they usually disappeared pretty quickly. When the Springfield contingent arrived, though, he immediately sensed a different stripe. There was nothing conceptual about their plans; they were extremely detailed and were backed up by reports and maps, and they clearly knew their position. The descriptions from Maha and the others were impressive, but it still didn't alter his reality. And Steve explained that reality in very clear terms: 'I have a limited budget and all of the region's funds for new and upgraded roads are committed for the next four years'.

Maha was alarmed. *Four years!* But he remained steady and replied, 'We would like to know when it is planned to happen and what *we* need to do to make it happen'. Steve immediately recognised the new element in this statement. It was the usual 'if' and 'when' about a new road, but the 'how' was different. The road through the area was a sound concept, especially if, as Maha suggested, it continued beyond the development site and linked up to other major road networks. This team had done their homework and had extended the original notion of a bypass into a major regional road connection. It was the type of strategic planning that appealed to Steve. And, as Maha repeatedly pointed out, it *was* rare that a single company had control of this amount of land. Being able to negotiate with one land owner instead of several was a huge benefit.

What the Springfield team were proposing was not just good for their development — it would open up the entire region. Steve knew that mass development was on the way. If it wasn't these guys pestering him about a dotted line on a map, it would be someone else. And if they ended up selling the land to a dozen different developers it would be more than one team of developers knocking on his door. Besides, he got the distinct impression that *these* developers were not going to go away.

The most immediate problem needing resolution was whether or not the Army would cooperate and allow this new road network to cross their land. Greenbank was an army training facility that discharged live ammunition, and if they said no this new road would be in trouble before it began. Also, as David pointed out, there was no way the Springfield team could successfully negotiate with the Commonwealth Government Defence Department. Any approach would have to come from government, not private citizens.

Two weeks later Steve, Maha and David met with the senior officer responsible for the administration of Army land around southern Queensland at the Victoria Army Barracks in Brisbane. Initially Steve had made contact alone to explain the significance of the road to the government and the wider region and had been told that access through the Army land was 'not impossible'. To Maha's delight, it turned out that the Army could see some benefits to the proposal. It could offer them an opportunity to solve a couple of their own challenges. For instance, for safety and security reasons the Army were keen to close a public track that crossed the training land. If Maha could get permission to close and line it with a high fence, the Army would find the proposal much more appealing. The new road would create an isolated slice of land that Maha would need to buy from the Army as compensation, *and* they would need compensation for the land the road would be constructed on. The site had been a live testing and training facility for decades, so a survey would need to be conducted to find and safely dispose of any unexploded shells, and this cost too would be borne directly by Springfield. It was reiterated that all work to do with the road would be their responsibility and all legal approvals would need to be secured by them.

Maha struggled not to shout out in delight. Although the Army approval conditions would prove to be quite onerous, at least it wasn't an outright 'No'. It also turned out that this road could be a blessing for the Army. They had been on the Greenbank site for decades, but increased development meant they now had residential neighbours complaining about the occasional explosion. The presence of a new road might introduce a little background traffic hum that would give them cover and reduce the number of complaints.

In true Springfield fashion, Maha agreed to everything the Army asked for and would work out how to deliver it later. The fact that the Army was listing demands was a huge step in the right direction. The road was now at least possible!

The Army's favourable response wouldn't be set in stone until the paperwork was complete, however, and as far as Steve Golding was concerned it didn't alter his position. Maha had taken the Army agreement as acknowledgement the road *would* happen, while Steve took it to mean it *could* happen when the time was right, and as far as he was concerned that time was *at least* four years away. Steve reminded Maha of the realities of his position: 'Maha, I have a large network of roads that need repair, replacement, extension, widening. And I have blokes like you, expecting me to find millions to suit their projects. Yes, I want this road. The opportunity is significant, but you will have to get in the queue like everyone else'.

Day after day the Springfield team sought ways to get bumped up that queue. After every knock-back they made new appointments and went back to the drawing board to address the points that had caused the rejection. It was an endless round of character-building stumbles! Maha and Bob had taken the hardest possible path.

To add insult to injury Steve Golding was transferred out of the department and his replacement made it very clear that he did not want to speak to or even see Maha. Faced with continued resistance, Maha decided it was time to go to the top. He would get an audience with the Premier. For months (as is related in the next chapter) he virtually stalked the Premier, and finally managed to catch him as he made his exit from a function. Although not pleased to be collared, he couldn't reasonably refuse the persistent developer's request for an appointment.

Eventually after much persistence from Maha, a call came through and an appointment was set for a month's time. The Springfield team expected to hear the same arguments... The development was in the wrong area. It wasn't a priority. There was no money to support an out-of-sequence development. They were prepared for battle, and as they entered the Premier's office the reception was frosty to say the least. The Premier was standing with a folder pressed tightly under his arm and he had the demeanour of a man preparing to say 'No' and escape as quickly as possible.

Having listened to Maha's outline of the opportunity he simply held up his hand and demanded, 'Why should I support a developer with public money?' Maha was taken aback, the emotion of the relentless struggle bubbled to the surface and tears pricked his eyes. 'Premier', he replied, 'you are not supporting a developer. You are supporting a region. Please do what is right'. The Premier was taken aback. He hadn't expected to see this sort of passion, which is very difficult to fake. While it was true that Maha needed that road more than anyone else in the room, the argument he so passionately presented was sound. The road *would* open up the region. Development was coming, whether people in and around government wanted it or not. This initiative represented a unique opportunity to take control of that development and create something that planning gurus such as James Rouse had dreamed of some 30 years before. Finally, some time after their allotted 20 minutes had passed, the Premier agreed to organise a meeting with the relevant government people so they could study the proposal further.

Another tiny little step forward.

Several weeks later Maha and David sat in front of 15 unconvinced and inconvenienced government officials keen to put the matter to rest once and for all. The chair and Main Roads Regional Director opened the meeting: 'Mr Sinnathamby, the Premier has asked me to see you. I know you want the Centenary Highway extended. However, we don't think that this will be needed for five years, 10 years, 15 years or 50 years.'

Fifty years! Maha resisted the urge to scream at the bureaucrats sitting before him. Instead he delivered *a performance.* He explained the unique opportunity at hand: a rare chance to master plan an entire region and to bring great status to Queensland. He took the tactic *not* to emphasise the highway, as he had to generate broad appeal for the project first. He told them, 'We could chop it up into a few pieces and sell it. Most people would do this and many think this is what we should do, but we see something different. We have a vision to accommodate future growth for generations ahead in a truly master-planned city'.

Slowly the people around the table started to ask questions, and Maha gained confidence and energy with each new question. The debate continued. The minister in charge found himself in a tricky situation. He *loved* the idea of this development and it was not his natural role to argue against expansion of the road network. In truth, he felt for the Springfield team. Maha was right: with one eager landowner and developer, they had a chance to punch a road through the area and ultimately link to other highways to the south and west, yet he had been asked to stand firm and deliver a message. The meeting had run on long enough. It was time to scare them off or slow them down. 'Mr Sinnathamby, if you think this road is so important we will have to do an Environmental Impact Statement. Will you pay half?'

Silence fell around the table as everyone expected him to say no. Environmental Impact Statements can be notoriously expensive and time consuming. They invite public scrutiny, which few developers relish, and yet if Maha refused the government had their 'out'. Maha recognised all this, looked briefly at David and announced, 'Yes, we'll do it'.

Bringing this critical piece of infrastructure to Springfield involved a series of tiny steps forward followed by a few large steps backwards. They were already under pressure from the council to upgrade the road leading into the development, and that would cost an additional $400 000 and that was just the start of it. They had to deal with newspaper articles that would quote the minister as saying the road was unlikely before 2000 and that there was no budget available for it for the next five years. It was a relentless struggle that required everyone to dig really deep and find a new level of determination and persistence.

The only glimmer of hope in a bleak 1994 was when Planning Minister Terry Mackenroth had decided he wanted a shake-up of planning that could have positive and far-reaching implications for Springfield. In short, he was proposing that if the council approved the DCP, then the Planning Department would coordinate other government departments in a sort of test case for comprehensively organising government expenditure. The DCP would then be supported by an infrastructure agreement between the developer and council that would define the responsibility of each party for infrastructure investment across the life of the development.

This would create a unique situation in which a private company would put in money with government to deliver roads, schools and services ahead of time so long as the developer agreed to bring forward costs between when the infrastructure was actually built and when the government had planned to build it.

It was an innovation that required endless meetings and negotiations. Finally a very rare letter arrived at the Springfield offices. On Queensland Government letterhead, it referenced a Cabinet minute granting the Springfield developers and their partners a mandate to extend the Centenary Highway to the Logan Motorway. This meant that the state government would guarantee the capital cost of the road. It was a critical next step in constructing a highway to Springfield.

From Springfield's perspective, the structure of the deal was no small matter, however. They had to find a road contractor prepared to finance, design and build the road on the assumption that government would guarantee payment. The contractor would be required to raise the capital based on the guarantee provided by the letter. All good news, because Maha and Bob couldn't possibly find the millions needed for this critical initiative. The money would eventually come from government, but Bob wanted the actual capital relationship to exist between the road contractor and government. Maha and Bob needed to pay the interest bill for three or four years and there was value in these 'bringing forward' costs, but there was no value in being the up-front banker for the capital works. It was progress, but there was still a long way to go before the wagons would roll in to lay the bitumen.

Maha had almost cried in exasperation when he was told the road would not happen for at least five years, yet in the end it took four. Years of struggle, years of little wins and backslides, hundreds of hours of meetings, planning and strategising, sourcing a construction partner and signing the infrastructure agreement, were fraught with heart-racing challenges. The battle to bring the road to Springfield was relentless, right up to the bitter end.

Even once it was built the drama didn't end. In July 2000 the Premier was scheduled to open the new Centenary Highway extension. The Ipswich mayor was to be there as well as MPs, councillors and other senior officials and dignitaries. But a few days before the official opening Barry discovered a problem—a *huge* problem that threatened everything.

The highway was physically complete. Miraculously Bob had worked out a way to fund the the whole undertaking with almost none of their own money. They had found road contractors, led by Peter Wood and Jason Malouf, who had set new industry benchmarks. The construction team were justifiably proud of their performance and put a bright copper plaque on one of their machines recognising an Australian record for the speed and volume of tar laid. The negotiations with government and contractors had been brutal and it took a great deal of smooth talking by Barry, and especially Bob, to get everyone over the line.

The importance of the highway and delivery schedule had been further emphasised when Maha contractually linked its completion by 30 June 2000 to the finalisation of the Delfin deal. Springfield would not be paid their second advance royalty cheque of $4 million if that road wasn't finished on time. The future of Springfield came down to an 8-kilometre stretch of bitumen, and against phenomenal odds it *was* completed on time.

The problem was, no-one was allowed to drive on it!

When construction began in 1999 the Army granted them access via a 'permit to occupy for the purposes of construction'. On completion they had to register it in the Land Titles Office as a dedicated road before the public could drive on it. When it was registered and the title was issued, all necessary insurances could be secured and the Army would officially release the land and, if desired, a thousand open-top limousines could freely cruise their way into Springfield.

Everything was progressing perfectly when Ian Keilar alerted Barry to a small, obscure policy change within the Titles Office. He now needed a written concession from the owners of a few metres of gas pipe and they could not track down who owned the easement over the gas pipe. For reasons Barry couldn't fully understand, the ownership of the easement was obscured through a series of sales or mergers of gas company interests. Meanwhile Maha was jigging around the office asking everyone which tie he should wear to the opening.

Eventually Barry was able to confirm that Santos owned the easement and was told by the Springfield lawyers that Santos's property manager would need to sign the paperwork. But he was somewhere in the South Australian desert, presumably peering into holes looking for oil or smelling for gas. He was uncontactable. When Barry called the Army to explain this slight administrative oversight he was told that if any member of the public attempted to drive on that road before the issue was addressed, there would be *extreme* consequences.

It was a nightmare. Everyone was lined up for the grand celebratory opening, Barry was being invited to join the convoy of open-top buses for the big day—and the Army were threatening 'extreme consequences' if anyone so much as put a wheel on the tarmac. And the only man who could prevent this disaster was location unknown in the Australian outback.

On his way home Barry called Springfield's dark horse, Ian Keilar. Unlike many surveyors, he had a practical way of getting things done. Ian said he knew some surveyors in South Australia and that one of them might know the Santos bloke and how to get a document to him. On the morning of the opening Barry called Ian. The Santos guy had been located. He was in Coober Pedy, a remote town in South Australia where the residents live underground because the heat is so fierce. Ian said he would call as soon as there was further news.

Barry felt physically ill. They needed to find this guy, get him to sign the document, fax the signed copy to the Springfield lawyers and have them sprint down to the Titles Office and lodge the paperwork. Outside his office he could hear that the go-carts had arrived. Maha and the Premier were going to have a race on the new road. Someone came by the office carrying orange pit crew suits and a chequered flag. Someone else came past with motorbike helmets speculating about the maximum speed of the go-carts.

Barry put his head in his hands. To think, only a week ago he and Bob had raced their cars along the new strip of road without a care in the world! In a rare moment of unbridled celebration they had even hired a bus, complete with driver and wait staff, loaded the back with booze and the Springfield team and road contractors had travelled back and forth on the new road toasting the miraculous achievement. Barry had dubbed it the Bus of True Believers. At the time no-one knew about the obscure change to legislation that was about to trip them up.

Barry briefly contemplated the possibility of chartering a helicopter in a last-ditch attempt to save the opening day from disaster. But it would all take too long. Everything depended on Ian. He looked at his watch. It was eight-thirty and the title had to be formally registered *before* the 1 pm ceremony.

For the next hour he tried to keep busy but found himself staring at the phone, willing it to ring. It was impossible to concentrate. 'Ring, you bastard!' Ten o'clock came and went, then 10.15, 11.00, 11.30. All over Brisbane and Ipswich people would be making their way to the ceremony. Even if he had all of their numbers, if he didn't get a phone call in the next few minutes it was going to be impossible to contact everyone and cancel. Besides, there was no way of knowing how many people Maha had invited personally. Very shortly they were going to find out exactly what the Army meant by extreme consequences.

Despondent, Barry left the office and drove to the start of the new highway. A bank of large orange plastic barriers blocked the road. Behind them, a cavalcade of cars was beginning to form, people were milling around and Maha was moving through the crowd shaking hands and patting backs. He came to Barry and expressed his pride and appreciation.

Barry stared into Maha's radiant face. Taking a deep, possibly career-ending breath, Barry began, 'Hey Maha, we have a slight...'. Just then his mobile rang. It was Ian. 'The bloke has landed. He has the signature.' After a moment, Maha was released from Barry's bear hug, looking a little rumpled and confused, but glad to see he was finally getting into the spirit of the day. Little did he realise that the title was officially registered as a 'dedicated public road' only at 12.15. The road had taken seven solid years of blood, sweat and tears and it had all come down to 45 minutes.

Everyone connected to Springfield, especially in those early days, had faced overwhelming challenges with incredible resilience and persistence. Each challenge they solved simply threw up a new set of problems to fix; the pressure was relentless. Yet no-one ever dreamed of throwing in the towel. They had character, individually and collectively, formed by a thousand stumbles.

Have you got the will to surmount mountain-high obstructions?
If the whole world stands against you sword in hand, would you
still dare to do what you think is right?

 ## The principle in action

In the modern world when it comes to strong character one man stands head and shoulders above the rest — Nelson Mandela. Born Rolihlala Mandela on 18 July 1918, his Xhosa name, literally translated, means 'Shaker of Trees', or more colloquially 'Troublemaker'. And he certainly was a troublemaker for the status quo in South Africa.

Given the name Nelson by a teacher who felt he was destined for great things, he began actively participating in politics following the 1948 election victory of the National Party, which enacted the apartheid laws that institutionalised racial segregation. Nelson became an anti-apartheid activist. Although initially influenced by Gandhi's approach of nonviolent resistance, he eventually became the leader of Umkhonto we Sizwe, the armed wing of the African National Congress (ANC). He insisted that armed resistance was a last resort, and the bombing campaign that followed always chose symbolic apartheid targets, such as pass offices, native magistrates courts and government buildings, and was carried out in such a way that no-one would be hurt. In 1962, after 17 months on the run, he was arrested and convicted of a series of capital crimes.

Mandela served 27 years in prison, 18 of which were spent on the infamous Robben Island. It was on Robben Island that he developed the character that is so universally admired and revered today.

The conditions on Robben Island — the tiny cells, daily hard labour and routine cruelty of the white Afrikaner guards — are well known, yet it was here that Mandela evolved from impetuous, risk-taking radical to mature leader and statesman. He used his experiences, many of them beyond difficult, to become the master of his own situation. If he was told to run he would walk, if he was told to slow down he would speed up. He knew he was in a place run by 'the most unrepentant racists in the world', and he came to appreciate that the relationship he had with those guards was a microcosm of the whole South African situation. If they could be taught to treat him with dignity, then he could take that understanding back into the outside world and change his nation. And that's exactly what he did. Through intelligence, charm and dignified defiance he won over even the most brutal prison officials.

Mandela is a big man in every sense of the word, and he always had presence and charisma, but it was the struggles and challenges he faced that shaped the man who in 1994 would become the first democratically elected president of South Africa, a role he had predicted he would fill decades earlier in a speech to the ANC Youth League.

It is not how someone handles success that defines their character, but how they handle failure and difficulty. In the same way, it is not always the big things that define a character but the little things. Jessie Duarte, Mandela's personal assistant for four years, tells the story of how she had asked him to break with his habit of making his own bed while they were staying in a hotel in Shanghai, China. The hotel cleaners were charged with cleaning the room and making the beds, she argued, and if they were unable to do this they could be insulted and might get into trouble.

Mandela listened and then asked her to call the hotel manager, who came to his room with the ladies who were to clean his room. When they arrived he politely explained why he had to make his own bed and that they were not to feel insulted. Jessie Duarte recalled, 'He didn't ever want to hurt people's feelings. He never really cared about what great big people think of him, but he did care about what small people thought of him. That used to amaze me. He didn't mind if he insulted a very important person, or said something to them that was unkind, because he said they could fend and fight for themselves. But he would never insult someone who did not have power'.

That's character.

One of Mandela's most strategically brilliant moves while in office was to encourage black South Africans to support the previously hated

Springboks when South Africa hosted the 1995 Rugby World Cup. Rugby had always been perceived as an elitist white man's game, a symbol of the apartheid era, and yet when he opened the tournament and walked onto the pitch in a Springbok jersey the mostly white audience erupted: 'Nelson! Nelson!' He felt sure that if the nation could unite behind *their* now racially integrated team, then more barriers between class and colour would be removed. And he was right.

The event is considered one of the most remarkable pieces of political theatre ever staged, and as the Springboks progressed to the final the country, black and white alike, were swept along with them. Former political prisoner Tokyo Sexwale said, 'It was the crossing of another Rubicon. Only Mandela could wear an enemy jersey. The liberation struggle of our people was not about liberating blacks from bondage, it was about liberating white people from fear. And there it was, fear melting away'. The Springboks won the World Cup and Mandela presented the trophy to captain Francois Pienaar, an Afrikaner, wearing a Springbok shirt—a move widely seen as a major step towards South African reconciliation.

Mandela stepped down from the presidency in June 1999 having fulfilled his goal of freedom for black South Africans. In his lifetime he received more than 250 awards including the 1993 Nobel Peace Prize.

> *Coming to great leaders of mankind, we always find that it was the personality of the man that counted.*

What this principle means for you

After decades of research on achievement and success, renowned psychologist Carol Dweck, of Stanford University, has concluded that where we end up in life has far less to do with genetics, environment, ability or talent than we might assume. Instead, she suggests that our mindset and approach to life are a far more accurate barometer of whether or not we will succeed. What is particularly interesting is that Dweck proposes that everything comes down to which mindset you have—fixed or growth.

If you have a fixed mindset, you believe that you have or don't have certain abilities, that the hand you are dealt at birth through some sort of genetic lottery predetermines your future and there is very little you can do to alter that. If, on the other hand, you have a growth mindset, you believe the hand you are dealt at birth is just the starting point and it is how you use it and play the game that really determines the outcome. The growth mindset is based on the belief that intelligence, personality and character are things you can cultivate through your own efforts, and that everyone can grow and develop through application and effort.

Most of us are taught the fixed mindset from an early age. As soon as we are old enough to evaluate ourselves, we realise that looking smart is good and we must do whatever we can to avoid looking stupid. As a result we stop learning, stop trying and stop asking questions because if we ask questions we will alert the world to what we don't know, and that means we might look stupid. Have you ever noticed how children ask millions of questions when they are very young and ask fewer and fewer as they grow older, until as adults they ask hardly any at all?

We are so busy trying to protect our fragile egos by appearing a certain way to the outside world that we fail to recognise that everything is up for grabs. Human beings are not born finished. The polishing process comes about through experiences, and the most valuable experiences are often the biggest failures and challenges. These are our opportunities to find out who we are, what is really possible and what we are capable of achieving when our back is against the wall. These are the experiences that form character. No-one has ever achieved anything meaningful without hard work, repeated failure and persistence.

It is this character-building process of trial and error that helps explain why so many of life's greatest accomplishments are made later in life. Mandela was in his mid forties when he went to prison. But he chose his mindset in prison; he studied and honed his character and evolved from revolutionary to statesman. He was 75 when he became president.

Maha was 52 when he and Bob bought the land at Opossum Creek and he began the project that would take many decades to complete and require herculean commitment, effort and persistence to bring to fruition. The type of resilience and strength of character required to accomplish something great is rare in someone in their twenties or even thirties, because they have rarely experienced enough difficulty to understand just how powerful resilience and determination are.

Pastor Robert H. Schuller said, 'God's delays are not always God's denials', and whether you are religious or not the sentiment is valid. When you try and fail it is not necessarily the end of the line—unless you have a fixed mindset. The universe is not saying, 'Sorry, you're not good enough', it's saying, 'Sorry, you're not good enough—yet!' When we can view setbacks from this context they become incentives to try again, and if we continue to try and try again, fine-tuning the process as we go, we will succeed.

> *Neither money pays, nor name pays, nor fame, nor learning; it is character that cleave through adamantine walls of difference.*

Maha's action plan

Character is established through a thousand stumbles! To help you shift your thinking and incorporate this principle into your life you will need to:

➤ believe it's 'No' until it's 'Yes'

➤ fail forward

➤ accept no compromise.

Believe it's 'No' until it's 'Yes'

If you were to ask Maha's family what philosophical ideas are most embedded into his character you will inevitably hear this phrase. It was and still is one of the abiding laws of Springfield.

And it was born at least in part out of ignorance. When Maha first moved to Perth in 1971 the first piece of real estate he bought was a beat-up old house near a petrol station. It was to be the Sinnathamby family's first home when Yoga arrived with their three girls. Maha assumed that because the house was near a commercial petrol station he would be able to rezone the property into a commercial lot, but his application to council was rejected. He set up a meeting with the planner and was rejected again. He called and was verbally rejected. He wrote emotional letters about how he had three young children who were distressed by the petrol fumes, and he was rejected again. He left it for a while to allow the planner to calm down, then after a few months he approached him again, only this time he didn't force his case directly. He would speak about other property and planning prospects. Eventually he built up a good rapport with the planner and again broached the issue of rezoning. 'I bought this property in ignorance. I am just a water engineer. My family is very distressed.' After a long silence the planner said he would have another look at the application. Several weeks later he received a letter of approval. And he realised then that it's always 'No' until it's 'Yes'.

Never allow a person to tell you 'No' who doesn't have the power to say 'Yes'.

— Eleanor Roosevelt (US First Lady)

Things change, people change, relationships and regulations change. If you need a yes, then keep asking, find new people to ask and different ways to ask, but haunt them and keep asking until you get the answer you need.

Nothing in this world can take the place of persistence. Talent will not; nothing is more common than unsuccessful people with talent. Genius will not; unrewarded genius is almost a proverb. Education will not; the world is full of educated derelicts. Persistence and determination alone are omnipotent. The slogan 'press on' has solved and always will solve the problems of the human race.

— Calvin Coolidge (30th US President)

Fail forward

Maha Sinnathamby obviously has a growth mindset and it is his ability to constantly challenge himself and stretch what is considered possible that has ultimately led to his success and wealth. Maha has always 'failed forward' — in other words, he has never allowed his failures to negatively affect his confidence or knock him backwards. Instead, he has used his mistakes to make himself stronger and more resilient. He has worked out what he did wrong and what he must therefore do differently in the future, and he has gone into action again.

Failure is the condiment that gives success its flavour.

—Truman Capote (American author)

Queen Street Down Under was a daring and innovative development in the heart of downtown Brisbane, but it didn't work. He was upset and disappointed. The effort had cost them a lot of money and time, but he drew valuable lessons from the experience that were instrumental in the success of Springfield. If he had not failed with Queen Street Down Under he would not have appreciated just how important it was to get political and community approval for a large development. And it was that important insight that helped make Springfield the success it is today.

Failure is truly failure only when you keep repeating the same mistakes and refuse to draw lessons from the experience. If your house burned down but inside that house was a 10-carat diamond ring given to you by your great-grandmother, would you throw up your hands and say, 'Oh that's terrible, I've lost the ring!' or would you rummage through the rubble until you found it? There is value in everything—even disaster—if you are prepared to look for it.

We need to teach the highly educated man that it is not a disgrace to fail and that he must analyse every failure to find its cause. He must learn how to fail intelligently, for failing is one of the greatest arts in the world.

—Charles F. Kettering (American engineer and inventor)

Accept no compromise

There is something deeply inspiring about someone who stands firmly by their convictions, whether or not you believe in their views. When someone stands up for what they believe in and refuses to yield that position, especially when it causes them personal distress and discomfort to do so, the world looks on that person with awe. It is the mark of greatness and is woven into their character so deeply that it's impossible to separate the individual from the cause or project.

Mandela's reputation grew while he was in prison not only because of the justice of his cause but because when the state offered concessions and even freedom if he agreed to compromise his stance, he refused. He never did.

Good character is not formed in a week or a month. It is created little by little, day by day. Protracted and patient effort is needed to develop good character.

—Sri Swami Sivananda (spiritual teacher)

Maha too has been uncompromising in his approach to life. He demands a great deal of others and more of himself, and he rarely backs down. There have been many opportunities for him and Bob to take the money and run, or to scale back the Springfield vision to make life easier or more pleasant, and yet they steadfastly refused to take them. When Delfin originally expressed interest in Springfield, the CEO spoke openly of the need to scale back the vision, but despite desperately needing that deal to keep Springfield solvent, Maha refused to even entertain the idea of compromise. As far as he was concerned nothing short of the full master plan would be delivered.

Don't compromise your vision. Keep your promises, especially those to yourself. Stand up for what you believe in and don't back away from your goal when the going gets tough. Use the challenges to foster even deeper resolve. Maintain your integrity and strengthen your character. Or as Maha's ancient wisdom advises, 'Above all, beware of compromises. Hold on to your own principles and never adjust them to others' "fads" through the greed of getting supporters'. Of course compromise is necessary in some situations, but never compromise your character.

All compromise is based on give and take, but there can be no give and take on fundamentals. Any compromise on fundamentals is a surrender. For it is all give and no take.

—Mahatma Mohandas Gandhi (political leader)

Chapter 8

Everyone is great in their own place

Each is great in his own place, but the duty of the one is not the duty of the others ... A good society is one in which every person works in their own way to uplift humanity ... We should never try to follow another's path for that is his way, not yours. Your way is the best for you, but that is no sign it is the best for another.

It is easy to look at the great achievers in life and conclude that we ourselves could never reach those lofty heights. It's easy to assume that those gifted individuals are somehow special and blessed. Ours is a world that honours and rewards soccer players over brain surgeons, pop singers over scientists, those who are 'famous for being famous' over those who make a useful contribution. The fact is, not everyone can be a world-class soccer striker or sing like an angel, nor can everyone become a leading brain surgeon or scientist, but we all have a place and a role to play.

At first glance, this principle might appear to contradict the first principle, 'Make one idea your life'. In chapter 1 we explored the idea that there is no such thing as 'natural' talent and that talent is the inevitable product of time, effort and practice. There is little doubt, however, that the process of developing talent is significantly more agreeable if you first find something you are interested in, or can at least imagine yourself being interested in. Maha didn't pluck real estate out of the ether. Yoga's father was a successful entrepreneur and property developer in Malaysia and planted a seed in Maha's mind, whether or not either was aware of the process.

Every conversation, experience, event, book, situation or outcome in your life plants seeds. Whether those seeds grow depends on you, your innate nature, and your ability and willingness to cultivate those tender shoots.

This principle is about acknowledging difference. As Maha points out, 'Success is never due to one individual. There are always many people who prop that individual up and who are involved in complementary roles. Successful people in all walks of life draw people around them who are supportive of their vision'. Nothing is achieved alone. Everyone has something to offer. Aristotle once said, 'Different men seek happiness in different ways by different means'. He also said, 'The whole is greater than the sum of its parts', meaning that when people of different qualities and abilities are brought together, they can collectively create something much greater than each could have created alone.

And that is what this principle honours.

The right partners

Maha Sinnathamby and his business partner, Bob Sharpless, couldn't be more different and yet it is that very difference that makes their partnership so strong.

Physically, Maha is about 5 feet 9 inches tall, of slight build and dark Indian complexion. Bob, on the other hand, is the stereotypical Aussie bloke—over 6 feet tall, well built with a pale Anglo-Saxon complexion. Maha is spiritual, Bob is not. Maha drinks green tea, Bob prefers a beer or a glass of red wine. Maha has a one-track mind—Springfield. Bob has other interests. Maha has one car and is not overly interested in money. Bob loves his toys, the well-earned spoils of his success, although he's not extravagant. Maha loves politics; Bob doesn't. Maha wants his children involved in Springfield; Bob wants his children to find their own path. Maha likes publicity; Bob likes to work behind the scenes. Maha is animated and energetic; Bob is stoical (he's known affectionately as Poker Face). Maha sees everything as possible, Bob is 'Mr Reality Check'. In short, you couldn't find two more different personalities.

And that's why it works.

Maha is a visionary. He looks at what's possible, not what's probable. It doesn't matter how difficult or unlikely the project is or even whether the world is really ready for it; he is motivated by what could be and how it could uplift other people in the process.

Like many entrepreneurial visionaries, Maha thinks in big-picture, broad-brush terms. If you want to get a sense of what Springfield will be like in 50 years' time, then Maha's the person best suited to painting you a picture. If, however, you were to ask him how much land they sold to Cherish and for how much, he'll know roughly but not exactly. If you ask Bob the same question he will tell you it was 293 hectares (725 acres) and it sold for $2.84 million. If you want detail, Bob's your man. Maha's daughter, and Springfield's deputy managing director, Raynuha Sinnathamby, often wishes that Bob had a USB port behind his ear so she could download all the data stored in his brain!

Maha is an engaging and charismatic man with the hide of a rhinoceros. His mind is always active. When in conversation with him, you often get the impression he is multi-tasking, and that another part of his mind is chewing over a problem or going through his list of things to do that day. If your conversation drifts away from Springfield, you will soon find yourself in conversation with yourself, as all his attention switches to other, more consequential matters. This can be disconcerting. There is an element of eccentricity about Maha Sinnathamby, no doubt born out of his singular obsession.

Maha is also very likeable, and because of this and his infectious enthusiasm he has a phenomenal ability to connect to people, to persuade them or to pursue them until he gets the answer he wants. His enthusiasm and belief in the project are contagious and you can't help but be affected.

Maha's persistent championing of Springfield, pushing the development along through informing and educating government officials and other stakeholders, is legendary. And he expects others to be as vocal and persuasive as he is. For example, when the DCP was being prepared Barry was expected to haunt the Planning Department. He was there or on the phone so often that most people probably thought he worked for the council rather than for Maha. But Maha himself elevated political networking to a whole new level. The Queen Street Down Under project had taught him that unless you present your case, convince, argue, befriend, persuade and remain in almost constant contact with the people who ultimately make the decisions, then the project will be at risk.

Bringing the highway to Springfield is a classic example of this. For years Maha and his team were unable to get any firm commitment, hitting brick wall after brick wall. He needed to get to the Premier.

For months he called the Premier's Office in an effort to secure an appointment, with zero success. He called in favours and hounded his contacts, but nothing worked. Maha knew he needed to see the state leader when his gatekeepers weren't around, so he studied the newspapers and asked for tips within his political and business networks to find out where and when he would be appearing in public. A list of opportunities came together. The Premier spoke regularly at events such as the opening of buildings and bridges in the local area, so Maha began to *haunt* him! For the next few months, he attended dinners, conferences and political functions where he knew that the Premier was a guest speaker, often paying extra for a front-row seat.

The Premier must have noticed. Whether the presentation was about water quality, literacy standards, health care, schooling or koala preservation, close to the podium was a familiar, intense-looking gentleman, who appeared to have universal interests!

Finally at one such event, as the Premier concluded his speech and acknowledged the applause, Maha leaned across and whispered to Yoga, 'Get your handbag. He's about to leave'.

As soon as the Premier was out of the room Maha broke into a sprint and caught up with his quarry at the escalator, 'Excuse me, Sir'. The politician spun round to the outstretched hand and beaming smile of a man who looked vaguely familiar. Clearly not happy at the interruption, he asked. 'Do I know you?' Maha introduced himself and told him briefly about Springfield and how he would like to schedule a meeting. Maha knew the Premier couldn't reasonably say 'No', however cool his demeanor had just become, and sure enough he reluctantly replied, 'You may', before turning and leaving abruptly.

These are the lengths to which Maha was prepared to go. He simply would not take no for an answer. He didn't like being away from his family and, like Yoga, would have much preferred a home-cooked curry and an evening with the children. But he was on a mission, and if that meant being out night after night to get an outcome then so be it.

Maha does not enjoy socialising for no purpose or sipping champagne into the small hours. He is on task all the time. He has an innate capacity to enter a room, quickly pinpoint the one or two people who might be able to help, and initiate the conversation with them. Once done he will then leave. This singleness of purpose has without doubt been instrumental in Springfield's success.

It's important to note that Maha's relentlessness in pursuing useful relationships and persuading the right people, and his ability to turn initial hostility into support, is not a strategy he adopts just when the chips are down. It is a constant theme in his approach to business. Over the course of his career Maha has hounded many people to get what he needs, and inevitably his tactics have upset and irritated some. He has always tried to network respectfully and maintained the utmost courtesy, but he is not a man who is easy to dismiss or fob off. And his likeability has helped ensure that people don't stay mad at him for long.

Maha is the glue that has kept the external people who are instrumental to Springfield's success engaged and on-side, and his single-minded focus and the force of his personality have ensured he does that job well.

Bob, on the other hand, is the glue that has kept the internal people who have been vital for Springfield's success engaged and on-side. And his multi-focused, down-to-earth style ensures he does *that* job well. It is Bob who will regularly socialise with other members of the team, have a beer in the office on a Friday night, go for a run or talk about the footy at the end of a busy day. He will go to sporting events or barbecues with the others, and he does it because he wants to. Maha rarely socialises, except for special occasions. He just isn't wired that way. Maha's pleasure in life comes from family — his wife Yoga and their five children, Uma, Raynuha, Meera, Naren and, the most demanding of the lot, Springfield. He loves spending time with his grandchildren and likes a regular game of golf, but that's the extent of Maha's interests. This disposition is almost certainly rooted in his upbringing and culture. As a child he didn't have the luxury of time to play. Life was hard and demanding and he was expected to pull his weight from a very early age. He was encouraged to use his time constructively and never waste a moment, while Bob is more western in his approach and enjoys working hard but also playing hard on occasion. Most of the Springfield team, especially in the early days, had more in common with Bob's approach than with Maha's. So it was Bob who kept the internal team ticking along, and it was that camaraderie, and a shared loyalty to the vision and the owners, that inspired them to stay — even during the tough times.

A typical straight-talking Aussie bloke, Bob has sometimes needed to act as the 'fire blanket' to Maha's passion. A classic example of this calming influence was when contracts were due to be signed for the road to Springfield.

In July 1999, after six solid years of negotiations plagued by setbacks, rule changes, authority changes, brick walls and bureaucratic apathy, the documentation that would make the road a contractual reality was ready to sign.

The agreement required 15 different contracts. The signing ceremony was due to start at 4.00 pm and would involve a minimum of eight sets of lawyers and representatives from a range of banks and other companies. By midday several large boxes had already arrived and the Ipswich Council CEO Jamie Quinn glanced at the top document. It was the contract for the council's section of the highway. Although the road through Springfield would ultimately be one continuous carriageway, the council had agreed to fund this section. There would be a separate contract between the Springfield Land Corporation (SLC) and the contractor for their section, and for reasons best known to the lawyers, 12 other contracts were necessary to bind all the parties to all their duties. The contract for the council's section alone was for $18 million.

Although the council had a large and growing budget, demand for capital works was vast across the city and this was a considerable investment. Bob and Barry had negotiated hard to get the council involved, arguing forcefully that it would be cheaper to complete the two sections at the same time while the equipment was on site. It made sense, and although the council wasn't obliged to get involved in the construction this early, there were considerable benefits to doing so. For a start the financial model for the Springfield development demonstrated the substantial returns council would earn through increased rates, and Springfield's recently signed deal with Delfin for a massive residential development now gave this forecast greater certainty. Delfin was the premier residential developer in the country and Forest Lake had demonstrated what they could achieve locally. The council was also aware that a major golf course developer was interested in Springfield, and this too would boost Ipswich's image. The region needed this new passageway and the developers were paying their way. But the council still conducted its own due diligence.

The construction went to tender and there was only one response. This was hardly surprising when you consider that the contractor was required to fund the road themselves and would be reimbursed only if it was completed *on time*, which meant they carried a great deal of risk. Notwithstanding the sole tender response, council had insisted on an independent expert's report to confirm that they were getting fair value. They also sought assurances and bank guarantees that Springfield could pay its share.

As vehicles began to gather in the council car park, it became clear that while everything was in place for signing, everyone with a pen within a half-mile radius of that meeting room was on edge. As Bob approached the building and tried to shepherd everyone inside, he heard raised voices behind him and turned. The head of the construction company and Maha were clearly getting into a last-minute altercation that was fast becoming heated.

The contractor was concerned about the risk they were carrying and was seeking additional last-minute assurances and security. For his part, Maha was keen to ensure that they didn't incur any additional debt they didn't need. The project manager joined Bob and they could hear his boss press his position: 'Maha, you're not putting any money into this deal. We only get paid by you guys at the end. We need to know that you are motivated to pay'.

Inside, Barry was also doing his best to ward off late changes. Bob had been in constant phone contact with Barry through the afternoon. The council wanted to alter the agreed payment routine. The initial structure required monthly instalments to the contractors, but now the council was seeking to hold back their payment until their section was started, following the SLC section. Council also wanted to change the order of signing: they now wanted SLC to execute documentation with the road contractor first to lock in this relationship before they joined. All of which was unacceptable because, as the road contractor was now emphasising, SLC did not intend to put any of their own money into the pot until the road was finished. In truth, the highway was of no value to them until it was completed and they had therefore intended that the council's progressive payments would tide the contractor over during construction.

Without doubt it was an innovative and complex deal. But the order of signing was crucial because the whole deal would work only if each party locked in their respective piece in precisely the right sequence. Yet as they stood metres from delivery the pieces seemed bent on moving out of order. There had never before been an agreement of this type in Australia in which council had partnered with a private company to deliver infrastructure, and everyone involved was understandably nervous.

Bob listened as the argument escalated. 'Your part of the deal is being backed by what is in effect another mortgage over part of your land,' the head of the construction company told Maha. 'There must be separate loans and mortgages all over your land. This project is like a quilt! We have to be cautious when we have a $30 million road to deliver.' Maha shook his fists. 'You knew the fabric of the deal before today. This is just stage-fright from a couple of nervous nellies. Just sign the contract and *get on with it.*'

Upstairs in the meeting room Mayor John Nugent arrived. It was now 6.00 pm and the contractors and the Springfield crew were late. Among the piles of documents and dozens of people Barry stood looking pale and exhausted. He could sense that the council and the contractor were not the only ones having second thoughts. People were in huddles, scribbling notes over the typed pages. It did not look good.

Below in the car park things were going from bad to worse, until eventually Maha exploded, stormed back to his dark Mercedes and sped away in a cloud of dust. Upstairs Council CEO Jamie Quinn wondered if it was time to send everyone home. As he looked down on the scene in the car park he could see Barry walking towards the shattered group. Bob was looking at his shoes shaking his head and the road contractors were returning to their car.

The deal hung by a thread.

The council were ambivalent about a delay so long as the contracts worked in their favour. Nor was the bank too concerned. They would have to sign away some of their security over the land to make this deal work, but if it didn't go ahead they would foreclose on Springfield and recoup their money regardless.

As it stood, the second payment from Delfin was dependent on the road being open by July 2000, only 11 months away. Many people were saying it was an almost impossible timeline. Any additional delay would certainly make it genuinely impossible. Bob knew it was now or never. The documents *had* to be signed tonight.

What followed was a masterful display of diplomacy, last-minute negotiation, reassurance and calm determination led by Bob. By the time everyone had settled their differences, reconvened at the council offices and signed their sections, it was close to 10.00 pm.

One of Bob's greatest strengths, apart from his ability to negotiate incredible deals while holding a pretty poor hand, is his capacity to extinguish brushfires caused by Maha's passion and volatility. Yoga shares this trait and helps to do the same at home. If Maha returns from work upset or cranky she takes care never to add fuel to the fire. Yoga too is intensely loyal, and that loyalty goes well beyond Maha to include others in the Springfield team, especially Bob. Yoga's quiet, unassuming strength has sustained Maha as he has pursued his dream. She has never interfered or complained and has always managed the household and supported her husband, while offering remarkably insightful solutions to problems that he has struggled with. Even at the height of his success in Perth, when Yoga would visit the office she would never make a show of being the boss's wife. Then and now she is a much-loved and deeply respected player in the Springfield story.

As in all solid long-term relationships there have been times when Maha and Bob haven't liked each other much. Certainly Bob wasn't exactly thrilled when Maha flew into a rage and sped out of the car park that evening. But although very different on the surface, they share a number of critical qualities, including loyalty.

They trust each other implicitly and recognise that each brings something special to the partnership. When other staff complained to Bob that Maha was being unreasonable or especially demanding, Bob would simply listen and apply the fire blanket. Even if he agreed with the complaint, he would never say so. Besides, according to Bob, Maha has a sixth sense. Over the years, whenever Bob had his doubts, even when he didn't verbalise them, just as the thought would arise Maha would call, work his magic and the thought would be forgotten as quickly as it arrived!

The other dominant characteristic they share is determination. They differ only in the way they express it—Maha through fire, passion and force of personality, Bob through silent, dogged focus on the end game and, if anything, the suppression of emotion. The outcome, however, is the same, because they are two hard-headed, fiercely determined, resilient individuals bound by a shared vision.

Maha and Bob also have very similar core values, and these are shared by their wives. Maha says, 'There is simplicity about the four of us. We all go out for dinner a couple of times a year. Last time the oysters were $36 and I was encouraging Belinda to order them because I knew she enjoyed them. Belinda refused, "I won't buy oysters for $36 when I can buy them for $14 from the market". She knew I was paying that day but it didn't matter, because for her it was the principle'.

Although Maha and Bob are now extremely wealthy, it has never been about accumulating money for the sake of it. To both of them, wealth is just a useful, universally understood yardstick of success, but above all they are driven to succeed, to do the right thing to the best of their ability, and the money they've earned is just a by-product of that drive. It's astonishing to consider the challenges the Springfield team have battled every day for close to two decades. It's hard to imagine why anyone would put themselves through that degree of unremitting stress, but perhaps part of the answer can be found in the words of Franz Kafka, who wrote, 'From a certain point onward there is no longer any turning back. That is the point that must be reached'. That point was reached by both Maha and Bob quite early. When you sink your heart, soul and financial future into a project, and you fight day in and day out to realise it, giving up becomes unthinkable. And every step beyond that point galvanises you, driving you towards success. Going through so much together creates a powerful bond, and that is what has made this partnership so special. Today if you asked Bob to describe their relationship he would tell you that Maha is like a brother to him, and that feeling is clearly mutual.

He who has a dogged determination shall have everything.

Build your team based on attitude as well as aptitude

Maha has always looked at the world a little differently. When he first arrived in Australia in 1971 he wrote 42 letters to prospective employers, but his approach was unorthodox to say the least. What he proposed was that the company give him 5 per cent of the business if they were happy with his performance after a year, in return for which he would give that company his life and undivided loyalty.

Maha was never interested in being an employee — going to work, putting in a few hours of effort and going home, and collecting his salary. He was always more driven. At the Water Board in Perth he was encouraged to opt for the minimum pay and maximum superannuation package. Superannuation for government employees was generous and led to a handsome pension. But Maha chose the opposite, because he had no intention of staying. He wanted to be out 'in the wild', under his own steam, where his effort and commitment would have a direct effect on what he earned and what he could create. That ideology has remained strong his whole life.

When he and Bob started the Springfield project he was interested in working with people like him, not in skill set but in attitude. David Henry was one of their first employees in Brisbane. He had a building degree and Maha and Bob needed a capable project manager, but it was his attitude and approach to life that made him stand out.

David was a visionary in his own right. It was David who would fuel Maha's interest in building a master-planned city, and it was David who was instrumental in liaising with government to bring the roads and the first school to Springfield. He was every bit as passionate as Maha as the two bounced ideas around and enthused about what could be achieved in Springfield. David was like the Energizer bunny—he would just keep going and going, and he had a tremendous capacity for getting things done. He also got into action very quickly, which soon made him an integral member of the Springfield team. By his own admission, however, David sometimes lacked subtlety and tact. He was usually blunt. He liked to attack, nag, cajole and encourage *with force*, but he got things done and his influence and contribution were immense.

Barry Alexander was another vital player in the Springfield story. Again Maha was drawn to him because of his attitude and his aptitude. Maha approached Barry to secure approvals for Springfield because he was the best man for the job. He had vast experience in and out of government and although at the start he considered the project impossible, he too was inspired by its scale and the opportunity it presented. Here was a project that could define his career, and in many ways it did.

Barry was another 'can do' individual. He was a true blue Aussie who combined likeability and a down-to-earth approach with resolute determination and breath-taking attention to detail. Take the DCP, for example. Once it was passed by council it was sent to the Department of Local Government and Planning (DLGP), where it would be reviewed to ensure it conformed with the department's planning standards, and they would seek input from other government departments. After a further year and a half of intense negotiation between the developer, council and a multitude of government departments, the DCP was very close to final approval at state level. This document would initiate the infrastructure agreement that the minister of planning had proposed several years before.

The details of the DCP would in effect be set in stone through new legislation so it was absolutely essential that it was perfect. Barry had called the DLGP officer in charge of the submission, who assured him the documentation was finalised, but a conversation with a senior planner set alarm bells ringing. Barry was a man who left *nothing* to chance and would ensure, wherever possible, that he was the last person a decision maker saw before making a decision. Yet it seemed that someone else had managed to get the last word.

Barry called the DLGP officer again and was reluctantly told there was just some last-minute 'tidying up' of the cabinet submission. The officer's reticence could be explained by the fact that he was to break for his well-earned Christmas holiday the next day and he knew from past experience that if Barry got wind of the changes he would be in his office in a heartbeat. And he was right. Within the hour Barry showed up.

What followed was a mammoth and at times strained exchange during which the DLGP officer finally agreed to return the document to what had previously been agreed. And leaving nothing to chance, Barry waited for a copy of the new cabinet submission, insisting it be officially stamped 'Final'. His hunch had been right. The late alterations would have been disastrous for the project, but the crisis was averted by his absolute refusal to make assumptions or leave anything to chance.

Although Barry was paid a salary for the crucial work he did, he was also part of Maha's 'no go, no dough' payment culture. More often than not, project-critical staff members and external consultants were paid on results rather than effort. To Maha and Bob this was essential, because they didn't have the money to splash out on huge salaries, and a success fee kept everyone focused and hungry. But the approach was unconventional and required a certain degree of faith on the part of the individuals—faith in their own ability to deliver and faith in the project. These people were known as the true believers, those who were prepared to put their own skin in the game.

For the true believers there was significant risk but also the possibility of significant financial reward. The road contractors took a major risk but it paid off. They built the highway in record time and secured the additional work at Brookwater as a result. SLC lawyer Andrew

Erikson also took a punt early on and reaped the reward. When he was trying to snag a large corporate account for his fledgling law practice, he accepted a no go, no dough arrangement against the advice of his partners. As a result Springfield is now one of his biggest and most lucrative clients.

Another true believer is Ian Keilar. Ian was a unique individual with a talent for getting things done and finding creative solutions to thorny problems. A respected surveyor and planner, he was also extremely well connected. When his advice on what to do with the land parcel was first sought, Ian suggested that all they could realistically do was to parcel it up into 16-hectare (40-acre) lots and sell them on for an $8 million profit. Despite that initial recommendation, he became a vocal advocate of Springfield. Often he would go months without being paid, and he too faced intense pressure from his partners to sever ties with Bob and Maha, but he always refused.

Springfield attracted passionate, productive and talented individuals who could appreciate the scale of what was being attempted and the potential rewards for being involved in something so audacious. And those rewards were not just financial. This was a small, tightly knit group of people who were focused on one goal and trusted each other to bring their own unique skills to the table to make it work. It was a living, breathing example of what is possible when the right people are doing the right things at the right time.

On the public side financial motivation was irrelevant. For these individuals the journey was equally tough, although for vastly different reasons. They were under constant scrutiny and were required as a condition of their appointment to do the best for the community they served. Getting involved with private enterprise was risky. Being seen to support private development was potentially career-ending risky, yet there were trailblazers and visionaries in government too—people who could see the long-term benefit such a project would bring to the area.

Mayor John Nugent was one of the first to really appreciate the possibilities, although when he first met Maha in 1991 he thought his talk of a new city sounded crazy. He expected requests for help or special treatment. But they never came. In their early dialogue Maha asked only for advice on how to advance understanding and support from the council. Occasionally John attended meetings with Maha, and he took some political flak for it. But the way he saw it, he wasn't supporting Maha or Bob, he was supporting a development that had the potential to bring great prosperity to his city. John was always grateful that Maha and Bob chose the hardest path and was fully aware that they could have taken their profit and moved on.

Maha, in turn, was grateful for John Nugent's uncompromising integrity. Despite a pronounced stutter, John had entered politics where he was frequently required to speak in public. He cared little for what others thought or said about him. So long as he was doing the right thing as mayor, nothing fazed him.

Another political visionary was Terry Mackenroth. Over the Christmas break of 1993 the Minister for Planning initiated a shake-up of planning arrangements. It was a radical initiative that aimed to stem the tide of ad hoc, unmanaged development that had already blighted the Queensland landscape. Springfield would serve as a test case for how the government would plan and fund future state services.

This idea represented a significant departure from old thinking. The government was suggesting that 'out of sequence' developments pay a penalty for the costs of bringing forward the state's investments. It was a brilliant idea that would set a precedent in Queensland, and Springfield became the first major development for which the government sought to negotiate such a partnership. It was this long-range planning initiative that effectively made the highway to Springfield possible years ahead of its time and opened up the western corridor.

Every project needs its visionaries, bulldogs and true believers, and attracting such people becomes possible only when you acknowledge that nothing can be achieved alone, and that everyone is great in their own place.

> *Brave, bold men and women, these are what we want. What we want is vigor in the blood, strength in the nerves, iron muscles and nerves of steel, not softening namby-pamby ideas. Avoid all these. Avoid all mystery.*

The principle in action

Winston Churchill's 'place' was not always that obvious.

Churchill served as President of the Board of Trade, Home Secretary and First Lord of the Admiralty before the First World War. It was while serving in the Admiralty that he pushed through his plan to invade the Dardanelles, in what became the disastrous Gallipoli Campaign. His decision was based at least in part on erroneous information. The heavy casualties inflicted on both sides, including major casualties by Australian and New Zealand soldiers, led to Churchill's first departure from government. He then served on the western front and returned to government as Minister of Munitions, Secretary of State for War and Secretary of State for Air. Following the end of the First World War Churchill became Chancellor of the Exchequer. He was never afraid of holding a minority or controversial view. He was, for example, strongly opposed to Gandhi's fight for Indian home rule and was against the abdication of Edward VIII.

But he was also a lone voice warning of the dangers of Hitler and campaigned heavily for British rearmament in the thirties. These were his 'wilderness years'. He was also a vocal opponent of British Prime Minister Neville Chamberlain's efforts to avoid war by appeasing Hitler in the lead-up to the Second World War. Churchill famously stated in a House of Commons speech, 'You were given the choice between war and dishonour. You chose dishonour, and you will have war'.

When the war began, as he had felt sure it would, he was again appointed First Lord of the Admiralty. Neville Chamberlain resigned on 10 May 1940 and publicly supported Churchill's appointment as prime minister. Like all of us, Churchill was great in his right place, and his place was war. Even today he is widely regarded as one of the greatest wartime leaders the world has known.

Churchill created for himself the additional position of Minister of Defence and controversially put his friend and confidant the industrialist and newspaper baron Lord Beaverbrook in charge of aircraft production. Churchill too recognised that everyone is great in their own place. Britain needed to gear up for war and needed to do so quickly; who better to lead that charge than a man with proven business acumen. Beaverbrook's strength was his ability to get stuff done, not offer military or political insight. Churchill himself was already proficient at that. What he needed was more aircraft, weapons and munitions, and it was these that eventually made the difference in the war.

Churchill's steadfast refusal to consider any outcome other than outright victory helped to inspire British resistance, especially at the beginning when much of Europe was occupied and Britain stood alone in its active opposition to Hitler. His speeches and radio broadcasts helped rally the British people and are a further testament to the power of words. Indeed, when John F. Kennedy made him the first honorary US citizen in 1963 he said of Churchill that he had 'mobilised the English language and sent it into battle'.

Although Churchill successfully led Britain to victory and was a powerful, revered and much-loved prime minister through the war years, within months of the peace his Conservative government was voted out of power. Winston Churchill's greatness shone during a crisis. But the people who had fought and suffered so long now demanded wide social and political reforms, and they did not believe Churchill's Conservatives were the ones to provide them. Consciously or not, the British people also believed that everyone is great in their own place.

What this principle means for you

No two people are the same—not even siblings from the same family raised in the same environment. This principle acknowledges and honours those differences. Everyone has a role to play, a place where their contribution can be maximised.

Whatever it is you seek to achieve, sooner or later you will need to involve others and to trust them to do what needs to be done. Too often business leaders seek out people who are replicas of their own nature and personality. They assume that if they can find others just like them they will be able to multiply their strengths, but if no-one is plugging the gaps this rarely works. As Maha's ancient wisdom reminds us, 'All the men and women, in any society, are not of the same mind, capacity, or of the same power to do things; they must have different ideals, and we have no right to sneer at any ideal. Let everyone do the best he can for realising his own ideal. Nor is it right that I should be judged by your standard or you by mine. The apple tree should not be judged by the standard of the oak, nor the oak by that of the apple. To judge the apple tree you must take the apple standard, and for the oak, its own standard'. Only when you understand that everyone is great in their own right place can you let go of the compulsion to do everything or control everything and allow others to shine.

Maha and Bob offer a classic example of the principle. When Maha asked Bob to join him in Brisbane they hammered out the 'rules of the game' early on, and both have remained true to those rules. Bob wanted to be a partner, not just an employee, a reasonable request considering he was moving home and taking a significant risk. Maha accepted Bob's terms but had a few conditions of his own. Maha needed to be the boss. Obviously Bob should have a say in the business decisions, but Maha knew himself well: 'I have to lead. I am the old bull. You are the young bull, but we must work together'. Bob was amused by Maha's colourful analogy but could see the logic and happily agreed. 'I have no great argument with that, old bull, but I ask that you consult me before you make any financial decisions. I want to be the bull responsible for the books.' That conversation set the tone and expectations for both parties and the arrangement remains to this day.

For Maha the union was perfect and after losing his first partner, Ken Law-Davis, he loved having someone to bounce ideas off again, and someone who could take on the tasks he wasn't so good at. This in turn would free him up to focus on his strengths — making connections, selling the vision and finding the deals. According to Yoga, Bob even looked a little like Ken.

For Bob too the partnership was ideal. He could learn from the 'old bull' and fast-track his education in property development. Bob would readily admit that he's no visionary, being more attuned to reality than possibility. He's very much grounded in the here and now, and how to structure and pay for what's before him without going broke. He supported the big picture and contributed to its creation, but his focus was always on working out how it could actually be executed. Left to his own devices, Bob would probably never have attempted a project of Springfield's magnitude. But together he and Maha were able to counterbalance each other's weaker areas to create a remarkable legacy.

Maha's action plan

Everyone is great in their own place! In order to help you shift your thinking and incorporate this principle into your life you will need to:

> ➤ foster strong relationships
> ➤ match the task to the person
> ➤ expect the best from others.

Foster strong relationships

People do business with people they like and are more forgiving of people they like, so likeability is an important factor in developing and nurturing relationships. Maha is an expert at seeking out the right people, learning from them, influencing them and developing strong relationships over the long term.

When Maha took the job as a water engineer at the Metropolitan Water Board in Perth he wasn't thrilled about it, but he had a young family to support and it was the right thing to do. Although he didn't enjoy the job, he used the time effectively with an eye on the future. He recognised that when he became a full-time developer he would need to understand such things as municipal water supply, sewerage, water regulation and local government. He needed to develop a network of people who could help him in this. With that end in mind, Maha would identify the right people with specific know-how or those who could help him with his future development plans.

He put a lot of effort into building a rapport with them so he could pick their brains, understand how everything worked and develop networks for future use. Maha knew he would need to deal with them at some point for approvals and information, so everything he did was designed to foster positive relationships for the future. This approach was inspired by necessity. To the casual observer it might seem selfish or calculating. It's not. It's simply efficient. Today, Maha is utterly focused on Springfield and is always seeking ways to deliver the master plan to the highest level possible, but it's never a one-sided quest. He believes that one of his greatest duties is to help others, and the more he finds ways to do that the more he helps his own cause. This is the nature of karma.

There is little doubt Maha's tenacity has put people off-side at times, but Maha firmly believes, 'If you keep knocking the door will open. And if you're nice about it people won't hate you for it.' Besides the force of his personality, his passion for the project and infectious good humour are hard to resist.

When Maha was at university and working as a taxi driver to pay his fees he often fell behind in his studies. Most semesters he would write to the registrar requesting an extension. Finally, after six years, Maha completed his degree and contacted the registrar again to ask for an appointment. As soon as his assistant heard it was Maha, she laughed. 'Are you calling about another extension?' 'No', replied Maha. 'I've finally finished, but I would like to see the registrar.' A short meeting was set up and the registrar was surprised to discover that all Maha wanted was to say 'Thank you'. In his position people only every contacted him when they wanted something, so to have a student visit solely to express heart-felt gratitude for his leniency and support was very touching. The two spoke for over an hour and he wished Maha well in the future.

Expressing gratitude to the people who have helped him is important to Maha, and he never forgets such support. Despite being insanely busy, Maha will always send an email thank you, card or note after an important meeting. If someone has taken the time to see him or support him in any way, he will thank them. If he learns that someone he knows has won an award or been promoted he will always send a note of congratulations.

It is not the big things but the little things that develop relationships and foster loyalty, and Maha is a master of both.

Whatever you are seeking to achieve you can't do it alone. You must find other people who are in *their* right place and develop positive, mutually beneficial relationships that advance your vision.

A spoonful of honey will catch more flies than a gallon of vinegar.

—Benjamin Franklin (US Founding Father)

When restraint and courtesy are added to strength,
the latter becomes irresistible.

— Mahatma Mohandas Gandhi (political leader)

Match the task to the person

Maha is a gifted judge of character and can quickly assess what someone is good at and where their key skills lie and match those skills to various tasks that need to be completed.

When he needed the government to open negotiations with the Army about the road across their land, the perfect person for the job was Steve Golding, the director general of Main Roads. If Maha or anyone else in Springfield had made that first approach the answer would have been a flat 'No', but because Steve Golding was a government official and, perhaps most importantly, also a senior officer in the Army reserves, he was the perfect person to make the approach, as he had both official authority and a commonality with the officer charged with making the decision.

Another perfect match between person and task was Peter Sissons. Peter had already been selling sites around Brisbane for Maha and Bob before Springfield and had proved a brilliant salesman. Peter's innovative and inspiring TV advertising helped to put Springfield on the map. And it was *not* an easy sell. Yoga recalls, 'Forest Lake was like a limousine and Springfield a 30-year-old rust bucket. In those early years there was just no comparison. Seriously, the first person who bought a plot at Springfield deserved a medal!'

Peter Sissons was absolutely the right person for that task. He was also instrumental in encouraging Maha to return to his real name. Maha had promised to take Peter on a first-class round-the-world tour of famous development sites if he sold more than 200 lots in the initial stage. Peter sold 305 plots. In May 1993 on the first leg of their world trip, halfway across the Pacific Ocean, Maha told Peter that he preferred his real name, Mahalingam, to his adopted name of Ted. Peter immediately said, 'Well, if you want to do it, do it now!' Peter pressed the button for steward service and addressed the young lady who arrived: 'Can you please get my colleague *Maha* here a green tea?'

By working together, pooling our resources and building on our strengths, we can accomplish great things.

—Ronald Reagan (40th US President)

Most people took a few weeks to get used to it, but everyone adjusted eventually. Maha's secretary, Mary Jago, was the only person who never once slipped up.

Maha has always had a knack for knowing what someone will excel at and directing their efforts towards that task. Finding the right people, putting them to work in their right place and trusting them to get on with their job are essential ingredients for success.

Everyone according to their talent and every talent according to its work.

—French proverb

Expect the best from others

If you accept that everyone is great in their own place and that for a certain task someone else's ability may be vastly superior to your own, then you foster appreciation and admiration in others. As a result, you begin to expect the best from people and they have a tendency to deliver. This phenomenon is sometimes called the Pygmalion Effect, after George Bernard Shaw's play *Pygmalion*, in which a professor makes a bet that he can teach an uneducated London flower girl to behave like a high-class lady.

The idea is that people will rise or fall to meet their own or other people's expectations. In other words, if you expect the best from someone and encourage them to excel, they will invariably rise to meet that expectation. If, on the other hand, you don't believe that everyone is great in their own place, and you expect very little from others, then they are again likely to meet your much more limited expectations.

In all things do your best. The man who has done his best has done everything. The man who has done less than his best has done nothing.

—Charles M. Schwab (American industrialist)

Maha's oldest daughter, Uma, is still amazed at how he focuses only on strengths and positive traits. As a parent herself, she can see the failings in her own children as well as their relative strengths. 'Papa doesn't see the negatives. I used to think he just ignored them, but I've come to realise that he genuinely doesn't see other people's weaknesses. He will focus entirely on a person's strengths and the things that make them special and leave everything else alone.'

Maha's ancient wisdom counsels, 'You should never try to follow another's path for that is his way, not yours. Your way is the best for you, but that is no sign it is the best for another'. In other words, it's never wise to enforce your best way or dictate how someone should do a certain task. Instead, hire good people and encourage them to bring their own best way to the table. Accepting that everyone is great in their own place also requires that you respect and honour those differences. Whatever you seek to achieve, always encourage others and expect the very best from them. You may be astonished by what they will deliver.

It's a funny thing about life: if you refuse to accept anything but the best, you very often get it.

—W. Somerset Maugham (British novelist)

Chapter 9

Create your own destiny

Blame none for your own faults, stand upon your own feet, and take the whole responsibility upon yourselves. Say, 'This misery that I am suffering is of my own doing, and that very thing proves that it will have to be undone by me alone'. Therefore, stand up, be bold, be strong. Take the whole responsibility on your own shoulders, and know that you are the creator of your own destiny.

A cornerstone of Maha's personal philosophy is that you are the creator of your own destiny—you are whatever you choose to be. You are surely familiar with the principle, but have you experienced the results that are possible when you genuinely believe it? If you are not as successful or happy or accomplished as you once thought you would be, then perhaps you are not as familiar with it as you might think. No matter where you are right now, whether or not you are living the life you want, the first and only place to start in your own transformation or journey towards what matters for you is an appreciation of this principle. Its importance is such that it could easily have opened the book. It is an idea that has been so thoroughly hijacked by the personal development industry that it is too easily dismissed as an empty platitude. Nothing could be further from the truth.

The principle has been deliberately positioned towards the back of the book because only through experience can you truly appreciate its power and relevance. Had you read it in the opening chapter you might have thought it overly optimistic or dismissed it as a cliché. Now you arrive at it after reading story upon story of its enduring expression. Maha is the personification of this principle and Springfield is the manifestation of the principle in action.

Because Maha believes he is the creator of his own destiny he has refused to accept any other reality. He was not born to privilege or money and could not call on any 'old boy's network' to facilitate success. As a Sri Lankan immigrant from Malaysia in a predominantly white country, he could easily have chosen to claim prejudice, racism and ridicule as an excuse for not succeeding, yet he never flinched from the task and refused to believe he was different.

You are the creator of your own destiny. If you're not happy right now, you and only you have the power to change it.

Battle for land

In creating Springfield's destiny Maha and Bob have had to battle long and hard to protect their land from various interest groups. The most acrimonious and contradictory was the virtually concurrent battles with the mining industry and the environmental movement.

The passing of the DCP by the newly merged Ipswich Council represented the first milestone in the full approvals process. The next milestone was state government review and approval, followed by agreements with council and government on infrastructure funding. Getting the DCP to this stage had been hard enough, but the state review posed a new set of challenges. At least at council level there was only one organisation to deal with, but at state level a plethora of largely independent departments were engaged, and if the various departmental agendas were uncoordinated, or if there were policy conflicts, then the DCP could disappear into administrative purgatory for years!

Barry knew their opponents would be lining up to halt the DCP and if he was to beat the enemy he first had to know them. There had already been submissions regarding the development, some positive, more negative. Anyone who was interested could review them, so Barry did exactly that. There were a few glowing letters and a positive submission from the Springfield Residents' Association, but mainly Barry read complaints. It was understandable in the context of such a large, transformational planning application. Most people don't like trees being knocked down or the encroachment of extra houses, people and cars around them.

Barry read submissions from a mining company, a mining union, the Queensland Mining Council and finally the Department of Mines. The mining company had rallied *all* of its backers.

When Maha and Bob bought the land at Opossum Creek they knew there were coal reserves under there and that a mining company had an exploration license over several hundred hectares in the far western portion, roughly eight kilometres from their initial residential site. The license was like a permit, allowing the company rights to explore for coal. If the company was satisfied the reserves were of sufficient quality and could be commercially extracted and sold, it could apply to government for a lease to mine.

Before they bought the land, Maha had spoken to the mining company, the council and advisers about the exploration permit. His best advice at that time was that the coal was good but deep and, given the abundance of ore closer to the surface across Queensland, it was unlikely the resource would ever be commercially competitive. So it wasn't considered a direct threat. In the preparation of the DCP submission, however, the mining company asked that the section covered by the permit be exempt from development.

Although directly affecting only 10 per cent of the total land area, a coal mine would adversely affect 100 per cent of the project. It would be devastating to sales. No-one wants to live near the pollution, noise and dust of a coal mine. The company was requesting that the council observe the mining legislation and allow extraction first, with development to follow when the mining was finished. The government was sure to be interested in royalty payments from any coal that was mined. Yes, this was a major enemy.

The other serious enemy was soon identified as Barry unfolded a map attached to another submission. There was a hand-drawn representation of the parcel of land with a thick black line across the middle. The submission was from the Department of Environment and Heritage (DEH) and apparently called for 60 per cent of the total land area to be retained for conservation.

So in opposing corners were government departments that wanted either to devastate the land and collect the coal royalties or to set aside half of it to be environmentally protected. At this rate Maha and Bob might have room to erect a small tent on their own land, but little else.

Of the two forces posing the biggest threat the coal-mining license was the most worrisome. Way back at the start of the process the mayor of Moreton Shire had suggested to Maha that he seek out the expert opinion of Lloyd Bird, a highly regarded local environmental guru. Maha took his advice. A former Ipswich miner, Lloyd had walked the land at Opossum Creek for more than 50 years collecting native tree samples, cultivating seedlings and then propagating them in the places where they used to grow. He could name every local species, including their Latin name, and was often contacted by universities when someone wanted to identify a plant. He even discovered two native olive species, which were subsequently named after him. Lloyd loved spending time in the bush improving degraded sections, and no-one knew the environmental value of that land better than him.

If Springfield was going to head off inevitable environmental opposition, then they needed to be fully briefed by someone who *really* knew the land. Lloyd produced a report showing that after decades of farming and logging the land at Opossum Creek was badly degraded. Native wildlife was limited and the trees were not suitable for koalas. Of the entire land parcel there were only a few small sections of natural habitat that were worth persevering with and restoring. It was this report, and the fact that it was produced by the man most qualified to write it, that was instrumental in getting the DCP through at council level.

Now at the state review the government had Lloyd's report and Barry was confident that the DEH were just trying their luck. The mining, however, was permitted by law and the government was always hungry for coal royalties. They were going to be tough to get off the land. Bob and Barry attended countless, often heated meetings with government and the mining company but nothing was resolved.

Bob remembers a meeting at which he and Barry were bringing Maha up to speed on progress on the mining issue. Maha looked exhausted.

The incessant work and pressure was taking its toll. He closed his eyes for a moment and Bob signalled to Barry that they should leave. Maha heard their movement and said, 'Just a moment… Can we find out what the government stands to make from the royalties?' Maha stood up suddenly. 'I also want a market price for coal per tonne. I want to know the depth and what it will cost to extract per tonne. Tell me about the extraction methods and whether there is possible contamination of groundwater and streams. If there is a sniff of any environmental issues bring it to me. After what the Environment Department is putting us through I dare the government to back this mine. I want to know about any safety incidents with coal mines. Get me books, reports, articles, professional journals, maps. I want to know the coal market better than they do!' Maha paused for a moment. 'No, on second thoughts forget all of that. *Just bring me a solution!*'

It was Ian Keilar who provided that solution. Ian was their consultant surveyor and a passionate advocate of Springfield. He was also the 'go-to' man when it came to curly questions or offbeat challenges that required an innovative solution. He was regarded as someone who had an 'elephant brain' and who knew all sorts of odd facts and figures and bizarre planning precedents. As related in the previous chapter, it was Ian, reaching out to his extensive networks, who saved the road project at the last moment, when it seemed doomed. Barry immediately assigned him the task of resolving the mining problem. 'Something tells me, Keilar, there is something you know or will find out that can help us.'

In Queensland, no business is bigger or tougher than coal, and finding a way to talk a coal company out of earnings, while at the same time denying the government the resultant royalties, was a big ask!

A long-term resident of the Ipswich area, Ian was old enough to recall the days of the working coal mines, when the air was full of dust from the mines and stockpiles. The coal was often moved at night by rail and you could hear the endless bumping of rolling stock being coupled and uncoupled and the unforgiving screech of metal wheels on tracks. At some mine sites, fires burned constantly. It seemed there was no safe way to extinguish deep underground fires, so they were invariably abandoned and left to burn themselves out.

Ian well remembered the smoke and ash. In some parts of the district, the women gave up trying to dry their clothes in the backyard and strung the washing under their houses. Underground methane was also a danger and explosions were common. He recalled looking over the Box Flat mine in 1972 following a massive explosion. He sat all night on a hill near his home watching the fire and the constant arrival and departure of ambulances and fire crews. Seventeen men died that day. The next day, he failed his high-school physics test mostly because of fatigue. He supposed mines were safer and cleaner these days, but it would be a hell of a job to sell real estate beside one. Ipswich mines conjured up images of dust, smoke, noise and tragedy.

Barry and Maha met with a government delegation comprising state planners, mining regulators and other senior people from across government. The mining company was also there and advised they were actively examining the resource, as they were entitled to, but wouldn't say when or if they would mine. They were standing their ground and the government was not prepared to intervene. Barry was desperate for Ian Keilar to find a solution.

The next day Ian drove to the state archives and a particularly helpful librarian led him down two flights of stairs to a vault-like room illuminated by dull fluorescent lights. There were rows upon rows of brown, crumpled boxes on steel racks. From memory, the original Springfield land titles were issued in the mid 1800s, quite soon after the colony of Queensland was established. If he started his research from 1859, he should be pretty close.

Eventually they found the box he was interested in — the Josey titles. Inside a small viewing room Ian was told he could look through the box but to handle the fragile materials carefully. He could make notes but not take away any original materials, and there was a photocopier on the ground floor if he needed it. Working his way through the thick old parchment documents inscribed with delicate calligraphy, Ian eventually came across the title for land assigned in the 1850s to the former convict James Josey, the first owner of the Springfield land. He held it delicately, realising that he was probably the first person to lay eyes on it in generations.

James Josey had been convicted of a minor offence in the UK in the 1840s, when he was 19 years old, whereupon he was transported to the Moreton Bay penal settlement. In his late twenties, having served part of his term, he was pardoned and sought a piece of land where he might take up a productive, honest life. He settled on the land now known as Springfield. Josey's homestead would have been the only structure for miles.

The government at the time had issued a freehold title but had assigned itself rights to resources 'for roads and bridges and ports for the purpose of transporting goods in the colony of Queensland'. Ian looked at the specific wording. The government declared that it had rights to the clay, gravel and timber. But there was no mention of minerals, presumably because the title had been drafted at a time when no-one knew of Australia's immense mineral reserves. But if the government didn't have rights over the coal, then, unless he was mistaken, it wasn't entitled to the coal royalties. Maha and Bob were. Surely this changed the complexion of the debate.

And change it, it did. In one final meeting, armed with this new information, Maha, Bob and Con Galtos, a former consultant with the Springfield Land Corporation, pushed through a resolution. Con reiterated that the development of Springfield would mean more jobs for the area and less environmental damage. The Springfield team had done everything that government had asked of them. If there was a study to undertake and pay for, a plan to draw or a process to follow, they had done so. The quality of the proposed development was impossible to ignore, and when push came to shove no legitimate grounds for stalling the project could be found.

The fight to convince the Department of Environment and Heritage (DEH) that they did not need 60 per cent of the entire land parcel for conservation was every bit as arduous. Following the demise of the Bjelke-Petersen government in the late 1980s the Queensland environmental movement had gained momentum and power. For several decades the government had rubber stamped some reckless and environmentally damaging development proposals. Suddenly, under the new regime, the conservationists had so much government funding that people were selling land to them rather than to the developers. It was this renewed optimism and enthusiasm for conservation, together with an instinctive dislike of developers, that the Springfield team now found themselves up against. Although it was no surprise that the

DEH would make a play for the land, Maha and Bob did not expect their bid for 60 per cent of it, especially when they had gone out of their way to commission the most qualified conservationist in the area to assess the land and make recommendations.

Eventually, after many fruitless meetings and conversations, Maha arranged to meet with the minister in charge so he and Lloyd could present their case at the highest level. Lloyd explained that he had done a thorough analysis of the land and the only sections of environmental significance worth preserving were a strip up in the hills and some of the better vegetation along the waterways. Maha explained that their plans reflected these recommendations and they were already funding Lloyd and his land-care group to rehabilitate the sections identified. Clearly there was a mismatch between what the minister's officials were saying and the expert observations of a highly respected local environmentalist.

The following day a senior official from DEH walked the land with Barry. All day he took photographs and made notes. He pointed out some excellent remnant stands of endangered habitat and that the waterways had the best vegetation, just as Lloyd had reported. There were some beautiful ghost gum specimens. It was a pity about the exotic species: red berry lantana, pine trees and a host of weed species.

As the men headed back to the truck at the end of the day, Barry pressed him for an opinion and was told that while there *were* many sections of high-quality habitat, some of those sections were too small or narrow to be sustainable in the long term. The only really viable tracts of five hectares or more were up in the hills. The DEH official had clearly hoped to find large pristine areas of high environmental quality land, but after generations of logging they were long gone. He told Barry that he was going to recommend that a section linking the hills be retained, along with the beautiful stands of ghost gums and rare remnant rainforest along the waterways. There was a species of epiphytes he hadn't seen in years. 'Besides', he added, 'I wouldn't dream of contradicting Lloyd!' Barry was thrilled. Finally the environmental battle was almost over.

There was now just one more hurdle to overcome—cultural heritage. At the very start of the project it was recommended to Maha that he speak to the local Aboriginal elders of the Jagera clan to establish the history of the land and whether there were any sacred sites on it. Again Maha took the advice. Now the DCP review was at state level, the government wanted a cultural heritage survey. The Opossum Creek area and beyond had been a major Aboriginal meeting place for ceremonies and it was likely that the survey would find Indigenous artefacts. The cultural heritage policy stated that significant and representative areas should be undisturbed, and where possible the artefacts should be left *in situ*. The survey would take months to complete and cost more than $100 000.

Maha believed the environmental claim had been watered down because of the state of the land, but he wanted to honour the Aboriginal claim; although he hoped the survey wouldn't turn up too much evidence.

Ian was to negotiate the process and he spent many days in the field with the university anthropologist and local tribal elders. Initially he wasn't allowed to watch the surveying but the elders soon considered him an 'OK fella' and let him join the group. One of the main challenges with the survey and consultation process was that the elders of different tribal groups didn't always agree on what land should be left undisturbed. After forming a plan Ian's last meeting was with Neville Bonner, retired federal senator and local elder. Neville lamented the rise of development but added that it was a sign of vast improvement in cultural understanding that these surveys were even required. Tapping the map Ian had brought to the meeting he added, 'I know that land well. I spent a lot of time there with elders. You have done a good job. A lot of the good areas will be left alone'. When Ian pressed for information about where those 'good areas' were Neville refused to say. 'There are secret and sacred places around the land and if I told you about them, they wouldn't be secret. You won't find out through me why your plan is good.'

In the end it was agreed that a selection of significant areas and some sections the experts called 'representative' of Aboriginal heritage would be left alone in perpetuity. Many of the areas identified by Aboriginal elders as historically important or sacred were already within the areas identified by Lloyd Bird and designated for conservation and regeneration or were simply incorporated into the plans for open space in the city.

The irony of the environmental battle was that there is probably not a conservationist alive who would dismiss Springfield's environmental pedigree. Springfield has dedicated 30 per cent of the total land area as open space, three times more than the minimum required. More than 850 hectares (2100 acres) have been set aside for public parklands, which meander across the whole development in a continual vein. This is the city's 'green lung', providing a natural setting for workers during the week and families over the weekend. Unique flora and fauna are being protected and most of the flooded gums in the area will be maintained. Two hundred and fifty thousand ghost gum seedlings have been planted in the waterways of Springfield. These native trees have brought back bird species previously forced out by logging. More than 170 native plant species (including 10 classified as rare) and 50 bird species now inhabit the land.

Springfield is also home to one of the world's most sustainable shopping centres, the Orion Springfield Town Centre, which has been awarded a 6 Star Green Star rating by the Green Building Council of Australia. The first high rise in the CBD, Springfield Tower, is one of Queensland's most environmentally advanced commercial buildings, has been awarded a 4 Star rating by the same organisation and is also registered for a 4.5 NABERS rating. As the first high-rise office tower in the 390-hectare CBD, the $60 million Springfield Tower has incorporated a range of environmentally innovative design principles that set the standard against which all future office facilities will be benchmarked.

There can be little doubt that their environmental approach and willingness to think beyond profit to the long-term sustainability and wellbeing of the community contributed to their winning the FIABCI Prix d'Excellence Award for World's Best Master Planned Community. In 2010 Springfield took out this prestigious award ahead of 54 other worthy entrants from across the globe.

The power of conditioning

In chapter 6 we explored the power that is generated when there is congruence between thought, word and deed. Whatever it is you want to achieve, whatever your goal or aspiration for your own life, you first have to believe it's possible. You have to believe in yourself, and everything you think, say and do must drive relentlessly towards the outcome. If you do that consistently then you will create your own destiny. But there is a caveat.

There is no doubt that thoughts have power and how you think has a significant and measureable impact on what you create in your own life. The challenge is that there are two different types of thoughts and, left unquestioned, one type has significantly more power than the other.

Scientific research has demonstrated that the human brain processes about 400 billion bits of information per second yet your conscious mind, the one reading this book, is aware of only 2000 of those bits. We use that information to make decisions and take action. Your subconscious mind takes care of the rest!

Science has already proven that if we take conscious control of our thoughts and direct them towards a goal, we massively increase our chances of success. This sort of focused intention, also known as visualisation, has been talked about in spiritual texts for centuries. Twelfth-century Persian Sufis wrote of altering and reshaping experience. Tibetan Tantric texts are filled with visualisation exercises. Indian Yogi Paramahansa Yogananda says, 'Proper visualisation by the exercise of concentration and willpower enables us to materialise thoughts, not only as dreams or visions in the mental realm but also as experiences in the material realm'.

That we can manage our thinking and direct those 2000 bits towards outcomes we want is good news. But the rest of those 400 billion bits of information is being stored in the subconscious, and that too has an impact, often a massive one!

We have just a little bit of sensuous consciousness and imagine that to be our entire mind and life; but it is but a drop in the mighty ocean of subconscious mind.

Biologist Bruce Lipton puts it this way: 'The conscious mind is the creative one, the one that can conjure up "positive thoughts". In contrast, the subconscious mind is a repository of stimulus–response tapes derived from instincts and learned experiences. The subconscious mind is strictly habitual; it will play the same behavioural responses to life's signals over and over again'.

Your subconscious mind is therefore a storehouse of information gathered over a lifetime. Not all of it is accurate, but it often directs our actions and behaviours and influences our results.

How we are brought up as children has a dramatic impact on who we become as adults. We learn what is acceptable, normal and 'right' from our parents or principal care providers, from our siblings, teachers and friends, and from the environment in which we live. This 'associative conditioning' is an extremely efficient and fast way to learn. The problem is that as a child our conscious mind, the neocortex or 'thinking brain', is not fully developed until the late teens. So the information we receive, either formally or informally, as children is taken on board as absolute fact, especially when it is repeated frequently or is learned in a state of heightened emotion. These 'facts' shape our own personal philosophy or belief system over time. They can become our liberator or our jailer.

> *First and foremost, we must seek to control the vast mass of sunken thoughts which have become automatic with us. The evil deed is, no doubt, on the conscious plane; but the cause which produced the evil deed was far beyond in the realms of the unconscious, unseen, and therefore more potent.*

In some parts of Asia elephants are trained to help farmers and contractors with heavy work in inaccessible locations. The training process starts when the elephant is very young and involves tethering the young animal to a tree with a rope. For months the little elephant will yank and pull and trumpet in rage at this constraint. He will try everything to escape, pushing the tree with his trunk and pulling on the rope with all his strength, but eventually he will give up. The elephant is conditioned into believing that he can't escape so he stops trying. Meanwhile he grows up into one of the strongest animals on the planet, so strong that he could easily uproot the tree, yet he does not. This conditioning is so powerful that his handler need only put the rope on his leg for the elephant to become docile. The tether is no longer necessary, and the elephant has become his own captor.

We are similar to that little elephant. Our conditioning, left unchecked or unquestioned, will become the road map of our life. For centuries the argument has raged about whether nature or nurture has the biggest impact on an individual. Are people born great or are they made great? By far the biggest influence on your life is conditioning, from the environment and circumstances in which you grow up.

Maha is a good illustration of the power of conditioning. Both his parents were strong individuals and had a profound impact on him. His mother Pavalaratnam was determined and fearless, quite unlike the traditional submissive Indian woman of her time. She never took no for an answer and through her words and, perhaps more importantly, her example she passed on that determination to her children. No matter what happened, she endured.

Valipuram's sister was just 35 years old when she died delivering her ninth child. From that day on Pavalaratnam and Valipuram took on responsibility for those children even though they had eight of their own and their resources were already stretched to the limit. Pavalaratnam even breastfed her brother's newborn baby while also feeding her own youngest child.

In 1975 Maha's parents left Malaysia and settled in Perth. Many of their children were now living in Australia and it made sense to be closer to them. In 1987 the whole family gathered as Valipuram and Pavalaratnam celebrated their sixtieth wedding anniversary. In Hindu tradition a marriage that has lasted 60 years is seen as especially blessed. Despite their humble beginnings, both Maha's parents were healthy, mobile and independent, and all eight of their children were healthy and financially secure. To celebrate their successful union Valipuram and Pavalaratnam decided to repeat the wedding ceremony they had undertaken 60 years before.

Valipuram insisted that all his children and their spouses arrive at the house two days before the ceremony so everyone could spend time together. The day before the ceremony Valipuram gathered his children and presented each with a book on Thrikular, a famous Indian sage. Inside each book he had inserted a single gold sovereign and a handwritten note, which said, 'As you go through life, it is important to realise there is much more to achieve other than financial success and I bless you all and I wish you all well'. Valipuram was immensely proud of his children and what each had accomplished, yet as a spiritual man he wanted to remind them that the real riches in life were not financial. Education, love, family, service and making a positive difference in the world were ultimately even more important.

To this day Maha is certain there was something prophetic about the gathering—that somehow Valipuram knew what was coming and had sought to make the parting with his children special and loving.

The marriage ceremony took place the following day at Maha's sister's home in Perth in front of 150 guests, and this time both Valipuram and Pavalaratnam were happy about the union. There followed a day of celebration, good food, laughter and happiness. As the day drew to a close Valipuram left quickly and he and Pavalaratnam drove the three kilometres to their home. Valipuram went straight to his favourite chair. Within moments he was experiencing chest pains, For about 45 minutes Pavalaratnam comforted her husband, repeating his favourite prayer over and over again.

She called Maha and the ambulance, and Maha and Yoga waited with them for its arrival. When it came Valipuram received immediate attention but he passed away in his wife's arms while she chanted the Lord's names in his ear and massaged his failing heart.

The next day Valipuram was cremated according to Hindu custom, and again family and friends gathered to say goodbye. Maha had told the Lord Mayor of Perth, Mick Michael, of his parents' upcoming wedding and he in turn had contacted *The Western Australian* newspaper, which ran an article on the wedding and what makes a successful marriage. Sadly they were now able to do a follow-up feature on the man who celebrated 60 years of marriage and died the following day.

Pavalaratnam stayed on in Perth. After Maha moved to Brisbane she would visit for three months at a time and he would travel back to see her as often as he could. On one such trip, in June 1992, Maha was reminded of his mother's no-nonsense strength, regardless of her advancing years. With the Springfield settlement date approaching, Maha and Bob were still unsure whether the Cherish deal would proceed. It was a stressful period and Maha decided to take time out to visit his mother. As soon as Pavalaratnam saw her son she knew something was wrong. No sooner had he set foot in the house than her phone rang. Maha immediately released her from his hug and said, 'It could be for me, Mum. The office has your number'. He ran inside.

For the next two days Maha was tethered to the phone. Pavalaratnam sensed a serious problem. Maha seemed to have the weight of the world on his shoulders. He would end his calls and try to force a smile. At dinner on the second night his mother could see her son was deflated. Maha and Bob *needed* a miracle. They didn't have the money to pay AFH the first instalment of $3 million. He had called everyone he knew, beating the drum. He had made presentation after presentation to potential investors, and watched their initial interest turn to indifference as the details of the deal were revealed. Maha knew it was a hard sell, but surely there was someone out there who had the vision to appreciate the opportunity.

It was a bleak time for Maha, and he had hoped this short break would act as a tonic, but as he watched his mother from across the dinner table he felt increasing guilt about his imposition on her. He had tried to keep his business conversations quiet but the stress was almost unbearable. The phone rang again and Maha's dull eyes lifted briefly, but this time he ignored it and turned to his plate. Pavalaratnam loved her son dearly but she had suffered enough in her lifetime. Finally she said, 'Mahalingam, I see the pain in you. I cannot watch it'. Her eyes filled with tears. 'You know I love you and what I have to say pains me deeply but I would like you to leave. I cannot bear to watch you suffer. Please don't come to me when your life is like this'. Pavalaratnam knew her children were the creators of their own destiny, just as she had been, and Maha clearly needed to get his house in order. She stood, hugged a tearful Maha and went to her bedroom. Maha left the next morning.

Maha is a male version of his mother. Their likeness is possibly more the result of conditioning than inheritance.

Maha's father too was also a strong individual. His was a quiet, spiritual strength, but when he decided to do something he would follow through no matter what. To this day Maha has no idea how his parents managed to save the money to send six of their eight children overseas to study. When it was Maha's turn to go, however,

Pavalaratnam fought against it. According to Indian custom, as the third son Maha was a gift and he had helped his mother all his life. After school he would tend the garden or milk the cows; from a young age he was constantly working. So when it was time for him to leave she was distraught and even threatened to kill her husband if he followed through with it. Valipuram was undeterred.

Maha's parents were not famous or wealthy, but they were extraordinary individuals in their own right. As his ancient wisdom reminds us, 'The greatest men [and women] in the world have passed away unknown'. They are both now long gone, but their strength of character and relentless spirit lives on in Maha. Never in his life did he see his parents back down or give up; it just wasn't an option for either of them. Like them, he doesn't know how to accept failure and walk away—he cannot imagine what that even looks like.

Maha and Yoga have gone to great lengths to instil that toughness and resourcefulness in *their* children and to positively influence their grandchildren. Determined that his grandchildren will never forget how powerful they are, like those little elephants tethered to the tree, Maha regularly has them repeat the Sinnathamby mantra: 'I'm the best, I can do anything, I never give up'.

We are all born powerful, complete human beings capable of incredible, impossible things, yet over time we are conditioned into believing that isn't so. For fear of failure we stop trying, and every time we give up or tell ourselves we can't be bothered or it's not important, we surrender that power, until like the elephant we stand, docile, watching life pass by.

We cannot control the conditioning we received as a child or where we grew up or what our parents were like, but we can control what we do about it. And though we inherit a genetic blueprint from our parents, that blueprint does not determine who we are and what we become. That is entirely up to us.

> *If the power of evil is in the unconscious, so also is the power of good. We have many things stored in us as in a pocket. We have forgotten them, do not even think of them, and there are many of them, rotting, becoming positively dangerous; they come forth, the unconscious causes which kill humanity. True psychology would,*

therefore, try to bring them under the control of the conscious. The great task is to revive the whole man, as it were, in order to make him the complete master of himself.

The principle in action

Throughout history the people who stand out for their accomplishments do so largely because they created their own destiny. These are individuals who were not bound by their conditioning, who cared little for convention, decided on a course of action, and refused to yield.

When Christopher Columbus first decided to explore the world by ship, people didn't just think it was crazy, they were convinced it was dangerous. Although the Greeks knew the world was round as far back as 570 BC, the notion of a flat world actually grew in popularity among uneducated medieval Europeans — testament to the power of a belief to influence reality. After all, if you believed that the Earth was flat and that if you sailed towards the horizon you'd fall off the edge, then you were hardly likely to begin such an expedition.

This 'fact' had been conditioned into people to such an extent that it didn't matter whether or not it was true for people to behave as though it was. This type of limiting belief can so easily derail dreams. Despite humble beginnings as the son of an Italian wool weaver, Columbus was an educated man and dreamed of discovering new lands. But he needed royal sponsorship.

Presenting his ambitious plans to the king of Portugal in 1485, he asked for three ships, governorship of any lands he discovered *and* one-tenth of all revenues derived from those lands. The king's counsellors rejected the proposal, declaring Columbus's estimates were wrong. But he wouldn't give up. Three years later he was again rejected by the court of Portugal. He approached Genoa and Venice and even had his brother sound out Henry VII of England. Still he received no support.

In May 1486 Columbus was granted an audience with Spanish monarchs Ferdinand II of Aragon and Isabella I of Castile and again was rejected. But he continued to lobby the Spanish court, until finally Ferdinand accepted his plan.

Columbus was made 'Admiral of the Ocean Sea' and given three ships, the *Santa Maria*, the *Pinta* and the *Niña*, with which he made his famous New World 'discoveries'. He also successfully negotiated a share in the wealth these discoveries generated for Spain.

Columbus once said, 'By prevailing over all obstacles and distractions, one may unfailingly arrive at his chosen goal or destination'. We may not all agree with Columbus's methods, motives or legacy but no-one can deny that he prevailed over all obstacles and distractions and in doing so created his own destiny and changed the world forever.

This world is neither good nor evil; each man manufactures a world for himself.

Mohammad Yunus is another individual who took this principle to heart and transformed millions of lives. In 1976 in a village called Jobra in Bangladesh, Yunus watched as a local woman wove a beautiful stool from bamboo. He learned that she made these stools, which required great patience and skill, to support her family, but that to buy the raw materials she had no option but to make use of an unscrupulous money lender. The woman worked hard yet she was virtually a slave of the money lender, who made by far the most money from her efforts. Yunus was appalled. He loaned $27 from his own pocket to 42 families living in the tiny village. And that single act sparked a revolution that is helping millions of people to break the cycle of poverty and create their own destiny.

Yunus founded the Grameen ('Village') Bank in 1983. This bank does not lend vast sums to people who are already wealthy by world standards. Instead it offers the poorest people in the world access to small amounts of credit, in many cases helping them to transform their lives.

In 2011 Grameen Bank has 8.34 million borrowers and has provided $11.21 billion in loans, predominantly to woman (96 per cent). The bank states that they focus on women because they are often 'neglected in society'. Studies have also shown that women work harder to pay back the loans than men and that 'women are more likely to use their earnings to improve their living situations and to educate their children'.

According to conventional wisdom it's bad business to lend money to the poor, yet Grameen Bank enjoys an unprecedented repayment rate of 97 per cent and has remained largely unaffected by the global financial crisis.

In 2006 Mohammad Yunus won the Nobel Peace Prize for his contribution to eradicating poverty and his micro-finance model has been adopted worldwide, giving the very poorest in society a genuine opportunity to break free from poverty and create their own destiny.

What this principle means for you

When you fully appreciate that you create your own destiny and that you can be anything you want to be, then you take full control over your life. We may be influenced by the way we are brought up, and the conditioning in our subconscious mind may have an impact on what we believe possible, but only if we allow it. There is no blueprint for success in terms of background or environment. Oprah Winfrey was born to unmarried parents in Mississippi and spent her first six years living with her grandmother in rural poverty. She nonetheless became an Academy Award nominated actress, media tycoon, talk show host, publisher and billionaire. Considered one of the most influential people of the twentieth century, Oprah has said:

> 'I don't think of myself as a poor deprived ghetto girl who made good. I think of myself as somebody who from an early age knew I was responsible for myself, and I had to make good.'

If you want to achieve something it's up to you to make it happen. There are no limits to what you can do except the ones you impose on yourself. There is no such thing as perfect parents or a perfect upbringing. Every life has ups and downs. The question is whether you allow the challenges to stop you or simply use them as fuel to try harder. What you believe about yourself and what you are capable of sets up what sociologist Robert Merton called the self-fulfilling prophecy. Merton says, 'The self-fulfilling prophecy is, in the beginning, a false definition of the situation evoking a new behaviour which makes the original false conception come "true". This specious validity of the self-fulfilling prophecy perpetuates a reign of error. For the prophet will cite the actual course of events as proof that he was right from the very beginning'.

Limiting beliefs and negative conditioning mask the truth and, unless you choose differently, will ensure a 'reign of error'. If you don't believe in yourself, you will engage in behaviour that actively sabotages your own efforts so you can prove yourself right. How flawed is that!

That you get what you expect in life was demonstrated conclusively by a famous experiment conducted by Harvard social psychologist Robert Rosenthal. In this study Rosenthal tested 18 classes of elementary school students in non-verbal intelligence. Following the tests 20 per cent of the students, selected randomly and *not* on test scores, were officially identified as 'intellectual bloomers'. Their respective teachers were told they could expect to see significant intellectual gains in the coming year from those particular children.

Eight months later the same children were tested again and the 'intellectual bloomers' were found to have increased in IQ points over the rest of the group. Remember, the 'bloomers' group was chosen randomly so would have included children of average and less than average intelligence.

Rosenthal concluded that the *expectation* of improvement set in motion a self-fulfilling prophecy that actively created that outcome. Meanwhile the teachers created their own 'false definition' regarding the children and, whether consciously or not, altered their behaviour around those expectations. A teacher told to expect great things from specific students was more likely to support those students, helping them when they got stuck and encouraging them to work hard. If they made a mistake or misbehaved, then the teacher simply put it down to a lapse of concentration or otherwise excused the behaviour. The teacher is far less likely to support those students who have been identified as of 'average' intelligence, especially in a busy classroom where time and effort could be more usefully directed towards the bloomers. If the 'average' kids did well or aced a test, then the teacher was more likely to be suspicious than to congratulate and encourage them.

The only difference between these children was their teacher's expectations of them. But it was enough to alter the teacher's behaviour and attitude, which in turn affected the IQ scores. In effect, the teachers became better teachers for the 'intellectual bloomers' and worse teachers for the rest. This 'specious validity' created a 'reign of error', which in turn created a self-fulfilling prophecy according to which the 'bright kids' were supported and encouraged to do better, which they did, but the 'average kids' were less supported and less encouraged and of course didn't improve. Had the experiment ended there, the teachers might have seen the results as proving that the bloomers really were more intelligent. Of course they were then told the truth!

The self-fulfilling prophecy happens in life all the time. This experiment offered a powerful reminder that unless you step up and create your own destiny there are plenty of people around you only too willing to do it for you. This is your life. Expect the best from yourself and, if necessary, take pride in proving the nay-sayers wrong. Twenty years after Maha and Bob bought the land at Opossum Creek, one of their guilty pleasures is the satisfaction of knowing they had achieved something that no-one believed they could. Everyone had expected them to fail.

Creating a new city from scratch is a mammoth task that involves thousands of people. Unlike building a company to sell widgets, it requires authorisation from countless people, departments and levels of government, and those people are constantly changing. It requires vast amounts of capital. Maha and Bob couldn't have chosen a more difficult goal, a goal with more vested interests wanting to control the outcome. Yet they refused to allow anyone to control their destiny. Buddha said, 'We are what we think. All that we are arises with our thoughts. With our thoughts we make our world'. If that is true, and it is, what world are you making?

> *We are responsible for what we are; and whatever we wish ourselves to be, we have the power to make ourselves. If what we are now has been the result of our past actions, it certainly follows that whatever we wish to be in future can be produced by our present actions; so we have to know how to act.*

Maha's action plan

Create your own destiny! In order to help you shift your thinking and incorporate this principle into your life you will need to:

➤ believe in yourself
➤ be resourceful
➤ manage your mind.

Believe in yourself

Self-belief is critical to success. If you don't believe in yourself, how can you expect anyone else to believe in you?

When Maha first began to talk about building a new city no-one believed it even possible. But he believed in himself and his ability to make it happen. Of self-belief, Maha says, 'Be your own best friend. You are the only person you are with permanently from birth to death; every moment of your life is spent with yourself. You can't leave and go somewhere else without your friend being there, so you need to be good to your friend, take care of him or her and love yourself'. Buddha reminds us, 'You can search throughout the entire universe for someone who is more deserving of your love and affection than you are yourself, and that person is not to be found anywhere. You, yourself, as much as anybody in the entire universe, deserve your love and affection'. So be your own best friend, support yourself and back yourself no matter what others around you may say.

Nothing is achieved without self-belief, but it can be a tricky and illusive attribute to harness. Too often in life we take on labels and limitations that other people impose on us. Maha is adamant that you must consciously expel anything that negatively affects your self-belief. If you think that you are the victim of racism, sexism or any other type of discrimination it is you who bring yourself down. Meera, Maha and Yoga's youngest daughter, says, 'I was never told that I needed to be better because I was Asian or because I was a woman. We were just expected to do our best full stop, not for any other reason. There was never any discussion of difference, and as a result we never thought of ourselves as different. I vividly remember my husband asking me if I'd ever experienced racism and I was 24 at the time. I can honestly say I've never encountered racism in my life'. Because Maha refused to see himself as different from anyone else his children didn't either. This outlook is instrumental in creating strong self-belief.

Maha believes that putting a label on yourself before you've even begun is like tying an unnecessary weight around your neck. If you believe you can't be successful because of the colour of your skin or because you're a woman or because of any other type of discrimination, then you will probably turn out to be 100 per cent correct. If, like Maha, you refuse to see yourself as any different, any less capable, any less worthy than anyone else, then you will also be 100 per cent correct. The choice is yours. The first choice leads to mediocrity and excuses, the second to freedom and self-belief.

Eleanor Roosevelt once said, 'No one can make you feel inferior without your consent'. Forget about what others think about you and focus on what you think about yourself. Self-belief starts with liking and trusting yourself, and making the conscious decision that no matter what life throws at you, you will be okay. Very often it is a process that occurs over time through the making and keeping of commitments to yourself. Be a person who does what you say you will do when you say you will do it. Demand more of yourself than anyone else can reasonably demand of you. And keep your promises, especially the ones you make to yourself.

Be a person of honour and integrity and always do what is right, not just for you but for the community you live in. Be ethical and honest and set a high standard for yourself and others.

It doesn't matter if others don't always believe in you or your vision, but you must believe in yourself. Every good idea will have its critics. As Gandhi so eloquently put it, 'First they ignore you. Then they laugh at you. Then they fight you. Then you win'. You will always achieve what you set out to if you believe in yourself and never give up.

Whatever qualities the rich may have, they can be acquired by anyone with the tenacity to become rich. The key, I think, is confidence. Confidence and an unshakable belief it can be done and that you are the one to do it.

—Felix Dennis (British publishing entrepreneur)

Believe in yourself! Have faith in your abilities! Without a humble but reasonable confidence in your own powers you cannot be successful or happy.

*—*Norman Vincent Peale (American pastor and author)

Be resourceful

If you are to be the creator of your own destiny you must learn to be resourceful. That means finding solutions, even when none are obvious or apparent. For most of Springfield's history money has been in short supply, and while this has been a constant challenge it has fostered a level of resourcefulness that would never have been realised had there been bucketloads of cash. As Roman poet Horace pointed out in the time of Caesar Augustus, 'Adversity has the effect of eliciting talents which in prosperous circumstances would have lain dormant'.

Maha and Bob were always looking for people who were willing to share the risk and would agree to be paid—at least partially—on success. It was important that everyone was truly accountable for their work. And the people who agreed to these terms needed to have the self-belief that they could deliver. Maha and Bob were very cautious with expenses and frugal. This had always been Maha's way. Back in Perth his children remember him going to his building sites and loading the surplus bricks into the back of an old station-wagon, until finally this regular overloading of bricks broke the axle! Even today, a wealthy man, Maha still cuts open the toothpaste tube to make sure he has used every scrap of toothpaste in the tube. Uma still does the same thing and will open her children's hair gel tubes so they can extract and use every last drop. The Sinnathamby family share a 'waste not, want not' ethic that has never changed through all the financial ups and downs.

Maha's resourcefulness and dislike of waste didn't just rub off on his children, it also influenced the team at Springfield. In-house accountant and true believer Malcolm Finlayson was one of the first staff members to live in Springfield and often he would walk home for lunch. On the way he would pick up seeds that had fallen from the trees and take them back to the office, where they would be allocated to the 'landscaping resources' for the new developments.

To be resourceful you must first believe that a solution exists. And that is facilitated by an optimistic mind. One of Maha's greatest strengths is his optimism. Nothing throws him for long. This can be explained by what American psychologist Martin Seligman calls his 'explanatory style'—that is, the way he explains the ups and downs of life to himself and others. There are three parts to a person's explanatory style—permanence, pervasiveness and personalisation—and by understanding these elements you can learn to be optimistic. Seligman believes we are not born optimistic or pessimistic but become what we are through conditioning and experience, and that we can therefore learn to be more optimistic by altering our explanatory style.

When Maha faces a crisis, he automatically believes that the situation is temporary and that the darkest day brings the brightest dawn. He never believes the crisis is permanent or that there is no solution. When one part of the project stalled or a decision went against them, he didn't automatically assume that the problem would have a knock-on effect in other areas. An optimist always sees setbacks in isolation and doesn't allow them to pollute other areas of their life. Finally, Maha never took anything personally. When someone turned him down, he never internalised the setback. Optimists never personalise failure or attribute it to some personal fault or weakness; they simply brush it off and try again. For a pessimist, on the other hand, failure is always personal.

Learn to be an optimist so you can access the full reservoir of your resourcefulness. When things go badly, accept the setback as a temporary glitch rather than a permanent outcome, accept that the failure is isolated to one event or situation and is not an indication of pervasive failure, and don't take setbacks and failures personally.

All the resources we need are in the mind.

—Theodore Roosevelt (26th US President)

Literally hundreds of studies show that pessimists give up more easily and get depressed more often. These experiments show that optimists do much better in school and college, at work and on the playing field.

— **Dr Martin Seligman (American psychologist)**

Manage your mind

You are the creator of your own destiny. You are what you choose to be, but only if you take conscious control of your thoughts and actively challenge negative subconscious conditioning. The order of creation is from thought to word to deed, but creation is an endless cycle and can begin at any point.

No-one has the time to lie about on a psychiatrist's sofa to ferret out all their unhelpful or negative conditioning. Everyone, even those who were brought up in supportive loving homes, has limiting beliefs and mountains of unhelpful and inaccurate information stored in their subconscious. The fastest way to dismantle negative conditioning and break the spell of limiting beliefs is to move straight into action and reverse the thought–word–deed process.

What it lies in our power to do, it lies in our power not to do.

— **Aristotle (Greek philosopher)**

Whatever it is you want to achieve, just do it. Plan your tasks and tick them off one by one. Take action and reinforce that action with new words and when you do that often enough you'll train your mind to think in a new, more constructive way. Say you want to start a business but you're nervous it won't work out. If you believed you couldn't fail you would start the business. It's the belief that's holding you back. But if you just start anyway, you grow stronger and more confident by doing the work required, until eventually you'll believe you can't fail. It's a self-fulfilling prophecy that is set in motion through action, not thought. We are defined not just by what we do but by what we don't do, so get into action now.

Your subconscious mind will throw up reasons and excuses for why you should not follow through. It may whisper, 'Don't be stupid, it will never work.' It may even accuse you of threatening disgrace and ruin by continuing. It will derail you with other 'urgent' tasks, such as cleaning behind the fridge, or fool you into thinking you're hungry or need a cup of tea. It will taunt you with impending failure and do it's best to maintain the status quo. When you move into action you may feel uncomfortable or fearful; that's to be expected, so welcome the feelings when they arrive and push on through. Your subconscious mind is just a storehouse of past experiences, opinions, events and information. Are you seriously going to let outdated information and past experiences, whatever they are, stop you from living the life you want? Your conscious mind is the boss, but only if you use it to take control of your subconscious thoughts and manage your mind positively.

To change a habit, make a conscious decision, then act out the new behaviour.

—Maxwell Maltz (American author)

Chapter 10
All power is within you

All power is within you. You can do anything and everything. Believe in that ... Stand up and express the divinity within you.

'All power is within you' expresses both a practical and a philosophical call-to-arms. This final chapter explores the power inherent in Springfield and the pillars that have underpinned and driven its vision and outcomes. It also introduces the ancient wisdom that has guided Maha Sinnathamby throughout his life.

This principle recognises that you are capable and powerful and that you already have everything you'll ever need within you to achieve your dreams. Nothing is written in the stars. Success is the product not of luck, chance, good timing or magic but of persistent, consistent effort towards a goal and a steadfast refusal to give up. Nothing in Maha's life has been easy. He's made many mistakes and turned many wrong corners on his life's journey. Great accomplishments, like great individuals, take time to mature. Struggle makes success all the sweeter.

When you truly believe that all the power you will ever need is within you *right now*, then the world looks very different—and nothing will stop you.

The critical pillars that underpin Springfield

From the start Springfield was planned around the three core pillars of education, health and technology and complemented by a strong culture of environmental sustainability.

Education transformed Maha's life. It allowed him to transcend a life of poverty and hardship to achieve success and prosperity. Maha inherited from his parents a belief in the transformational potential of education and was determined that this value would be embedded in the Springfield way of life—that it would be a place of lifelong learning.

The fruition of that vision is a work in progress, but the foundational piece of the education puzzle was undoubtedly the opening of the first Springfield State School. Like most milestones in Springfield, securing the school was a hard-fought battle.

Normally a new residential development will simply tap into existing infrastructure and services. As the population grows the residents, new and old, will put pressure on government to upgrade or build new facilities. But Springfield was a greenfield site. Local children had to travel to nearby schools, which were fast overcrowding. It needed its own brand-new school. Needless to say, government, with a finite budget and other pressing priorities, was reluctant to build one.

The social infrastructure agreement meant that, in theory, Springfield could pull forward the construction of critical services such as roads and schools as long as they agreed to pay the interest on the loans required to build them until such time as the government would have built them anyway. In reality, the building project was merely added to the state's list for consideration each year, and each year it was rejected.

In January 1998, five years after the first residents moved to Springfield, the Springfield State School finally opened its doors, but it wasn't the glistening grand opening that Principal Nev Smith had hoped for.

When he had been given the brief and budget to build an innovative, contemporary learning institution, Nev was thrilled. The government's planning allowed for an initial intake of 200 students, which it considered would be a little over capacity, but the developers and many parents were already saying that would be insufficient. To make his own judgement, Nev took a tour of the new Springfield development and looked at the distribution of local primary schools and their likely catchment areas. The Springfield estate was huge and the local Camira School was already bursting at the seams. Alarm bells started ringing for Nev. The school was being built to the planners' estimates yet the enrolment assumptions looked to be way underdone!

In an effort to establish real needs, Nev announced an enrolment day for the new school. He and a colleague sat at a desk in the partially constructed car park and watched in disbelief as the queue of parents continued to grow. After two hours they had accepted 180 enrolments. A subsequent day tipped the student numbers over 300.

The last-minute spike in enrolment meant the Education Minister and local media arrived to open a school dominated by temporary, second-hand demountable buildings. Although it wasn't the prestigious start Nev had hoped for, he would ultimately create a dynamic and revolutionary campus where technology and learning materials took centre stage, teachers were more like guides and facilitators, and students progressed on the basis of educational attainment, rather than by year. Nev Smith was a visionary, and his school would in time be regarded as one of the best in the state. Nev's input was also important when Maha and Bob sought to lock in another key piece of the educational puzzle by bringing a university to Springfield.

Bringing a university to Springfield

Attracting a university to Education City was central to Maha's plans from day one, yet he was told time and again that it would *never* happen. He first pursued an alliance with one of the biggest and most prestigious universities in Australia, the University of Queensland (UQ). Springfield offered UQ 121 hectares (300 acres) free of charge on which to build their campus. Negotiations progressed well and the Springfield team were invited to present to the university senate. Following some political twists and turns the deal was finally blocked and the new UQ campus was subsequently built close to the Ipswich CBD instead. Despite this last-minute blow, securing a university was never taken off the Springfield agenda.

In 2003 the right opportunity finally presented itself when Maha was invited by the Premier to join a state delegation to India. He accepted without hesitation. In truth it mattered little to him where the delegation was heading; what was important was that it represented at least 15 hours in which he would be in an enclosed space with people who could positively influence Springfield, especially the Premier himself. On the trip Maha also met Bill Lovegrove, the Deputy Vice Chancellor of Griffith University. Bill explained to him that all the universities operated within certain geographic catchments and took great care not to enter into 'turf wars' with each other. As Springfield was outside Griffith's catchment, Bill suggested that Maha approach the University of Southern Queensland (USQ) instead.

And that's exactly what happened. Contact with USQ was established and discussions progressed well. Then, frustratingly, the principals involved in these positive discussions left the university around the same time the Vice Chancellor's term came to an end, so the project was put on hold. In a rare stroke of good luck, Bill Lovegrove was then appointed as the new Vice Chancellor of USQ. Since it had been Bill who had suggested that Maha speak to USQ in the first place, this put him in a tricky situation. But to his credit he reviewed the proposal fairly and facilitated a presentation to the University Council. Nev Smith's representation on the team was strategically important given the very high level of respect he was held in across the education sector in Queensland. His opinion was valued and there's little doubt he helped the Springfield team get USQ across the line.

Today the University of Southern Queensland operates its 'Brisbane campus' out of Springfield, where it is the jewel in the crown of Education City. But of course it wasn't all plain sailing. The project was a huge undertaking. The Education City vision had always been bold and called for a six-storey building with a 350-seat auditorium. The university needed status, so it needed substantial and impressive buildings. Maha and Bob engaged the very best architects and planners to design the precinct. Adding to the pressure, it was important that the entire campus be constructed concurrently, including the student accommodation, the cafeteria and the childcare facilities. All at a time when there wasn't even a road to the university site!

After finalising the agreement with USQ, the Springfield team negotiated a landmark deal with the James Fielding Group to joint venture Education City, and things began to move forward quickly. Towards the end of 2004 a spanner was thrown in the works when James Fielding Group was taken over by Mirvac. The positive for Maha was Mirvac's early decision to appoint James Fielding's former

CEO to head up the merged group. However, other key Mirvac personnel showed little interest in the project.

The construction timeline had been initially estimated at 15 months and the campus would cost about $85 million to complete. *And* the project was not staged — everything needed to be finished at the same time. With every week of delay these estimates looked more improbable. In January 2005 Mirvac sought a delay to the start of construction of one year. But Springfield had already announced publicly that the university would be open for students in 2006, and there was no way they were going back on their word. Once again the team dug in and fought to keep the deal alive. Miraculously, despite the holdups and delays, the builders finally managed to reduce the already ambitious 15-month schedule and the university was built in record time. The whole Education City campus opened as promised in January 2006.

In the first year USQ enrolled 300 students — a remarkable intake considering that when students had to make their university selections there was no campus to walk around.

It was particularly rewarding for Maha. He had always wanted to create an educational environment that would uplift people, inspiring them to expect and demand more of themselves and their lives. In this the university is already a huge success. The typical enrolee is a first-generation tertiary student. In other words, these are students whose parents and grandparents never advanced beyond high school. In 2011 the university taught 1500 students in law, business, engineering and surveying, psychology, arts and education. USQ has already purchased more land and has plans to construct a new building that will effectively mirror the existing one — 6000 square metres (1.48 acres), six stories high.

Education City is a unique, 18-hectare integrated learning community that currently hosts a range of early childhood educational providers, schools, private learning institutions and the university, and is able to cater for the lifelong learning needs of the city and region. In 2011, however, Education City was only 10 per cent developed so the potential is enormous. Of significance also is the combined presence of a university with other learning institutions in the same precinct.

Outside the Education City precinct, Springfield boasts six schools, a state golf academy, an English training school, a language school and other education facilities with a total current enrolment of almost 5000 students. In total there are more than 8700 students in some form of education, giving the area the highest student to resident ratios of anywhere in the country. Springfield has about one student for every three residents, making it a living expression of Maha's dedication to education.

That dedication also extends to underprivileged children. Less than 25 per cent of Indigenous children finish school and, like anyone else without an education, they are often doomed to a life of hardship and poverty as a result. To help rectify this situation, Maha and Bob recently donated land to the Hymba Yumba Community Hub, an $8-million school for Indigenous Australian girls. Hymba Yumba will encourage students to strive to achieve academic, sporting and creative excellence while honouring their proud traditions and heritage. Often these girls are young mothers and finishing their education offers them the best opportunity to break the cycle of poverty.

There is no money in this project for Maha and Bob. They donated the land to allow the project to move forward. But Maha feels very strongly about the negative impact of isolation on any community. 'We are all influenced by our environment. My daughter Raynuha is fond of saying you are the average intelligence of the people you spend time with.' If you are a single mother on welfare and the only people you mix with are others on similar benefits, then you may not aspire to more. If, on the other hand, you have opportunities to witness and experience other life choices, you will find that we can all learn from each other and pull each other up. In Hymba Yumba many of the girls are young mothers who have resigned themselves to a certain life because they didn't believe they could finish their education and didn't know anyone who took learning seriously. With access to child care and a positive supporting environment, they come to realise that their past does not dictate their future and that wonderful things are possible.

Maha adds, 'If I can get one girl a year to believe in herself and realise that her circumstances can be changed for the better, then it will all have been worth it'.

World-class health care

The second pillar of Springfield is health. And here too Springfield has never shied away from big ideas. Again the vision was bold and innovative. In true Springfield style, the team visited other similar projects around the world, sought the input of leading consultants on international best practice, then set out to create the best healthcare facilities possible. Senior officials from the NHS in the UK were consulted and several million dollars were spent on two separate reports completed over two years by specialists from Harvard Medical International. More recently, Maha and Bob have entered into a strategic alliance with Mater Health Services, which will be the major provider of hospital services within Health City.

According to the Harvard reports, one of the main challenges in health care is that medical specialists, doctors and personnel are underutilised because they are often compelled to travel between facilities or conduct non-medical duties. In addition, hospital resources are chronically overextended because of lack of space and beds. Health City will solve these problems by having all the facilities in one location. Once patients have received hospital treatment they will be discharged to an acute nursing facility, where they will receive state-of-the-art aftercare. Alternatively they may be transferred to the luxury five-star hotel in Health City, where they will be closely monitored by medical personnel. Either outcome will free up valuable hospital beds. There will also be a three-star hotel to provide accommodation for visiting family members during treatment and recuperation.

Spread across a 52-hectare (128.5 acres) campus, Health City will incorporate an integrated approach to primary, acute and aged care and wellness. Deliberately planned to be adjacent to Education City (via Sinnathamby Boulevard), Health City will be a research and education hub as well as containing a public and private hospital and every kind of health facility from physiotherapy to alternative therapy clinics. Aged-care and retirement living facilities will mean Springfield residents will remain close to family members after they reach retirement age or need care. National statistics suggest aged-care residents seldom see relatives (the average across Australia for an 80 year old is sadly once every three months). Part of the problem is that aged-care facilities are often located a considerable distance from those relatives. At Springfield, however, community members can ensure their aged loved ones live close by and share the amenities of the emerging city. Forward planning has made allowance for 2500 aged care beds within the Health precinct by 2026.

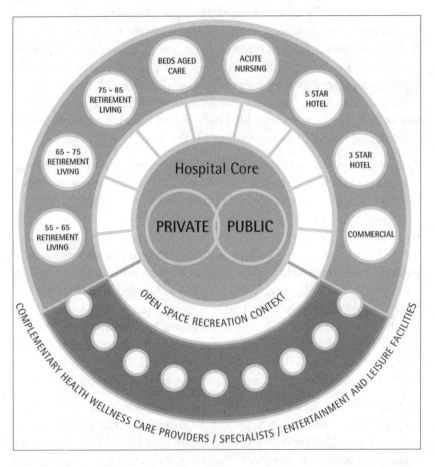

Health City will also provide 'real innovation' in health care. The use of new technologies across the board—from pathology through hospital services to monitoring the aged—combined with e-health and telemedicine will ensure health services leverage the community's dark fibre and data centre infrastructure. For example, using reliable high-speed connectivity it is now possible for a doctor in New York to supervise an operation on your brain in Brisbane. Watching the operation in New York, the specialist advises the on-ground surgeon while the operation is in progress.

The digital city

The final pillar that supports Springfield and is closely linked to both health and education is information technology. Today it's easy to see the importance of IT in the modern world, but it was less obvious back in the early 1990s. When Maha and Bob first bought the land, internet and mobile phone technology were still in their infancy. Even then, though, they knew that technology would play an increasingly important role in our daily lives and they wanted Springfield to be ready when that day arrived.

Twenty years later that vision is a reality. We now live in a world utterly dominated by technology. It is now an everyday part of life, especially in the fields of communication, teaching and learning. When Barack Obama won the US presidency in 2009, defying the odds to become the first African-American to enter the White House, many commentators said it would never have been possible without new technology. He used technology to communicate directly with his supporters and mobilise huge numbers of apathetic and disenchanted voters, especially the young. He used social media sites such as Facebook and Twitter to counter media attacks in real time and gather feedback and opinions on real issues of importance to people. He broke records for fundraising and rewrote the rulebook on campaign advertising. The official campaign recordings created for YouTube were watched for 14.5 million hours—air time that would have cost many hundreds of millions of dollars had the campaign team used traditional advertising channels.

Internet, and particularly social media communication is now commonplace but that was not the case in the early 1990s, when Springfield became the first fully computerised community in the world. Through a system called Springfield Community Net, every home had a computer that was linked to every other home in the area, as well as to all shops, schools, hospitals and the emergency services. Other developers had put cables in the ground to allow this sort of connectivity, but Springfield was the first to put a multimedia computer in every home as part of the purchase package. Although this technology became largely redundant with the almost universal adoption of the internet, it emphasises the forward thinking that has always been central to the design and development of Springfield.

Springfield State School was the first school built from scratch in Australia, and only the eighth in the world to set up an Apple Classroom of Tomorrow (ACOT). The program sought to integrate computers into the learning environment and support teachers in combining technology with traditional teaching methods.

Springfield has become the definition of a digital city. With a private investment in fibre-optic cables and geographically diverse fibre links to Brisbane, in 2006 the information superhighway arrived. This innovation, together with the delivery of environmentally sound buildings, led to development of the $220-million Tier 3+ Polaris Data Centre, Springfield's first data centre and ICT hub, which opened in January 2009. Untouched by the 2011 Queensland floods, Polaris delivers primary, secondary and disaster-recovery data centre capabilities for all levels of government, national and multinational corporations, and Springfield's key IT infrastructure services. Complete with bullet-proof glass, biometric security systems, and multi-carrier and dark-fibre connectivity options, Polaris is the largest, most secure and most advanced purpose-built data centre in Australia.

Even the 24-hectare (59.3 acres) Robelle Domain (named after Bob and Belinda Sharpless), the core of the Springfield Central Parklands in the heart of the CBD, is a technological innovation costing $30 million. The park includes all the conventional public open-space features, with 11 kilometres of boardwalks, walking and cycle tracks, sports fields, water play areas, exhibition gardens and picturesque picnic areas. But it also offers free WiFi, Australia's first ICON on GALAXY play equipment that combines play with the excitement of electronic gaming, and a stage and amphitheatre that caters for up to 10 000 people and features lighting including nine-metre-high artistic light towers and interactive surround sound audio.

Springfield was designed from the start as a digital city but is perhaps better described as a 'Big Idea City'.

Environmental protection and sustainability

The Springfield project has always been driven by a strong and consistent culture of good environmental behaviour and a genuine respect for the principles of sustainability. At every stage—from the distribution of green space throughout the city to protecting sacred Aboriginal sites to wildlife and plant life regeneration to the innovative use of technology to the creation of environmentally friendly buildings in the commercial and residential areas—the goal has been to minimise the environmental damage and increase long-term sustainability. Notwithstanding the protracted battle with the environmental lobby detailed in the previous chapter, Springfield's track record in this area is impressive and the city is home to some of the most environmentally advanced buildings in Australia, including its innovative shopping centre.

An unprecedented 32 per cent of the land in Springfield has been set aside for parks, gardens, waterways, conservation and open spaces. The full length of Springfield's 7.75-kilometre north–south axis is now connected through a series of wide and sensitively landscaped walkways, with interconnected access also to the east–west axis and to the pristine Spring Mountain.

Orion Shopping Centre

Springfield CBD is a massive 390 hectares (963 acres), and already 8000 people work there. When it's complete it will be twice the size of Brisbane's CBD. Thousands more will pour into Springfield every day, brought to work by the $1.2 billion extension to the rail network, which will open in 2013, or one of the five major arterial roads that intersect at the CBD. It is expected that 30000 new jobs will be created for people in the local community, who will have the opportunity to work in one of many purpose-built commercial premises such as Springfield Tower or the Parkside Business Precinct. During their lunch breaks they will be able to stretch their legs in Robelle Domain or go shopping in Orion Shopping Centre, which, when finished, will be the largest shopping centre in the country. In fact, it was the shopping centre deal in 2002 that finally secured Springfield's future.

Finding a partner for the retail section had taken almost 10 years. No-one wanted to build a shopping centre where there wasn't the population base to support it. The only serious contender was Greg Paramor, CEO of the James Fielding Group. Maha and Bob had wanted $40 million for the shopping precinct. Maha and Greg traded figures over coffee one afternoon, and in no time $11 million was taken out of the deal. Maha knew Bob wouldn't be happy, but money now was always better than possible money—even if more of it—later. Besides, a confirmed commercial partner would massively boost the city.

In September 2002 Maha, Bob and Greg met for the final exchange of contracts and a nice fat cheque for $29 million. The cheque, it turned out, wasn't nearly as fat as expected. Greg said he wanted to pay in two instalments. He assured Maha and Bob of his commitment to the project. Handing over a payment of $15 million with a promise of the rest in a year's time, Greg uttered the deal-clinching words: 'Please hang in there'. How many times had Bob said the same thing to other people! This was their karma. Although not what they'd hoped for, Maha and Bob knew only too well the mutual trust needed for long-haul relationships so they accepted the deal. Maha took the cheque, which was quickly snared by Bob. After 11 long years of financial stress and struggle Springfield was *finally* safe. 'This deal allowed us to become pretty much debt free and to start breathing again', Maha said. 'And on completion, the Orion Shopping Centre gained an unprecedented 6 Star Green Star rating, of which we are very proud.'

The future of Springfield

Springfield's critical pillars, of course, support the residential communities, as do the commercial precincts and improved access and public transport networks. The residential communities are flourishing: at the time of writing there are more than 23 000 residents across five suburbs of Springfield. Within these suburbs there has been a deliberate attempt to enhance the community by attracting all types of residents and families. There are homes suitable for first-time buyers, for families looking for space to grow and for professionals looking for luxury living. Children play together whether they come from a cash-strapped single-parent home or an affluent two-parent family. The old and the young live side by side to encourage everyone to learn positive lessons from one another. 'Our planning has always been influenced by a desire to foster good open communication and add value and dimension to human capital', Maha says.

Springfield has come a long way since 1991. As a consequence of the DCP and the special legislation all the power to complete the city is within the development now, but the struggle to fully realise Maha's vision is not over. While the DCP locks in place the areas of Springfield designated for each specific purpose, the execution of those plans is still fluid. Maha has always envisioned the 'beautiful face' of Springfield. Like sculptors, he and his team have chipped away at the rock to unveil the face of the city, but many of its features are still only roughly drawn.

Maha insists on the highest possible specifications; it is this principle that continues to exercise his mind most. After a 20-year journey he is every bit as obsessed by Springfield as ever. So early retirement is not on the horizon for him, although he would like to find just a little more time to spend with Yoga and his grandchildren.

Maha is a passionate man who has lived, breathed and dreamt Springfield for decades. He is a seasoned networker who makes this valuable skill look easy. But how will the next generation handle these challenges? Will they maintain and foster the important relationships with the same passion and drive? Will they apply the same sense of urgency? Will they be as hungry to manifest and drive the vision and to protect the integrity of the planning scheme?

In fact, there is little doubt that the answer to all these questions is 'Yes'. At almost 20 years his junior, Bob knows Maha as well as he knows himself and has that drive. All Maha's children have been brought up on the dream and are every bit as passionate as their father. Raynuha and Naren work full time in the business. Uma and Meera are busy raising families but are still involved part time. Raynuha especially has played a very significant role in almost all of Springfield's key milestones and is her father's most likely successor.

In 1997, with a Law and Arts degree and an MBA behind her, Raynuha was happily working in a Brisbane law practice. By his own admission Maha put a great deal of pressure on her to join the company, and reluctantly she agreed. It's fair to say that at first she hated it, but she stuck it out for her father's sake and after two years she was hooked. Raynuha realised that as a lawyer she would only ever have been involved in part of the project, whereas SLC offered her an opportunity to embrace every aspect of it, from start to finish, and that prospect was exciting and challenging. Ever since, Raynuha has dedicated her life to fulfilling her father's vision. Naren completed a Commerce degree with a Marketing major and joined SLC in 1999, although by his own admission it took him a while to find his niche. As Director of Marketing, Naren now plays a pivotal role in spreading the word on Springfield.

In many ways the Sinnathamby family is a living expression of the tenth principle. They are an incredibly tight unit. Although all the children are married the six of them still attend monthly family meetings, and there is no doubt that to varying degrees they will all continue to act as guardians to the integrity of the Springfield vision.

Sir Francis Drake once said: 'There must be a beginning of any great matter, but the continuing unto the end until it be thoroughly finished yields the true glory'. It may be many years before Springfield yields its true glory.

Introducing Vedanta

Throughout this book there are references to Maha's ancient wisdom. That wisdom is Vedanta. All these quotations and those that are otherwise unsourced through the book are from the writings of Swami Vivekananda, a man who, alongside Gandhi, has had an especially profound influence on Maha's life and outlook.

Swami Vivekananda was the chief disciple of the 19th-century Bengali mystic Ramakrishna Paramahansa and is considered a key figure in bringing Vedanta to the west.

Maha's father introduced him to Vedanta. While not realising his ambition to become a monk, Valipuram raised a family in his spiritual teachings and passed his passion for Vedanta and education to his son. Maha's subsequent efforts have brought education to many thousands of people, both through the schools and university he has helped to create, and through his practical support for the Vedanta Society in Australia.

Although Maha and his siblings attended a Catholic school in Malaysia, and Valipuram was supportive of the Christian doctrine, at home he would teach the children Vedanta. One evening Maha asked his father if they were Hindu in the evening and Christian during the day, and whether they were allowed to pray to the Christian God during school time. His father simply laughed and said, 'It doesn't matter whether you are Buddhist, Muslim, Christian, Hindu or whatever. I think humans have complicated it too much. I don't think there are dozens of different gods or fellows up there, but pray to whoever you like. It is what is inside you and your qualities that matter. Follow whatever or whoever you like, as long as it makes you a better person.'

To someone of different conviction that idea might seem incomprehensible or even blasphemous, but one of the most profound aspects of Vedanta is that it makes no claim about who is the 'right' God. There is no central figure or prophet. Vedanta doesn't even originate from a single source. Rather, it is the collective knowledge of the Vedas, the Upanishads, the Brahma Sutras and the *Bhagavad Gita*—all ancient Hindu texts. But Vedanta is not Hinduism; rather, it is the root of all Hindu sects—indeed some suggest it is the root of all world religions. The word *Vedanta* itself means 'the conclusion of all knowledge'.

Above all, Vedanta is a practical philosophy that prescribes a way of being rather than a way of praying. As Maha describes, 'Vedanta tells of a constant universal truth. Just as the sun will always rise tomorrow the wisdom of Vedanta is always relevant, real and true. It is like gravity. Apples will always fall from trees because of the forces of gravity. There is nothing unusual about it. The fact that Newton discovered this does not mean that he invented gravity. He simple witnessed the truth and gave it a name.'

We are all divine, but we are tricked into believing we are not. The challenges and difficulties in our life are not punishments but opportunities to rise up, shrug off illusion, manifest our divinity and understand our true nature—that of Brahman. Brahman is the one absolute reality, the life force behind everything. That is why Valipuram was happy that his children were taught in a Catholic school—to a Vedantist everything is the same. We are all the same, all religion is the same, and we are all connected and all part of the same infinite whole. This is why all power is within you. According to Vedanta there is no God outside of you that you need to coerce or appease because God is in each of us as the divine self or Atman.

The Atman is like the sun behind the clouds. It is always there; you may not realise it and you may not always feel its warmth and power, but it is *always* there and is completely unaffected by the ups and downs of life.

> *We believe that every being is divine, is God. Every soul is a sun covered over with clouds of ignorance, the difference between soul and soul is owing to the difference in density of these layers of clouds.*

In Vedanta we are always connected to the infinite because we are the infinite. You sculpt that 'life force' by your thoughts, words and deeds. If you don't do that consciously to create what you want it will happen anyway, subconsciously, and you'll probably end up with something you don't want. It is your thoughts, words and deeds that determine what you create, not luck or chance or even prayer. Like electricity this power is there for the taking and can accomplish great things. Whether you plug into positive or negative thoughts, words and deeds is up to you, but you can expect to get back exactly what you plug in.

> *Do not hate anybody, because that hatred which comes out from you must, in the long run, come back to you. If you love, that love will come back to you, completing the circle.*

In Vedanta this is karma. In Christianity this idea is expressed in 'As ye sow, so shall ye reap'. Christianity also counsels, 'Love thy neighbour as thy self'. Vedanta suggests the same, not because you should be nice to your neighbour, but because you and your neighbour are essentially part of the same whole. If you hurt your neighbour or treat him or her badly, you are effectively hurting yourself.

Whether or not you buy into the Vedanta philosophy is entirely up to you. For Maha it is a way of being that is fundamentally hard-wired into his nature and his beliefs have guided him through exceptionally difficult times and moulded an extraordinarily creative individual.

Ultimately Vedanta is simply a collection of universally relevant principles or ideas on how best to live your life. They encourage self-belief, hard work, persistence and the uplifting importance of striving for a meaningful goal. Vedanta is the simple acknowledgement that regardless of the circumstances of your birth, your upbringing, your skin colour or your gender, you have within you a sleeping giant: you are infinite and all the power you will ever need to achieve your dreams is already inside you now. All you need to do is wake that giant!

> *You must remember that all work is simply to bring out the power of the mind which is already there, to wake up the soul. The power is inside every man, so is knowing; the different works are like blows to bring them out, to cause these giants to wake up.*

The principle in action

There are countless true stories of incredible courage and commitment that raise questions about individual beliefs and attitudes. One such story is of an extraordinary young man named Aron Ralston. In 2003 Ralston decided to go hiking in Utah's Bluejohn Canyon. As he was climbing, a 400-kilo boulder dislodged and crushed his right arm, pinning him against the canyon wall. He was alone, had not told anyone of his plans and did not have a mobile phone. After five days he was dehydrated and delirious. He had run out of water and he expected to die. But all power is within. The following morning Ralston was surprised to find himself still alive and experienced an epiphany — a radical solution to his predicament had come to him ... He would use the boulder to snap his own arm, then he would amputate the arm with his penknife.

And that's exactly what he did. After freeing himself he climbed out of the canyon he had been trapped in, abseiled down a 20-metre sheer wall and hiked out of the canyon in searing midday heat. Luckily he met a holidaying Dutch family, who raised the alarm. Ralston's family had alerted authorities that he was missing and a helicopter was already in the air looking for him. Six hours after amputating his own arm he was airlifted to safety.

There can be little doubt that the drive to survive is a powerful motivating force, but there was something more at play here. In an interview with *National Geographic* Ralston was asked why he made the decision he did. He said, 'After having enough sleep-deprived, meandering thoughts about how I arrived in the canyon, I realised that my situation was the result of decisions that I had made. I chose to go out there by myself. I chose to not tell anyone where I was going. I chose not to go with two climbers I had met in the canyon on the first day. But I also realised that I had made all of the choices up to that point that had helped me survive. I took responsibility for all of my decisions, which helped me take on the responsibility of getting myself out'.

Ralston took responsibility for where he was. He accepted his part in the catastrophe and in doing so accepted his part in finding the solution. That sort of thinking is helped dramatically when you believe all power is within. When we come full circle and face ourselves—good and bad—and accept both, we have the power to do extraordinary things and tap into extraordinary resources.

Another man who tapped into extraordinary inner resources was Shun Fujimoto. His is probably not a name you are immediately familiar with, but what he did at the 1976 Montreal Olympics in Quebec still beggars belief. As a member of the Japanese gymnastics team Fujimoto won gold, but did so with a broken leg!

During the last moments of his floor routine he broke his kneecap, but completed his routine without alerting anyone to his injury. Such was his loyalty to the team and his commitment to gold that he continued to the pommel horse, an apparatus that requires supreme upper body strength while keeping the lower body perfectly straight. Fujimoto had to keep his broken knee straight through the entire routine, which he did, scoring an almost incomprehensible 9.5.

Yet there was more to come. Fujimoto also had to complete his rings routine and his performance was going to be crucial for Japan to win Gold from the Soviet Union. For this round of the competition the athlete is lifted up to the rings, where he must complete a routine that combines superlative strength and grace with a perfect landing from two and a half metres in the air. Incredibly, Fujimoto landed squarely on both feet, with his hands elevated and scored 9.7, the best rings score of his career. His actions and his faith and belief in himself to find a way meant that Japan won Gold by four-tenths of a point.

After the gymnast had received medical attention, one doctor said, 'How he managed to do somersaults and twists and land without collapsing in screams is beyond my comprehension.'

The goal is to manifest the Divinity within, by controlling nature, external and internal. Do this either by work, or worship or psychic control or philosophy—by one or more or all of these—and be free.

What this principle means for you

This principle is not a new idea. Indeed it underpins all world religions. For example, the Bible says, 'The Kingdom of God is within us'. The person who genuinely believes this will think and act very differently from the person who believes they do not have access to the resources they need. If you choose to believe that you are divine, perfect and undamaged just as you are, regardless of the past, then you hold the reins that permit you to direct your own life. When you come to believe this principle as Maha does, you can begin to part the clouds of ignorance and negative conditioning, and the world begins to look very different.

US spiritual activist and author Marianne Williamson puts it beautifully:

'Our deepest fear is not that we are inadequate. Our deepest fear is that we are powerful beyond measure. It is our light, not our darkness that most frightens us. We ask ourselves, Who am I to be brilliant, gorgeous, talented, fabulous? Actually, who are you not to be? You are a child of God. Your playing small does not serve the world. There is nothing enlightened about shrinking so that other people won't feel insecure around you. We are all meant to shine, as children do. We were born to make manifest the glory of God that is within us. It's not just in some of us; it's in everyone. And as we let our own light shine, we unconsciously give other people permission to do the same. As we are liberated from our own fear, our presence automatically liberates others.'

There is both a spiritual and a practical element to this principle and which aspect you choose to focus on is up to you, but it's worth knowing that this concept of Brahman or inner divinity is now borne out by science.

David Bohm, one of the world's most highly respected quantum physicists and a protégé of Albert Einstein has proposed that at some deep level of existence everything is interconnected and is part of the same whole or source. This view is shared by many other scientists and resonates with Vedanta teachings. Brahman is the philosophical equivalent of the deeper, more profound order of existence that Bohm refers to. As the name would suggest, the universe ('uni' 'verse') is playing one song and we are all part of that song. If you hurt others you hurt yourself. If you love others you love yourself. In this context the notion of karma seems not only plausible but logical.

This is why Gandhi was such a remarkable individual. Winning independence for India was less amazing than the *way* he achieved it. His philosophy of nonviolence was not a political trick, tactic or strategy; it was the only possible course of action open to a man who believed with every fibre of his being that we are all one and that all power is within us. Gandhi followed the teachings of Vedanta and is perhaps the most astonishing example of their manifestation. It was Gandhi who famously said, 'An eye for an eye will make the whole world blind'. This wasn't a sound bite cooked up by a media team for maximum impact; it was the expression of his fundamental belief. Gandhi believed that we could never end violence with violence. War will never bring peace. Hate will never foster love. He knew that fighting and bloodshed would not secure Indian Independence and would simply perpetuate the violence. Everything we do to others comes back to us. Gandhi knew it so deeply that he was prepared to die for the principle, and he changed the world as a result.

> *All these extraordinary powers are in the mind of man. This mind is a part of the universal mind. Each mind is connected with every other mind. And each mind, wherever it is located, is in actual communication with the whole world.*

Maha's action plan

All power is within you. In order to help you shift your thinking and incorporate this principle into your life you will need to:

➤ find your own motivation

➤ recharge your batteries

➤ aim for no anger, no desire, no fear.

Find your own motivation

One of the most liberating aspects of Vedanta is that it does not seek to convert anyone, because we are all one, we are all connected anyway. In the end it doesn't matter what you believe, or who is right or wrong. It doesn't matter what your colour, religion or creed are. It doesn't matter if you draw inspiration and motivation from Vedanta, the Bible or any other religious or spiritual text. It doesn't matter if you are an agnostic or atheist and choose instead to draw your inspiration from success stories, movies, books, biographies, mentors and advisers. What matters is that you find a way to believe in yourself, to dedicate yourself to one idea and put everything you have behind it.

Maha's inspiration is Vedanta. One of his most treasured possessions is the nine-volume *Complete Works of Swami Vivekananda*. Maha's set is dog-eared and worn from more than 25 years of use. He has scribbled notes all over these books, and passages of special significance have been underlined. These notes and markings are like a personal biography of a volatile life. It's easy to see how he used these words to refocus his efforts and maintain strength through the bleak days.

Maha found what he needed to find in the pages of Vedanta. This is probably what his father meant when he said, 'Follow whatever or whoever you like as long as it makes you a better person'.

As an expression of gratitude to the philosophy that has been instrumental to Maha's life, Maha and Bob have donated 20 hectares (49.4 acres) of Springfield land to Vedanta Society in Australia.

Regardless of what philosophy you choose to follow, find your own motivation, draw strength from that source, use it to foster self-belief, plant your feet on the ground, run steel through your veins, lift your eyes to the sky and never, never give up.

We must not discriminate between things. Where things are concerned, there are no class distinctions. We must pick out what is good for us where we can find it.

— Pablo Picasso (Spanish artist)

By believing passionately in something that still does not exist, we create it. The nonexistent is whatever we have not sufficiently desired.

— Nikos Kazantzakis (Greek writer)

Recharge your batteries

When life is frenetically busy it can be hard to feel connected to anything and the pace and noise of daily existence can be exhausting. It's important therefore to take time out to recharge your batteries. And the busier you are the more important this is.

Maha recharges his batteries by rising early to enjoy the still, quiet hours of early morning, taking time to stroll through his garden and to meditate. Meditation allows you to slow the internal chatter of everyday life and helps you to disperse the clouds of ignorance and illusion and experience your own divinity.

It doesn't have to involve hours sitting in the lotus position in silent vigil. If it is unfamiliar territory then you may want to start gradually. Begin by spending five minutes alone without any distractions — no music, no TV, no noise of any kind. Be conscious of your thoughts as though you were watching them on a TV screen and let them drift past. Don't hold on to any or start thinking deeply about what springs to mind. Just notice the thoughts, emotions and anxieties and let them melt away. This is the art of meditation. Slowly but surely you will gain greater control over your own mind, which in turn will allow you to reaffirm that all the power you'll ever need is within you.

However you choose to recharge your batteries, you must take time out to re-energise. Not only will this process sharpen your mind and increase your energy but it will also help you access greater creativity.

Learn to get in touch with silence within yourself, and know that everything in this life has purpose. There are no mistakes, no coincidences, all events are blessings given to us to learn from.

— Elisabeth Kübler-Ross (Swiss–American psychiatrist)

The time to relax is when you don't have time to.

—Sidney J. Harris (American journalist)

Aim for no anger, no desire, no fear

One Vedanta mantra is 'No anger, no desire, no fear'. According to Vedanta these feelings are cyclical and interwoven. It isn't possible to be angry unless someone has done something or not done something that you desired. If you have no desire, you can't be angry. If you have no desire, you can't experience fear because you are not attached to the outcome.

This is not to say we shouldn't care about the outcome or strive to achieve goals, but that we should do so without attachment to the outcome. All we can do is all we can do. Your job is to put everything you have into a task. You won't always get the result you hoped for, but if you aim to rid yourself of anger, desire and fear, you don't then waste time and energy arguing about the failure or blaming others; you simply regroup and get back into action. Swami Vivekananda says, 'Desire, want, is the father of all misery. Desires are bound by the laws of success and failure. Desires must bring misery. The great secret of true success, of true happiness, is this: the person who asks for no return, the perfectly unselfish person, is the most successful'.

How people treat you is their karma; how you react is yours.

—Wayne Dyer (American author)

Maha readily admits that this particular goal is a work in progress. He has mastered fear, certainly, but he still has an overwhelming passion for Springfield and a deep desire to see it come to fruition, and this can spill over into anger when things don't go according to plan. Aristotle once said, 'Anyone can become angry — that is easy. But to be angry with the right person, to the right degree, at the right time, for the right purpose, and in the right way — that is not easy'. For the most part Maha has used anger in the right way to achieve his goals and although he has mellowed over the years, he still has fire in his belly. It doesn't, however, stop him from aiming for the ideal of no anger, no desire and no fear.

You will not be punished for your anger, you will be punished by your anger.

—Buddha (spiritual teacher)

Conclusion

In his 1961 inaugural address in Washington, DC, John F. Kennedy said, 'All this will not be finished in the first 100 days, nor will it be finished in the first 1000 days, nor in the life of this Administration — nor even, perhaps, in our lifetime on this planet. But let us begin'.

By 'All this', Kennedy was referring to his determination to end world conflict, 'explore the stars, conquer the deserts, eradicate disease, tap the ocean depths, and encourage the arts and commerce'. A tall order, but JFK was a visionary president.

When Maha stood on the rough land at Opossum Creek decades ago he saw a new city. He didn't think about how it would be created or when it would be finished; he rallied his team and began. As they progressed collectively, the original vision that inspired Maha evolved into something grander and finer than anyone, even Maha, could have foreseen. Springfield is a wonder. It has been an endless sequence of problems and solutions, and the problems never disappear. As Martin Luther King Jnr said, 'All progress is precarious, and the solution of one problem brings us face to face with another problem'.

Barry Alexander used to say something similar, about your strengths becoming your weaknesses and your weaknesses becoming your strengths. In the early days the biggest 'weakness' Maha and Bob faced was a lack of money. But out of that weakness grew their greatest strengths: they were endlessly resourceful and innovative; they negotiated like bulldogs; and they never accepted the first offer or first price. Of course that source of strength has since been weakened by Maha's appearance on the *BRW* Rich List! With suppliers now convinced they are rich, deals are harder to negotiate and employees are perhaps a little less frugal than they would have been in the early years. Maha and Bob are both wealthy men, but that wealth is not squirrelled away, propping up a very high mattress; it is tied up in the land and Springfield assets. The machine that is Springfield is a ravenous monster that devours millions of dollars a year. The GFC brought the same challenges to Springfield as it did to so many others.

Everyone involved in the project has been aware that creating a city from scratch is a project that cannot be completed in 1000 days, perhaps not even in a lifetime, but they nonetheless pursue the goal relentlessly. Everything great takes time. Success requires disciplined effort over the long haul.

> *If you really want to judge the character of a man, look not at his great performances. Every fool may become a hero at one time or another. Watch a man do his most common actions; those are indeed the things which will tell you the real character of a great man.*

Success also leaves clues.

The secret of Maha Sinnathamby's success lies in the 10 simple principles examined in this book. Each principle offers a powerful reminder of how to live well and achieve what you want to achieve. Their collective and cumulative potency can transform lives.

If you make one idea your life, arise, awake and stop not till the goal is reached, then you will succeed. If you work relentlessly, doing what needs to be done whether or not you feel like it, then you will gain strength and self-respect, which will foster success. If you choose courage in the face of difficulty, stay fearless and face the brutes when you have to, then you will survive the difficult times in the knowledge that tomorrow is another day and that the darkest night always brings the brightest dawn. If you stay true to your vision and maintain purity in thought, word and deed, then the inevitable stumbles of your journey will develop character, perseverance, resilience and self-confidence, and add to the satisfaction of achievement. When you come to appreciate your own strengths and weaknesses and celebrate diversity, you will realise that no-one is better or worse than you. We are all just different parts of the same puzzle and everyone is great in their own place. You are the creator of your own destiny because ultimately all the power you'll ever need is within you already. Your job is to disperse the clouds of illusion so you can manifest your own divinity. These 10 principles, practised daily, will help you do that.

Aristotle once said, 'The only way to achieve true success is to express yourself completely in service to society'. Maha is successful not because his wealth now exceeds $800 million. His success is not measured in dollars and numbers. It is measured in his relationships: the love he has for his wife and family, his enduring business partnership with Bob Sharpless. It is measured in the little things: the laughter shared with the family at their local Chinese restaurant, where everything not eaten is taken home for later. It is measured in time spent with his grandchildren. It is measured in his extraordinary ability to inspire people to surpass what they had believed possible of themselves. Real success can be measured in a close and loving family, ethical and moral strength, and a deep desire to create something that lives on long after he is gone. Through Springfield he has found a way to express himself completely in service to society.

When asked if he had a message for humanity, Gandhi replied, 'My life is my message'. For Maha and Bob, Springfield is their message. What will yours be?

Final reflections from Maha

Life is full of opportunities, regardless of your origins or where you live. The bottom line is that there will always be something you can excel at. In the end achieving your goals simply boils down to having a strong sense of self-belief, taking finite action day in and day out, and just never giving up. So my message is go and make your dreams come true regardless of your passion.

Clearly my passion has been Springfield and I can truly say, hand on heart, that we are creating something unique and extraordinary there. It has been an unrelenting struggle. We have had to fight tooth and claw to ensure the integrity of the master plan and we have constantly had to push for what is right over what is expedient. At times doing the right thing has been extraordinarily difficult. But it has also been the greatest adventure of my life. It's been fun and exciting. Most importantly, it's never been about the money, only the thrill of creating something great.

I hope you've enjoyed the story of our struggles, setbacks and successes. Most of all, I hope you now feel inspired to pursue your own goals and adventures. Whatever you want to achieve in life, I know that following the principles outlined in this book will help you accomplish it. If the book helps inspire just 10 people to action, then I will feel I have achieved my goal.

If there is one thing of which I can be very sure, though, it is that there is less difference between you and me than you may think. We are born fundamentally the same. But you'll find that highly successful people in life are driven to their very core by unrelenting persistence. Everything they do, say and think is focused on achieving their goal and every ounce of their energy is driven towards that attainment, be it raising a wonderful family, reaching the peak of Mt Everest or getting that promotion.

Calvin Coolidge said:

> 'Nothing in the world can take the place of Persistence. Talent will not; nothing is more common than unsuccessful men with talent. Genius will not; unrewarded genius is almost a proverb. Education will not; the world is full of educated derelicts. Persistence and determination alone are omnipotent. The slogan "Press On" has solved and always will solve the problems of the human race.'

Book knowledge will give you a good foundation and you know how much I value education, but in isolation it will only take you so far. It may get you that job or open a door, but beyond that the difference between good and great is what you then decide to make of yourself. 'Persistence and determination alone are omnipotent.'

My final message is that nothing good comes easy. Embarking on your chosen goal and thinking otherwise is foolish. So have the self-belief and determination to face the hurdles each and every day of your life. Surround yourself with people who uplift you; people who have bold aspirations, who challenge themselves and you. Read things that motivate and inspire you towards your chosen goal. Watch programs that teach you something new.

And know that there are no short cuts or fast tracks to success in life. You must believe in yourself and never, never give up, no matter what life throws at you. It doesn't matter where you live, there is opportunity everywhere. People say, 'But it's different now—there were more opportunities in the 1970s'. That's rubbish. Stop making excuses. Think positive, decide what you want to do and go for it. Be persistent and never, ever give up.

You really are the creator of your own destiny.

Best wishes,

Maha

Timeline

1939 (December) — Maha Sinnathamby born in Rantau, Malaysia

1944 (July) — Valipuram Sinnathamby becomes a Japanese prisoner of war

1945 (August) — Yoga Thambaiya born in Seremban, Malaysia

1945 (September) — Valipuram released from prison camp

1959 (February) — Maha begins studies at the University of New South Wales (UNSW) Sydney

1966 (April) — Maha graduates with a Bachelor of Civil Engineering

1968 (March) — Maha and Yoga marry in Malaysia

1968 (December) — Uma Sinnathamby born

1970 (July) — Raynuha Sinnathamby born

1971 (October) — Maha arrives in Perth, Western Australia

1971 (December) — Meera Sinnathamby born

1972 (January) — Yoga, Uma, Raynuha and Meera arrive in Australia

1972 (April) — Starts work at Perth Municipal Water Board

1976 (March) — Starts Murdoch Projects with Ken Law-Davis

1977 (July) — Naren Sinnathamby born

1982 (May) — Ken Law-Davis leaves partnership to live overseas

1983 (April) — Trust collapses; Maha fights to pay off debts

1984 (November) — Bob Sharpless begins working for Maha

1985 (September) — Sinnathamby family fly to Brisbane for fresh start; Bob Sharpless joins Maha as business partner

1987 (July) — Valipuram Sinnathamby dies

1987 (December) — David Henry joins Maha and Bob as project manager

1991 (October) — Secures land at Opossum Creek on option contract for $7.84 million

1992 (November) — Planning expert Barry Alexander joins the team

1992 (August) — Springfield launched by Deputy Premier

1995 (March) — Morton Shire and Ipswich councils merge and John Nugent elected mayor

1997 (January) — Local Government Springfield Rezoning Bill 1997 passed unanimously by Queensland state government

1997 (September) — Final payment made to AFH for Opossum Creek land

1997 (December) — Maha undergoes heart bypass surgery

1998 (January) — Springfield State School opens

1999 (January) — Bank gives Maha 30 days to pay back $9 million

1999 (June) — Delfin deal to extend residential community confirmed

1999 (July) — Road construction agreement signed for extension of Centenary Highway to Springfield

2000 (July) — Final stage of Centenary Highway opened

2002 (March) — $21 million Greg Norman–designed Brookwater Golf Course opens

2006 (January) — University of Southern Queensland Campus opens in Springfield

2006 (April) — Education City opened by Prime Minister John Howard

2007 (March) — $143 million Orion Springfield Town Centre shopping precinct opens

2008 (November) — $60 million Springfield Tower opens in Parkside CBD

2009 (February) — $220 million Tier 3+ Polaris Data Centre opens in Parkside CBD

2010 (May) — Springfield wins FIABCI award for World's Best Master Planned Community

2011 (May) — $30 million Robelle Domain opened

Index